60s!

60s!

John and
Gordon Javna

St. Martin's Press · New York

Photo Credits

Pages 16–17, *Surfer Magazine;* pp. 18–19, National Automatic Mechanics Association; p. 19, Grand Union Co.; p. 24; *Special Interest Autos* magazine, Volkswagon of America, *Car and Driver* magazine; p. 26, *Special Interest Autos, Car and Driver* magazine; pp. 27–28, *Special Interest Autos;* p. 30, *Special Interest Autos, Car and Driver;* p. 31, Jim Wangers, *Special Interest Autos, Car and Driver; p.* 32, *Special Interest Autos,* Rolls-Royce Motors Ltd.; pp. 34–35, George Barris; p. 35, Cooper-Hewitt Museum (Smithsonian Institution's Museum of Design); p. 36, Mercedes-Benz of America, *Special Interest Autos, Car and Driver;* p. 37, *Car and Driver, Special Interest Autos,* Coca-Cola Company; p. 38, American Petroleum Institute; p. 39, Colorforms, Inc.; p. 40, NASA, John Cavanaugh; p. 41, NASA, General Foods Corp., Buitoni Foods; pp. 42–43, Photo Co. of Atlantic City, Sol Abrams; p. 44, General Electric; p. 45, Campbell's Soup Co.; p. 56, Miles Laboratories, Campbell's Soup Co.; p. 57, Tom Smothers; pp. 58–59, Dick Martin; p. 62, Jay Ward Productions; p. 63, Stratolounger, pp. 64–67, National Archives, Kennedy Library, Smithsonian Institution; p. 68, U.S. Department of Defense; p. 69, F.E.M.A.; p. 70, National Archives; p. 72, Arlington Hats, Nat Sherman Cigars; p. 73, courtesy Chubby Checker; p. 74, Oster Co., Hoover Co.; p. 75, Frigidaire Co.; p. 76, A.T.&T., E.R. Squibb; p. 77, General Electric Co., Motorola, Zenith, Kelvinator; p. 78, Proctor and Gamble; p. 79, Proctor and Gamble, Colgate-Palmolive, Jane Withers, Kimberly Clark, Union Carbide, Lester Lewis, Inc.; p. 80, Amana Co., Eastman Kodak Co., Inc., Lavern Chair Co.; p. 81, A.T.&T., IBM, Austin Deflaun; p. 82, Kennedy Library; p. 84, National Telefilm Associates; p. 85, U.S. Department of Defense, pp. 86–87, National Telefilm Associates; p. 88, Jack Regan; p. 92, Hanes Hosiery, Sally Tuffin, Thom McAn Shoe Co.; p. 93, Pauline Trigere, William Claxton; p. 94, Thom McAn Shoe Co., J.C. Penney, Golo Shoe Co., Herbert Levine Shoes, Mike McGrath; p. 95, Scott Paper Co., Herbert Levine

Shoes, Colorforms, Inc.; pp. 96–97, Donald Brooks, William Claxton, Butterick Fashions, Eleanor Lambert, Hanes Hosiery; p. 98, William S. Claxton; p. 99, Exquisite Form Industries, Herbert Levine Shoes, William S. Claxton; p. 101, Max Factor and Co.; p. 102, Foster Grant Corp.; p. 103, Jantzen, Inc., Foster Grant Corp.; p. 104, Colgate-Palmolive, NASA, CBS Records; p. 105, Hoffman Apparel International Corp.; p. 106, Vidal Sassoon; p. 107, National Cotton Council of America, Sulton, Inc., Vidal Sassoon; p. 108, Hart, Schaffner, and Marx, Men's Fashion Association, Joseph and Feiss Co., J.C. Penney; p. 109, Mike McGrath, Levi Strauss, Co., Butterick Fashions, Don Snyder; p. 110, J.C. Penney, Pucci Perfumes, Andres Courreges, p. 111, Donald Brooks, Coty; p. 112, Alpha Beta Co., McCrory Stores, Nixon Project, Garden State Plaza; p. 113, Campbell's Soup Co., Leo Castilli Gallery; p. 114, Leo Castilli Gallery, Sidney Janis Gallery; p. 115, Papermate Co., A.T.&T., Leo Castilli Gallery; pp. 116–117, Bob Overstreet, D.C. Comics, Marvel Comics Group, *Mad Magazine;* pp.118–120, NASA, Leni Sinclair, Don Snyder, Personality Posters; p. 121, Paramount Pictures; pp. 124–125, Smithsonian Institution; p. 127, Tom Smothers, Smithsonian Institution; pp. 130–131, United Features Syndicate, Determined Productions, Ford Motor Co., ConAgra, NASA; pp. 132–133, NASA, John Cavanaugh; p. 140, NASA, Filmways; p. 141, Johnson Library, Nixon Project; pp. 142–143, McDonald's Corp., Taco Bell, KFC Corp., Burger King Corp.; pp. 144–145, The Kellogg Co., Quaker Oats, General Foods, General Mills; pp. 146–147, ITT Intercontinental Baking Co., Drake Bakeries, Hershey's Chocolate Co., Nabisco, Inc., W.P. Ihrie & Sons, Proctor and Gamble, Burry's Inc., Wise Foods, Ovaltine Co.; pp. 148–149, Anhaeuser-Busch, Inc., Stroh Brewing Co., Miller Brewing Co., Jos. Schlitz Brewing Co.; pp. 150–151, Coca-Cola Co., Pepsi Cola Co., Royal Crown; p. 152, Seven-Up Co., Stokely/Van Camp; p. 153, Pantry Pride Enterprises, Inc.; p. 154, Drackett Co., Pet

Foods; p. 155, Nabisco, Inc., Kitchens of Sara Lee, General Foods; p. 156, Campbell's Soup Co., ITT Intercontinental Baking Co., Pillsbury Co., United Brands Co., Nestle's Co., Inc.; p. 157, Ovaltine Products, Inc., Buitoni Foods, Wm. Wrigley Inc., and Co., General Foods, Libby Foods, Borden; pp. 158–159, Smithsonian Institution, Nixon Project; pp. 160–161, Personality Posters; p. 162, *Rolling Stone* magazine; p. 165, *Sixteen* magazine; p. 171, American Guitars/-Tom Wheeler; p. 178, Duncan Yo-Yos; p. 179, Don Snyder; p. 183, General Electric Co., Inc.; pp. 184–185, Herman Darvick; p. 187, Dr. Eugene Schonfeld; p. 189, Don Snyder; p. 190, Leni Sinclair, Rick Swinger, General Electric Co., Levi-Strauss Co.; p. 191, Ripoff Press; pp. 196–197, Mattel Corp., Jefferson Mfg. Co.; Tonka Toys, Milton Bradley Co., Parker Brothers, Kenner Products, Wham-O; p. 198, Wham-O, Duncan Toys, Co., *Surfer Magazine;* p. 199, Milton Bradley Co., Lloyd Ralston; p. 200, Mattel Corp., Estes Industries, Lloyd Ralston; p. 201, Lloyd Ralston; p. 202, Ideal Toy Co., Lloyd Ralston; p. 203, Hasbro, Inc., Mattel Corp.; pp. 204–205, Candy Barr, Mattel Corp.; p. 206, Pat Smith; p. 207, *Mad Magazine,* Famous Monsters of Filmland; p. 208, Mattel Corp., p. 210, Leni Sinclair; p. 211, Don Snyder; p. 214, Colgate-Palmolive; p. 217, General Electric Co.

Batman is a registered trademark of D.C. Comics, Inc., and is used with permission. Mr. Natural © R. Crumb. Miss Chiquita is a registered trademark of United Brands Co. Tony the Tiger, Snap Crackle, & Pop, Puffa Puffa Rice, Apple Jacks are registered trademarks of the Kellogg Co. Alpha Bits, Crispy Critters, Honeycomb, Sugar Crisp, Kool Aid, Tang are registered trademarks of General Foods Co. Page 162 is from *Rolling Stone* magazine, 7/16/68, by Straight Arrow Publishers, Inc., © 1968. All rights reserved, reprinted by permission. Car photos not credited above courtesy Ford Motor Co., General Motors, Chrysler Corp., and American Motors Corp. Additional photos by the authors.

Design by Hal Morgan

Library of Congress Cataloging in Publication Data
Javna, John.
    60s!
    1. United States—Civilization—1945–
2. United States—Popular culture. I. Javna, Gordon.
II. Title.   III. Title: Sixties.
E169.12.J37   1983   973.92   83-428
ISBN 0-312-72752-6 (pbk.)

First Edition
10 9 8 7 6 5 4 3 2 1

GORDON: It's dedication time.

JOHN: Oh, no, who ever reads those things anyway?

GORDON: I do.

JOHN: Then you write it.

GORDON: Okay. I'd like to dedicate this to Mr. Krolick, who ran the toy store in Tenafly.

JOHN: That's dumb. You gotta take these things seriously, Gordon. After all, a lot of people bent over backward to make it possible for us to write this book.

GORDON: Yeah. Maggie's gonna kill me if I spend any more time on it.

JOHN: You're lucky she hasn't killed you already.

GORDON: Okay, so we dedicate the book to Maggie . . . and Mom and Dad.

JOHN: Lorrie and Lowell should be included too. And I'd like to make sure Jim Abrams and Joann are in there. And Doug Ottati and Scott Huston.

GORDON: Who?

JOHN: They're the only friends I've got left from the sixties.

GORDON: That figures. Anyone else?

JOHN: How about Johnny Carson? If we dedicate it to him, he might put us on his show.

GORDON: Hey, yeah! And what about Merv Griffin? . . . and Mike Douglas . . .

JOHN: . . . Oh, and "The Today Show" . . . Barbara Walters . . . Ed Sullivan . . . Dick Clark . . . Howard Cosell . . .

Contents

ACKNOWLEDGMENTS

It would have been absolutely impossible to have written this book without help. Lots of it. And we did have a lot of help from a lot of nice people—people who trusted us on the phone without knowing who we were, people who let us come into their homes to take pictures, people who sent us photos, people who typed all night and worked overtime for us, people who put up with our incessant badgering, and people who held our hands. Down the stretch, our editor, Bob Miller, really came through for us. Thanks, Bob. Here are some of the people who made this book possible.

FAMILY AND FRIENDS: Mom and Dad (Hi, Mom), Maggie, Lorrie and Lowell, Joann McCracken, Bardin Levavy, Jim and Chris Abrams, Randy Flint, Walter Schneller, Linda Hogan, and Chip Stone ("Hey, Chip—listen to this one. . . .")

SPECIAL THANKS TO: Tom Canariato, Jan, Ellen, and Sharon at Pinewood Studio, Alfie Custom Lab, The staff at Kellogg-Hubbard Library, Montpelier Vt., Aldrich Public Library, Barre, Vt., Hackensack Public Library, Hackensack, N.J., Bob Cereghino, Carol Mann, Howard Kady, Lori Solensten, and, of course, Hal Morgan, of Steam Press

STARS OF THE SIXTIES: Sol Abrams, George Barris, Connie Boucher, Donald Brooks, Harry Chapin, Chubby Checker, Julie Cooper, Andres Courreges, Austin DeFlaun, Fabian, Bill Gaines, Marty Geisler, Rudi Gernreich, Deedee Kinnebrew, Eleanor Lambert, Herbert and Beth Levine, Dick Martin, Peter Max, Peggy Moffitt, Pat Paulsen, Dr. Eugene Schonfeld, Del Shannon, Tom Smothers, Sally Tuffin, Bobby Vee, Jim Wangers, Jay and Billie Ward, and Jane Withers

60s RESEARCH DEPARTMENT: Joanna Gilbride, Lynn Milich, Lois Scott, Dennis and Sharon, Nancy Boulanger, and Hilda Fleming

PHOTOGRAPHERS: Many thanks for the use of your priceless records of the sixties. Candy Barr, John Cavanaugh, William Claxton, Mike McGrath, Leni Sinclair, Don Snyder, Rick Swinger, and Jack Régan

COLLECTORS AND EXPERTS: These people shared their knowledge with us, and allowed us to photograph their prized possessions. Candy Barr, Bob Cereghino, Bill Christianson, Herb Collins, Chick Darrow, Herman Darvick, David E. Davis, Jeff Divine, Corky and Carroll of *Surfer* magazine, Tony Ellington, Maxene Fabe, Judy Fireman, Bob Forlini, Len Frank, Audrey Garvey, George at the Relic Rack, Goldmine Magazine, Steven Green, Ted Hake, Bruce Hamilton, Gary King, Roger Kirkpatrick, Mark Lapidos, Andy Levison, Strother McMin, Jerry Osborne, Bob Overstreet, Michael Pender, Lloyd Ralston, Herb Regan, Charles Reinhart, Artie Rickun, Ken Rudin, Sharon S., Sid Sackson, Lee Saegesser, Paul Seagord, Dick Sikes, Kiki Smith, Pat Smith, Speakeasy's Bob and Rita, Jeff Tamarkin, Ed Verga, George Wahlert, Tom Wheeler, Charles Reinhart, and Bob Dalley

CORPORATE CONNECTIONS: Thanks to these folks and many others at businesses who assisted us in obtaining photos and product information which would have been impossible to include otherwise. Murray Altschuler, Don Baumgart, David Carroll, George Chartier, Mae Clark, Bob Connors, Jim Crellin, Bob Cross, Carla Drake, Evelyn Dallal, Diane Dickey, Lynn Dragomier, Helen Early, Mauri Edwards, Jerry Einhorn, Susan Graham, Virginia Graves, Herbert Hoffman, Marion Ingram, Bill Jefferson, Pat Jent, Lou Jewell, Madryn Johnson, Suzanne Kautsky, Noah Kislevitz, Stella Labor, Jeff Lamb, Ervine Laverne, Juliet Lewis, Robert Lewis, Norman Liss, Warren McDermott, Pat McIntyre, Rita McKay, Barbara McLaughlin, James Maxwell, George Meredith, Michelle R. Milne, Phil Mooney, Goldy Norton, Robert Norwood, Jenny Oparski, Robert Patillo, Helen Perlman, Michael Quinn, Walter Reed, Pam Robertson, Emmett Robinson, Susan Rudolph, Mary Louise Ryan, Hank Scheibner, M.J. Schroeder, Deloria Smith, Lois Seulowitz, Chip Talbot, Lisa Wasser, Lois Zeigler, Jennifer Zook, and L. Craig Zuke

There are literally hundreds more people who assisted us with this book—more than our limited space will allow us to list here. But we want them to know how much we appreciated their help. The book would have been impossible without you, folks. Thanks.

INTRODUCTION

We grew up in the fifties in Tenafly, New Jersey, an affluent little town about fifteen minutes away from New York City. It was full of old houses and big shade trees, and it felt like nothing ever changed there. We were "protected" from Real Life. We lived in a world of television, modern appliances, baseball cards, rock and roll, an elementary school we could ride our bikes to, peaceful streets. We went to summer camp. We got drunk with our friends in the woods, smoked pot when it appeared in town. We hung out at the Dairy Queen.

In 1980, it suddenly dawned on us that the sixties were more than a decade gone, and that traces of the everyday world of our adolescence were disappearing fast. It would not be too long before the sixties were considered "ancient history," and people would begin reminiscing about them. People would be collecting the things we had during our youth, calling them "artifacts."

Up to this point we—like the rest of America—considered civil unrest, the war in Vietnam, and the counter culture the only history of the sixties worth taking seriously. But when we thought about it, we realized that breakfast cereal and mini-skirts were as much—or more—a part of what we personally remembered as any "great issue" of the day. So we decided to write about that part of our experience before it was completely lost.

The story of a popular doll or an unpopular car is no less significant than a story about a riot and it tells as much about the American people—and it's a hell of a lot more fun.

We've assumed you already know something about the incredible changes that America went through during the sixties. But in case you don't, or need a quick refresher course, here's a summary of the important trends of the decade:

• Youth. The post-World War II baby boom grew up and for the first time more than half the population was under thirty. Youth was in and everybody wanted to look young, feel young, act young. Young people dictated style and fashion: mini-skirts, long hair, dancing, music.

• Loss of innocence. The perfect society we were taught to believe in had flaws. It can't happen here? The death of JFK, Robert Kennedy, Martin Luther King. Racism. Poverty. America was losing a war for the first time. What other lies would we uncover? Stay tuned for Watergate.

• Affluence. Americans had more money than ever before, and we used it to buy ourselves a "better" standard of living. More dishwashers, more color tv's, more electric can openers. The result: a whole generation of middle class kids who didn't know what poverty was.

• Social activism. President Kennedy encouraged young people to get involved. It set the tone for the sixties: the civil rights movement, the Peace Corps, the War on Poverty, CORE, SNCC, Ban the Bomb, the Free Speech movement, Beautify America, Medicare, Vista, folk songs, rock music in politics, protests, demonstrations. Do it!

• The sexual revolution. The Pill freed women from the fear of pregnancy and gave them a chance to say "yes" if they felt like it. That meant women—heretofore defensive—could now be agressive. Whoops! There goes the traditional man-woman relationship. Enter mini-skirts, unisex, long hair for men, free love, love-ins, the bra-less look, "living together" (as an alternative to marriage), and a whole bunch of angry traditionalists who thought it meant the end of the world.

• Traditional values. People began to reject them. Bye bye apple pie and Motherhood. Here are some alternative life styles: communes instead of suburbia; mod clothes instead of gray flannel suits; hippies instead of young professionals; druggies instead of alcoholics. During the sixties traditional values were questioned and rejected by masses of young Americans who would have been the heirs-apparent to their parents' life styles. It was a shock to the parents, and an exciting trip to the kids, though it didn't last long.

• High technology. The real lasting revolution of the sixties was that America entered the Atomic/Computer Age irrevocably. We can never turn back now. Space travel, nuclear power plants, color tv, video tape, atomic subs, computers, push button phones, weather satellites, freeze-dried food, plastic clothes, paper clothes, the Pill.

• Experimentation. During the sixties it seemed like people would try just about anything. Let it all hang out. Do your own thing. Long hair. Men's jewelry. Going bra-less. Back to nature. Taking LSD. Pop and op art. Body painting. Communes. Astrology. Yoga.

• Television. By the beginning of the sixties, almost everyone in America who had electricity had a television. It's an awesome thought. Suddenly it was possible for a single source to reach almost everyone in America with a single message at the same time. It had never been possible anytime before this in the history of the world. When businessmen realized this was true, selling changed forever. So did politics. So, in fact, did everything in our culture. The whole society was geared around television. And it hasn't gotten any better. Want to play a video game?

We hope you enjoy this book as much as we did. And as you read it, remember . . . *this was your life!!!*

60s!

How to Talk Like a Surfer

Beach bunny: bikini-clad blond beauty. Doesn't surf, but doesn't have to.

Gremmie: beginner

Cowabunga: WOW!

Hang ten: hang all ten toes over the front of your surfboard. Very tricky.

Kook: beginner

Hodad: fake surfer; has a woodie and a board, and cold feet

Wahini: Hawaiian for girl—a real surfer girl

Wipe out: get knocked off your surfboard

Boss: great ("we're going to see a *boss* surfing movie")

Pop out: lousy

Baggies: long-legged, loose swimsuit

Ding: small damage to a cherished object, such as surfboard or car

Woody: vintage station wagon with real wood panels

Hot-dogging: showing off

Shoot the curl: do something really boss

Great Moments of the 60s
Nixon Gets Surfboard

Father's Day 1969 (a true story)
The surfing bug has finally bitten America's first family: today, Richard Nixon received a surfboard from his daughters. The Father's Day gift, says daughter Tricia, is a custom-made blue job with the President's name inscribed on it.

Nixon, fifty-six years old, seemed undaunted by the prospect of going one-on-one with the Pacific Ocean at his San Clemente palace. "I rode a surfboard thirty years ago," he said with a grin, "it doesn't impress me a bit."

But don't hold your breath waiting to see Mr. Nixon hang ten. He has no immediate plans for public display of this prowess. "I'll never ride it," he commented.

Six Things You Didn't Know about Surfing

1. The first national exposure of surfing was in the film *Gidget* in 1960.

2. Less than 1 percent of the population ever really surfed.

3. "Real" surfers didn't drive woodies; they drove panel trucks.

4. Surf music got its start at Surfer Stomps, California dances featuring performers like Dick Dale and the Del-Tones.

5. Many surfers didn't like the Beach Boys at first because they started too many people acting like surfers and crowded up the beaches.

6. At home in L.A., surfers were regarded as derelicts who didn't work. But when the top surfers went to the East Coast to give demonstrations, they were celebrities. "I remember one time in New Jersey," says a former champion, "there were seventy thousand people to watch us surf. It was unbelievable."

TOP TEN
Boss Surfin' Songs

"Surfin' Safari"	The Beach Boys	1962
"Let's Go"	The Routers	1962
"Surfer's Stomp"	The Marketts	1962
"Surfin' USA"	The Beach Boys	1963
"Pipeline"	The Chantays	1963
"Wipe Out"	The Surfaris	1963
"California Sun"	The Rivieras	1963
"Surf City"	Jan and Dean	1963
"Penetration"	The Pyramids	1964
"Surfin' Bird"	The Trashman	1964

Surfing

The Inside Story: The Origin of the Beach Boys

The Beach Boys did more to make surfing a national craze than anyone. You think they were surfers who sang about the life they loved, right? Guess again. Only one of them surfed at all. Here's how it really happened:

In 1961, songwriter Murray Wilson arranged for his three sons, his nephew, and one of their friends (all teenagers) to record a folk song just for fun.

The producer at the recording studio was unimpressed with them, but he respected Wilson, so he asked if the sons had written any original songs. That was a historic question. They hadn't, but one —Dennis—mentioned an idea he'd been saving up. As a surfer he knew that lots of kids were involved in the "surf scene." He knew also that surfing music was becoming popular in the L.A. area, but it never had any words. Surfers had their own language—why not use it in a song? Everyone agreed. Right there in the studio they made a list of surfing terms and wrote a song with them. It was called "Surfin'."

The boys still didn't have a name. They thought that if they called themselves the Pendletons, they'd get free shirts from the Pendleton Shirt Company. But at the recording studio, the name "Beach Boys" was selected, and the record was released that way. (The group didn't even know it until they heard the song on the radio. Then they got so excited that one of them threw up.)

"Surfin'" was a local hit that reached number seventy-five on the national charts and earned the group nine hundred dollars. It also attracted Capitol records, which signed them to an exclusive contract. Their next release, "Surfin' Safari," was the first major national surfin' hit. It

established the Beach Boys and made surfing a household word from Maine to Montana.

What Surfers Wore

Left to right: Windbreaker, shorts, bare feet; alligator shirt, Madras shorts, white socks, huaraches; Madras shirt, chinos, tennis shoes with white socks; baggies and flippers; wet suit, baggies, flippers; Oxford shirt, chinos, tennis shoes with white socks; sweat shirt, swimsuit, flip-flops. Not shown: bleach-blond hair.

Bikinis

The Mechanical Way of Life

Machines these days will sell you almost anything you want, from ice cubes and hot meals, to hardware and drygoods. To keep up with the public's willingness to do its shopping at machines, makers of the automatic vendors are building models ever larger, ever fancier and more versatile.
— *Business Week*, November 12, 1960

In 1960, it seemed like the sky was the limit for vending machines. After all, robots—machines that made life simple and left people with lots of leisure time—were the ultimate dream of the industrial age. "In America today," said the head of a vending machine company in 1960, "nobody wants to be a servant, and vending machines keep people from being servants." But a funny thing happened on the way to automation. As vending machines turned up doing more and more things, people seemed to get more and more selective about what they would buy from them. An all-vending machine restaurant that offered hot items fell flat on its face; automated grocery and department stores were a failure; gourmet foods dispensed by vending machines seemed unappetizing. Apparently, some things just couldn't be replaced by machines. Still, vending machines were here to stay—by the end of the decade, Americans were buying over five billion dollars worth of merchandise from vending machines.

Everything but a touchdown may soon be sold automatically at football games. A new Vendo unit sells frosty malts and piping hot hamburgers within inches of each other in the same cabinet—a companion vendor offers fresh corsages. Here Roli Kilman, Dartmouth rugby captain, pins a mum on Mimi Izzard, Scripps College junior, and gets a bite of her hamburger.

— *Press release, Vendo Company, 1960*

"Dial-A-Sale," the world's largest vending machine. Five feet wide, five feet deep, and nine feet high, it offered up to 204 different items. Merchandise was delivered to a door by elevator after the proper amount of change was deposited and a number dialed. It was designed to be an entire department in a retail store, or for convenience shopping in residential areas and apartment buildings.

A recent venture that flopped was that of Grand Union Co., which built coin-operated machines into several of its storefronts. The chain tried perhaps twenty different items, and finally gave up the project. When the stores were open, customers bought inside. When the stores were closed, the vendors didn't generate enough traffic. But the biggest headache was the rate of mechanical failure.
—Business Week, January 7, 1961

═══ 60s Selects ═══

The Five Most Creative Uses of Vending Machines in the Sixties

1. A London vending machine dispensed whiskey with water or soda for thirty-five cents a drink. It turned itself off automatically to conform with "legal hours."

2. In 1965 in Arkansas, a distributor had machines with live trained chickens, rabbits, and ducks that danced, played piano, or dispensed a fortune card after a coin released a morsel of food to the animal.

3. A machine that took five-dollar bets was installed at racetracks.

4. The Cinebox, imported from Italy, was "a jukebox with a twenty-one-inch movie screen mounted on top." A movie of a vocalist, band, or dancers accompanied every song.

5. Peanut butter vending machines made their appearance in Los Angeles in 1965.

It was inevitable that someone would think of it, and now it is here. A paperback book vending machine has just been introduced, and it has exciting possibilities for libraries. The U.S. in 1962 is an affluent society where very few of the adults using a library cannot afford the price of a paperback—often less than the cost of a hamburger and coffee.
—Library Journal, December 1, 1962

Four Vending Machine Ideas That Didn't Work

1. Credit cards for vending machines were introduced in 1965. A special plastic credit card was designed to be inserted into a slot in the vending machine. While the customer made a selection, the machine checked his credit.

2. Kansas City saw a new type of fast-food restaurant in 1961—an automatic drive-in. Machines doled out french fries, hamburgers, and other foods and drinks to the hungry-and-hurried shoppers.

3. A Miami ad agency planned to sell singing commercials that would play on jukeboxes automatically every thirty minutes.

4. In the summer of 1960, Macy's installed a men's underwear vending machine. It was national news! Throngs of people swarmed into the store to get a look at the contraption—so many, in fact, that Macy's had to move it from the ground level to the fifth floor to avoid store traffic jams. But unfortunately for Macy's, the bare facts were that nobody wanted to buy boxer shorts from a machine. It was just another flash-in-the-panties.

1965 Pontiac Catalina—$3,133

1960 Mercury Montclair—$3,465

1960 Pontiac Catalina—$3,116

1962 Chevrolet Bel Air—$2,698

1961 Plymouth Fury—$2,841

1965 Chevrolet Nova—$2,410

1962 Dodge Dart—$2,257

1962 Ford Galaxie—$2,687

1965 Rambler Ambassador—$2,777

1960 Pontiac Ventura—$3,461

1966 Rambler Ambassador—$2,648

1960 Edsel (that's right, Edsel)—$3,636

1960 Ford Fairlane—$3,843

1969 Buick LeSabre—$4,107

20

Cars! Cars!

1962 Chevrolet Bel Air—$2,750

1967 Oldsmobile 4-4-2—$3,426

1968 Chevrolet Caprice—$3,561

1969 Plymouth Fury—$3,095

1969 Pontiac LeMans—$3,301

1969 Pontiac Bonneville—$4,421

1968 Pontiac Tempest—$2,799

1968 Buick GS 350—$4,255

1962 Chevrolet Impala—$2,850

1963 Chevrolet Impala—$3,849

1964 Oldsmobile Vista Cruiser—$3,595

1968 Buick Electra—$4,330

1967 Pontiac Grand Prix—$4,321

21

Died in the Sixties

1960 Chrysler Imperial

Fins Are Finished

Fins first appeared on Cadillacs in 1948, but hit their high point in 1957 when Chrysler introduced the "Forward Look"—large, upswept fins, as "high as a driver's eye," dripping with chrome. The look caught the public mood perfectly. It was modern—almost futuristic ("Suddenly it's 1960" said Plymouth ads), and it was a good way to show off. Cars were America's number-one status symbol, and people in cars with enormous fins had more status than anyone. Carmakers planned the gaudiest, most conspicuous automobiles in history.

But in 1958 something happened. Public taste seemed to change overnight. One theory: The success of the first Russian satellite, Sputnik, in 1957 made Americans painfully aware that their priorities were screwed up. While they worried about having the fanciest cars on the block, the Russians were pioneering in space. Fins became an embarrassment, and car sales dropped drastically.

In a panic, Ford and GM revised their designs, incorporating the clean, austere lines that the public seemed to want. By 1961, fins had almost completely disappeared from their cars.

But not from Chrysler's. That was a different story . . .

1960 Chrysler New Yorker

The Chrysler Story

While Ford and GM were employing emergency measures to restyle their automobiles, Chrysler kept on producing cars with fins. Chrysler's design department, still headed by the "father of fins," Virgil Exner, was committed to producing cars with "classic lines." Maybe cars with fins were classic, but nobody wanted them. It was an incredible marketing blunder that turned off customers and demoralized dealers.

Great Moments of the 60s

Khrushchev on Fins

On a visit to the United States, Soviet premier Nikita Khrushchev derided American automobiles by placing his hand on a Cadillac tail fin and asking, with seeming innocence, "What does this thing do?"

1960 Buick LeSabre

1960 Dodge Dart

1960 DeSoto Adventurer

De Endo' DeSoto

November 18, 1960—Chrysler announced that after thirty-two years of production, the DeSoto had reached the end of the line. The announcement took place about a month after the 1961 DeSotos had been introduced—3,034 of the 1961 models had already been made (whatever happened to them?). Advertising billboards had to be taken down, and the DeSoto exhibit at the Pittsburgh Motor Show was closed the same day.

1960 Chevrolet Bel Air Sport Coupe

Valiant—Designed by the "father of fins," Virgil Exner—Cost: $2,053

Essentially a full-size Ford reduced to compact size. The most successful of all compacts, with 460,000 sold in the first year—but surveys showed that most people who bought Falcons would have bought Fords anyway. Phased out, 1969. 1962 Ford Falcon—Cost: $1,985

The first American compact 1960 Rambler American—Cost: $1,929

The first compact convertible. Gone by 1965. 1960 Studebaker Lark Regal—Cost: $2,267

1960 Pontiac Tempest—Cost: $2,248. It's hard to believe, but this car turned into the G.T.O.

THE COMPACT STORY

Part I: Let's Get Small

In light of the auto industry's troubles in the seventies and eighties, the story of compact cars is incredible. After all, who remembers that in 1960, major American manufacturers were already producing cars that got 30 mpg? It wasn't that they believed in cheap, fuel-efficient cars—they just couldn't ignore the fact that Americans were buying them.

Until 1959, the Big Three (Ford, GM, Chrysler) continually made bigger and more expensive cars, forcing anyone who wanted a small car to buy a Rambler or a European import. But in 1959, that amounted to 16 percent of all new car sales—a huge share of the market. So in self-defense, Detroit announced that for 1960, they would make "compact" cars, too ("small" had offensive connotations for Americans). Gas-efficient, low-priced compacts were a success; foreign car sales plummeted. That left the American market wide open for Detroit again.

Now comes the crazy part of the story. It's hard to say whether car-buyers demanded a change or automakers created the demand with advertising, but somehow compact cars got a little bigger and more luxurious each year. By 1965, "compacts" were practically as large as the full-size cars of ten years earlier.

1961 Buick Special, luxury compact—Cost: $2,358

The immortal "bug." While imports were going down, VW was going up. Volkswagen—Cost: $1,595

Part II: Kamikaze Carmakers

Meanwhile, the Japanese were building their auto industry, making small, cheap cars. And American manufacturers made the same mistake all over again. American compact cars had been phased out, so people who didn't want the expensive gas-guzzlers had to buy an import, giving Japanese and European carmakers over 10 percent of the American car market. Japanese car sales in America jumped from 6,000 in 1964, to 130,000 in 1968 . . . and they were growing!

So in 1969, a decade after they introduced their first small car, Ford had to bring out a small car again. For the same reasons. It was called the Maverick, and it was the first of a group of cars that the Big Three depended on for their comeback. But this time, they couldn't shake the imports out of the market. While they had spent the sixties making big cars, the Japanese had developed an ability to build small, low-priced cars that the American public kept buying.

Maverick—The "Saviour"

Flop of the Decade

Corvair

The Corvair was *the* bomb of the auto industry in the sixties. It caused more problems and created more controversy for GM than all of its other cars put together. Yet today it still has a fanatical following and is one of the prized cars of the sixties. Here are some highlights of its colorful ten-year history:

• It was the first air-cooled, rear-engine car ever produced in America. At the beginning, that meant a whole new set of mechanical troubles. "The Corvair is the perfect economy car," said a newsmagazine in 1960. "It never starts."

• Its odd "coming and going" look was too strange for American mass taste. It sold less than half of what Ford's compact, the Falcon, sold in 1960. Its future was precarious.

• In 1960, a lucky accident saved the Corvair and helped its inventor become president of GM. He customized a Corvair for his daughter, adding bucket seats and other sporty extras. Then on a whim he took it to a Chicago auto show. He was overwhelmed by the favorable reaction. Monza, the first car to cash in on the sixties formula for success—sex and youth appeal—was born. It made a lot of money for GM.

• In 1965, Ralph Nader's *Unsafe at Any Speed* used Corvair as an example of deathtrap cars. He said that a sharp turn might make it flip over. According to GM, that problem had been eliminated in 1964, but the unfavorable publicity made Corvair a dead issue.

• The Corvair was put to its final rest in

The Immortal Corvair

1969. Only three thousand were produced that year. The last one ever made was colored Olympia Gold and remains on display in the GM archives.

THUNDERBIRD: The Personal Luxury Car

1963 T-Bird

The Thunderbird was so popular that in 1961, when President-elect John F. Kennedy requested twenty-five of them for his inaugural parade, Ford had none to supply—they were sold out! And none of the buyers would relinquish his claim to a new T-Bird. (After some desperate juggling, Ford finally had to ask some of its customers to wait until after the inauguration for delivery.)

For a while, Ford had the profitable "personal luxury" field to itself, but only because none of its competitors could figure out exactly why people bought the Thunderbird. It was not a practical car—it was a gas-guzzler that could barely fit four people and almost no luggage. It was not a performance vehicle, despite the illusion created by the many dials on the dashboard.

But what the Thunderbird offered was status. It had originally been marketed as a "prestige sports car." Now, as a full-size vehicle, it was filled with unnecessary options, gadgets, and touches that suggested luxury. It made the owner feel successful. And better yet, it made his neighbors think he was successful.

It was a car to park proudly in a suburban driveway. It was the perfect image of suburban success.

THE CHALLENGERS

Avanti

A shockingly avant-garde car in 1962, Avanti was years ahead of its time. Its body was fiberglass, dashboard controls were overhead like an airplane cockpit, and there was no grille or fins. It was designed under the auspices of famous industrial designer Raymond Loewy as Studebaker's last effort to save its ailing auto division.

Riviera

Originally scheduled as Cadillac's "luxury compact," it was transformed into a Buick in 1962 and given a single mission: destroy Thunderbird. Its designer was aiming for a cross between the Ferrari and the elegant Rolls-Royce. A measure of his success: It was one of the most popular American cars in Europe. Riviera was a success in America, too, from the moment it appeared.

Toronado

Toronado represented the cutting edge of technology, and it looked the part. Modern, sleek . . . obviously the latest! It was the first front-wheel drive American car since the Cord of the 1930s. It began as a project called the "Red Car" that so excited Olds executives that they gave it their support even before a model was built. *Motor Trend's* Car of the Year, 1966.

MUSTANG
The Car of the Decade

Enter the Mustang, the car for the young, the automobile that showed Detroit *the simple truth of the sixties:* Everyone wanted to look young. Mustang was not only a new type of car, but *the* new type of car. Here is Lee Iacocca with his creation.

The Inside Story: Secret Project T-5

Mustang was the pet project of Ford General Manager Lee Iacocca, who, the story goes, kept notes on new car ideas in a little black book. Based on letters from car buffs who wanted a car like the 1955 T-Bird, Iacocca felt there was a market for a new "personal sports car" waiting to be developed. Research showed that the population was getting younger, and that young people bought more cars per capita than any other segment of the population.

Based on these findings, and Iacocca's instinct, Ford decided to create a car that was sporty yet low-priced, so young people and middle-income groups could afford it. It also had to be capable of taking enough options to make it a luxury car. The new project was dubbed "T-5." Ford engineers and designers worked under maximum security in a windowless room, known as the "Tomb." Even the wastepaper had to be burned under supervision. Over a three-year period they came up with many two-seat prototypes—XT-Bird, Median, Mina, Allegro, Aventura, and Mustang I (loved by car enthusiasts, but considered too

sporty by Iacocca)—but all were scrapped in favor of a four-seat model with a large trunk. It was completed in spring 1963.

It was designed to be versatile. The buyer had options: two different engines, air conditioning, whitewalls, power disc brakes, racing hubcaps, sports console, and on and on. Dr. Seymour Marshak, Ford's market research manager, said of the Mustang's option package, "That flexibility makes this car the greatest thing since the erector set."

Since Ford figured the T-5's market was the young sports car buyer, the name "Torino" was chosen because it sounded like an Italian sports car. The projected ad campaign called it "the new import . . . from Detroit." But last-minute market research showed that this car could appeal to *all* buyers, and a new name had to be chosen. Colt, Bronco, and Maverick (all used for later cars) were considered. But "Mustang" seemed best for T-5, bringing to mind cowboys, adventure, and the Wild West. As one Ford man put it, "It had the excitement of the wide-open spaces, and it was American as all hell."

Great Moments of the 60s

April 17, 1964: The Mustang Arrives, and America Runs Wild

• Mustang is the pace car for a stock car race in Huntsville, Alabama. When it drives onto the track, thousands of people scale the retaining wall to get a better look at it. The race is delayed for over an hour.

• The Hollywood jet set crowds into their local Ford showroom to see the Mustang. This group, owners of the world's most expensive cars, calls the car "glamorous." By the end of the day, Frank Sinatra and Debbie Reynolds are among the luminaries who've ordered Mustangs.

• A cement truck crashes through the plate-glass window of a Seattle Ford dealer when the driver loses control of his vehicle. The reason: He is staring at the new Mustangs on display there. They look "like some of them expensive Italian racers," he explains.

• A Chicago Ford dealer is forced to lock the doors of his showroom models because too many people are trying to get into them at the same time.

• A dealer puts a new Mustang on a lift to show a prospective customer the underside of the vehicle. By the time his demonstration is over, the showroom is filled with people, and he has to leave the Mustang up in the air for the rest of the day.

• A New Jersey Ford dealer has only one Mustang and fifteen eager buyers, so he auctions it off. The winner of the auction insists on sleeping in the car to be sure the dealer doesn't sell it out from under him before his check clears.

• Over 4 million people visit the 6,500 Ford dealers across the country, purchasing some 22,542 Mustangs.

• A record 100,000 Mustangs are sold in the first three months of production. Ford's "young people's" car turns out to be an "everyone's" car.

TWO MUSTANGS THAT NEVER WERE

Two designs that Ford considered on their way to the Mustang: Aventura and Allegro (right).

A PRODUCT OF *Ford*

THE TOTAL PERFORMANCE MUSTANG HARDTOP

If they're still waiting for Agnes down at the Willow Lane Whist and Discussion Group, they'll wait a long time. Agnes hasn't been herself since she got her Mustang hardtop (with its racy lines, bucket seats, smooth, optional 3-speed automatic transmission and fire-eating 200 cu. in. Six). Mustang is more car than Willow Lane has seen since the last Stutz Bearcat bit the dust. (And Agnes has a whole new set of hobbies, none of which involves cards.) Why don't you find out if there's any truth in the rumor–Mustangers have more fun?

Best year yet to go Ford
MUSTANG!
MUSTANG!
MUSTANG!

29

INSPIRED BY MUSTANG'S SUCCESS

Firebird. John Delorean, head of Pontiac, announced the Firebird as "the Pontiac of the personal sports car field." Interpretation: A GM car designed to attract the young buyers who were turned on by Pontiac's image as a maker of "macho, high-performance machines." Firebird was originally scheduled to be named the Banshee. The press releases were out, the initial announcements had been made, and then someone at Pontiac discovered that a banshee is "a supernatural being whose wailing foretells death." That, of course, would have been a disaster. It would have been like calling a car "the Grim Reaper." Who would dare buy it? The name was changed and like everything else Pontiac did in the sixties, it was immediately successful. It outsold Cougar and moved into the number-three spot behind Mustang and Camaro after only three months on the market.

Camaro. What, exactly, was "Camaro" supposed to mean? According to GM, it meant "pal" in French, a fitting name because "the real mission of our automobile is to be a close companion to its owner." But that was nonsense. A French auto executive pointed out: "It doesn't mean anything in English, and it doesn't mean anything in French either." Actually, it reflected confusion. The original name of the car was to be Panther, but GM was in the middle of its problems with Ralph Nader and shied away from "offending him" with aggressive names. They were sorry—the unexciting name was blamed for slow sales.

Barracuda. When news first leaked out that Chrysler planned to offer a car called the "Barracuda," they were flooded with requests for pictures. But they didn't want anyone to know what the car would look like yet, so they answered each letter with a photograph—of the fish. The first Barracuda in 1965 was a Valiant with a fastback roof. It was a loser, with less than a tenth of Mustang's sales. But by 1967 Chrysler had time to rework the car into a masterpiece.

Here's what American Motors said: "How to tell Marlin '66 from any other fastback. Put your family in it." Here's what the American public said: You put *your* family in it. If we want a family car, we'll buy a Chevrolet. A total bomb.

AMX. American Motors high performance car. A real comeback from the Marlin.

Cougar. "Untamed elegance! That's Cougar—an entirely new kind of road animal from Mercury." Translation: If you want a Mustang, but can afford something more expensive, this is for you.

MUSCLE CARS

1965 GTO

The Origin of the GTO

In the mid-fifties, when America was into cars with pizzaz, Pontiac had a reputation as a "grandmother's car"—reliable and DULL. Pontiac was not a hot item.

Solution: Change the image. Pontiac got rid of its old emblem, an Indian called Chief Pontiac; they widened the car and called it a "wide-track"; and they raced in stock car races. No "grandmother's car" could win races the way new "wide-tracking" Pontiacs could. Sales took off.

Then, out of the blue, in 1963, GM's top brass decided they didn't want GM cars racing anymore and they issued an edict prohibiting any of their divisions from participating in races. Pontiac people were furious. They felt they *had* to have racing to maintain their image!

Enter Jim Wangers, who ran Pontiac's ad campaign. He loved cars, he loved racing, and he knew a lot of tricks. His idea: Put a big engine in a standard car and offer it as an option instead of calling it a new model. That way, Pontiac wouldn't have to get GM's approval, but they'd still have a racing machine that could blow any American car off the road. So in 1964, a group of options that made up the LeMans GTO was listed in small print on the Pontiac's option sheet. It was America's first muscle car.

Here's how the public found out about it: Wangers convinced *Car and Driver* magazine to run a test-drive comparison between the world-famous Ferrari GTO and the Pontiac version. They did, and to everyone's surprise they rated the Pontiac favorably in a cover story. Overnight, Pontiac dealers—who hadn't even known the GTO existed—began clamoring for it. GM had to go along with it —they couldn't very well admit that they had never heard of the car. Soon other GM divisions demanded and got powerful cars and the muscle car became part of automotive history.

G.T.O.

words & music by
JOHN WILKIN

as recorded by
RONNY & *the datonas*
ON
mala records

1968 Plymouth
Road Runner

1969
Dodge Charger

1969 Firebird
Trans-Am

1969 GTO

31

LUXURY CARS

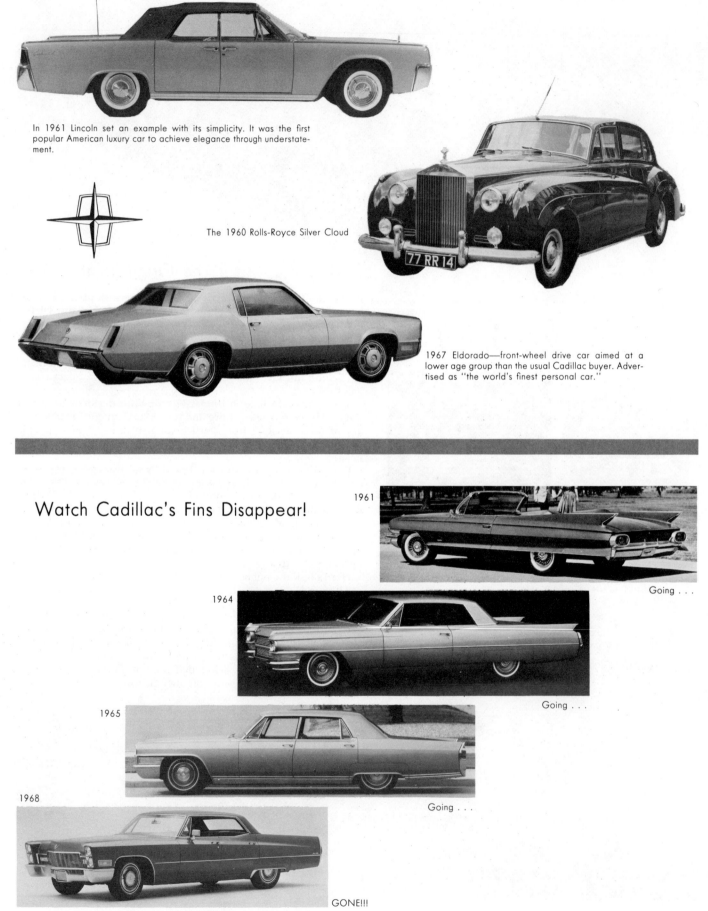

In 1961 Lincoln set an example with its simplicity. It was the first popular American luxury car to achieve elegance through understatement.

The 1960 Rolls-Royce Silver Cloud

1967 Eldorado—front-wheel drive car aimed at a lower age group than the usual Cadillac buyer. Advertised as "the world's finest personal car."

Watch Cadillac's Fins Disappear!

1961

Going . . .

1964

Going . . .

1965

Going . . .

1968

GONE!!!

Cadillac

THE CADILLAC "V" AND CREST interpreted in Diamonds and Platinum BY CARTIER

Maybe this could be your "someday"!

Most people say that someday—if events keep pace with their dreams—they hope to own a Cadillac car. And among these are many who do not yet realize that Cadillac has become for them a present-day practicality. For Cadillac's economies have never been more real—or more convincing—than they are during the current year. The initial cost represents a sounder investment than ever in terms of value-received. The car's operation is practical almost beyond belief—and, as always, it is in a class of its own as far as resale is concerned. Isn't it time you found out how close these facts bring *you* to the car of your dreams? Then we urge you to visit your Cadillac dealer—take a demonstration drive—and hear the 1960 story for yourself.

CADILLAC MOTOR CAR DIVISION • GENERAL MOTORS CORPORATION

CARS OF THE STARS

Sonny and Cher's "His and Hers" Mustangs

Zsa Zsa Gabor's $150,000 gold-plated Rolls-Royce

Bob Hope's Golf Kart

John Lennon's Rolls-Royce

The Green Hornet's car, The Black Beauty

The Munsters' Cars

If you wanted an extraordinary car and could afford the best, where would you go? To George Barris (shown here with one of his better-known creations, the Batmobile). Barris has built and designed more unique cars than anyone else in his field. He is truly the master of the custom car. In fact, all of the cars on these pages (except Lennon's) are by Barris.

SEXY! SEXY! SEXY!: Sports Cars of the Sixties

Mercedes-Benz 300SL "Gullwing"

MGA

Sunbeam Tiger

Volvo P-1800 D

Renault Caravelle

Austin Healy Sprite

Porsche 911 L

1962 Chevrolet Corvette

Jaguar XKE

Ferrari 242

UNUSUAL CARS

The Amphicar

Somebody got the idea that there might be a use for a combination boat and car, and proved it could be done. They built it with a sealed engine that could be immersed in water, and gave it propellers in the back that were activated by flipping a switch. You could drive it right off a dock and into the water. A great idea. Unfortunately, that's all it was. It needed costly special maintenance; it wasn't a great boat (it couldn't move very fast because the wheels dragged it along—it did something like five miles an hour) and it wasn't a great car. As the editor of *Car and Driver* magazine said, "they took the worst features of a car and the worst features of a boat and combined them into one extraordinary vehicle."

The Isetta

If you had been able to find one, it would have been at your Buick dealer's. This strange-looking vehicle had four wheels, but the two rear ones were so close together they gave the impression that there were only three. It was an extraordinarily clever idea—an excellent urban design—but it was ahead of its time and out of place in a decade when people longed for luxury. Plus, the Isetta pigeonholed its owner as a nonconformist without Macho. No speed. No power. No sex. On the highway, the Isetta was fragile—a huge semi passing it could make the car pitch dangerously—and its short wheelbase gave it a bumpy ride.

Chrysler "Perfects" the Jet Engine for Cars

Chrysler's reputation for kamikaze projects was offset enough by their reputation for engineering excellence that no one was really sure whether or not to believe that they were close to perfecting the jet engine for cars, as they declared in the early sixties. True, GM and Ford had given up on the project, but . . . anything was possible.

To prove their point, Chrysler announced in 1963 that they were going to produce fifty hand-tooled turbine-engine cars, and lease them to two hundred families over a two-year period. From this project, they said, they would learn enough to refine the engine and make it available to the public within five years. So in November 1963, the first turbine-powered car was driven from the Chrysler plant by Richard Vlaha, a twenty-four-year-old Chicago engineer. The car attracted attention on the street—Chrysler engineers left the whine in the jet engine untouched, believing that some day it would be a status symbol.

The project was carried out according to plan, and it was a great publicity gimmick that got extensive press coverage. Unfortunately, the car wasn't economical. Too bad.

The Comuta

The 1960s electric car that Ford thought would be on the market by now. When the government started cracking down on automobile pollution, everyone thought that electric cars were the logical next alternative. General Electric, Westinghouse, and others began experimenting furiously, trying to come up with a battery that was feasible. They all predicted it was just a matter of seven to ten years until electric cars were common. Wouldn't that have been nice.

REMEMBER THESE ... ?

Great Moments of the 60s
Pollution Solution

In 1965, Albert Verley and Co., of New Jersey, announced a new product aimed at alleviating the growing smog problem created by bus and truck exhaust. It was something you added to the fuel called Malabate PR105. It was an interesting way of dealing with pollution—make it smell good. It supposedly made exhaust smell like talcum powder. It never caught on.

A 1960 promotional giveaway—a post-card-size puzzle featuring a 1960 Chevy.

— NARROW TRACK
— PONTIAC'S WIDER TRACK

JOIN THE DODGE REBELLION

Dullsville falls.

Dodge Coronet rises.

Check out those prices: 32.9¢ for regular, 34.9¢ for "plus," and 36.9¢ for "extra." And no no-lead.

A Twiggy Thermos

A Twiggy thermos

A Twiggy biography

A Twiggy Colorforms set

The Inside Story:
The Origin of Twiggy

Lesley Hornby left school at fifteen (1965) and went to work in a hair salon. She met Nigel Davies (who later changed his name to Justin de Villeneuve) and told him of her dream of becoming a model. Justin, twenty-five, promoted her and worked at getting her named "Girl of the Year" by the *London Daily Express.* He remade her by having her hair cut very short, like a boy, and having it streaked "the color of lemon squash." She weighed only ninety-one pounds with a boyish 31-23-32 figure, so, for the final touch, de Villeneuve changed her name. "Skinny as you are, like a twig," he said, "I'll call you Twiggy."

What People Said about . . . Twiggy (1967)

HER MANAGER: "I think on American teenagers she'll have the same effect as the Beatles. She's sort of a mini-queen of the new social aristocracy in England and I feel that as the Beatles come across, Twiggy will have the same meaning."

BARBARA THORBAHN (vice-president of Stewart Models): "The whole world wants to do a story on Twiggy. There's been nothing out of England like this since the Beatles and the Stones."

NEW YORK TIMES: "Looks like your next-door neighbor, if he happens to be a skinny twelve-year-old boy."

BRITISH VOGUE: "She's exactly the right look at the right time."

NEWSWEEK: "Seventeen and starved."

TWIGGY: "I'm a bit of a freak, but I can't spend my life crying about it."

VOGUE: "She is the mini-girl in the mini-era. She's youth and freshness."

MARSHALL MCLUHAN: "Her power is incompleteness."

WOMEN'S WEAR DAILY: "It's all a massive publicity stunt."

CECIL BEATON: "Today's look comes from below. The working-class girl with money in her pocket can be as chic as the deb. That's what Twiggy is all about."

PRISCILLA PECK (of *Vogue*): "It's history. It's a revelation. The skull . . . lots of things." (Describing Twiggy's first haircut.)

SEVENTEEN: "It's like watching poetry. She's Harlow, Garbo, and all kinds of people."

LOOK: "Is it a girl? Is it a boy? No, it's Twiggy."

TWIGGY: "I am five feet six and terribly thin. It's not really wot you call a figger, is it? I have two thin sticks, quite comic for legs. My eyes are very large, and my nose is freckled."

A Skinny Twiggy ballpoint pen

The First Man in Space

On April 12, 1961, one of man's impossible dreams was realized: After centuries of fantasizing, we finally had a *real* spaceman! Yuri Gagarin, a twenty-seven-year-old Russian test pilot orbited the earth, becoming the first man in history to see our planet.

His 108-minute flight for the Soviet Union made him a worldwide hero. But he returned to testing new aircraft and was killed in a plane crash in 1968. He did not live to see man walk on the moon.

The Inside Story:

How They Picked the Astronauts

President Eisenhower decided that the first spacemen had to be military pilots. Several conditions had to be met before a pilot could qualify: He had to be younger than forty, under 5 feet 11 (the capsule couldn't take a bigger man), in perfect physical shape, and an expert jet pilot with over 1,500 hours of flying time.

In 1959, NASA found 110 men who satisfied their standards. Of these, fifty-six were picked to travel to Washington for interviews. After intelligence and physical tests, the number of qualified candidates was reduced to seven. Though NASA was originally looking for six, they took all seven.

But what would the pilots be called? To stimulate the public's imagination, NASA wanted a romantic name that would suggest daring, dedication, and heroism. So they created the term "astronaut," inspired by the Argonauts—a legendary band of Greek soldiers who sought and captured the Golden Fleece—and by the "aeronauts," pioneers of balloon travel.

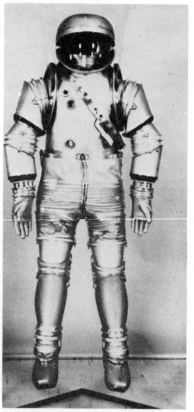

Suit of armor, circa 1964

Great Moments of the 60s

In Ankara, Turkey, farmers marched to the American and Soviet embassies and demanded compensation for flood damage to their crops. The floods, they charged, were caused by Russian and American spaceships, which had torn "holes in the sky." The Russian ambassador suggested that if they really thought there was a hole in the sky, they should be trying to figure out how to fix it, not complaining to him about it.

Telstar

Telstar was a satellite that revolutionized transcontinental broadcasting. It was also the inspiration for a song by an English group called the Tornadoes. This instrumental was better known to many young people than the satellite—the record sold 5 million copies in 1962.

Space Race

Tang was chosen for the Gemini astronauts

...and for the Ryans.

On every American space flight since Gemini IV, the astronauts drank Tang. Tang is the instant breakfast drink that Mrs. Ryan and Mrs. Turner and Mrs. Moore have used for years. Tang has more vitamins C and A than any orange juice you can buy. With natural orange flavor, Tang...chosen for NASA's Gemini Astronauts. Why not choose it for your family, too?

The NEW FRONTIER
MAN of the YEAR
Astronaut John Glenn

60S! HALL OF FAME
John Glenn

• John Glenn was the first American to orbit the earth (February 20, 1962).

• He was America's biggest hero since Lindbergh. He received 85,000 letters and telegrams in six months, and addressed a joint session of Congress to a standing ovation. He said he took "honest pride in his great achievements," but modestly added that his role was only one small part of a big program.

• Despite two handicaps as a candidate for Project Mercury—he had no college degree and was thirty-seven years old—he became an astronaut through sheer determination and perseverance.

• He was cool. At lift-off his pulse rate was 110 beats per minute, as compared to Shepard's 139 and Grissom's 170 at lift-off (60–70 is normal).

• He became a good friend of John Kennedy and decided to enter politics when Kennedy was shot. But running for U.S. Senate from Ohio in 1964, he slipped and fell in the bathtub, severely injuring himself, and had to withdraw from the race.

Suit of armor, circa 1464

TOP TEN
Products from Space

(Ten things you wouldn't have without NASA)

1. Freeze-dried foods
2. Solar collectors for solar heating
3. Cordless electric hedge trimmers
4. Airline instant reservation systems
5. Video games
6. Pocket calculators
7. Corningware
8. Rechargeable electric pacemakers
9. Live TV from other countries
10. Aerial photos on TV weather reports

BUITONI
SPACE MEN
20% Protein Enriched
MACARONI
Highest in Protein
Lowest in Starch

National Obsession No. 5

Heeere She Comes . . .

Beauty contests are as American as apple pie. Over five thousand times a year in the sixties, young ladies competed for such titles as Miss Universe, Miss America, Mrs. America, Little Miss America, Miss Reingold, Miss Gum Spirits of Turpentine, Miss Enriched Corn Meal, Miss Frankfurter, Miss Watermelon, Maid of Cotton, National College Queen, Miss Polish America, Miss Connecticut Sweater Girl, Miss Don't Rock the Boat, and Miss American Secretary.

Beauty contests didn't make it through the sixties unscathed; they lost some of their magic when feminist groups charged them with exploiting women, and black groups charged them with racism. But the majority of their audience kept applauding as they paraded through the decade.

Beauty Contest of the Decade

The Sixties Album salutes the National College Queen Pageant, a little-known beauty contest that awarded some lucky college girl a title, prizes, and a little fame for excelling in the most mundane activities imaginable. "We are idealizing the well-rounded average," explained the show's promoter in 1962.

Here are some of the events in which contestants had to compete:

• Blouse-ironing

• Cooking hamburgers

• "Doodling designs with colored inks on electric blankets" (How did they ever think *that* one up?)

• Carrying coffee cups and pots across a room to the judges' table and pouring (to evaluate "skill and poise as a hostess")

• Sandal decoration

• A fierce debate on "right and wrong hairstyles"

1960—Lynda Mead   Mississippi

1961—Nancy Fleming   Michigan

Who's that coming out of the water? Why, it's Miss American Secretary! Sure she's proud, but does she have to go *everywhere* holding that banner?

1962—Maria Fletcher   N. Carolina

1963—Jacquelyn Mayer   Ohio

1964—Donna Axum   Arkansas

1965—Vonda Kay Van Dyke   Ariz.

Beauty Contests Build Character in Young Women.

They teach:

• *The value of high moral standards.* During the 1965 Miss USA contest, the judges asked Miss Ohio, Sue Ann Downey, this question: "If you saw a friend cheating on a test, would you report it?" Her answer: "No. If they want to cheat, that's their business, but I couldn't do it myself." She was selected Miss USA.

• *The importance of taking a stand on social issues.* When a reporter asked Debbie Bryant, Miss America 1966, what she thought about the fact that there were no black women in the Miss America contest, the director of the Miss America contest abruptly ended the press conference. "She shouldn't have to answer a question about a national problem," the director said; "she's not the president."

• *Good nutrition.* The Armour Meat Co. sponsored the Miss Teenage America contest to try to get teenage girls to eat hot dogs instead of pizza.

• *To be well-rounded, relying on more than just good looks.* In Cairo, Egypt, in 1960, when the rules of a beauty contest were changed so the winner was going to be selected on the basis of brains instead of beauty, twenty-three of the twenty-five contestants dropped out. "Men are scared of brainy girls anyway," said one of the former contestants.

• *How to win gracefully and honestly.* When judges in a Nottingham, England, beauty contest announced that Nancy Harwood had won second prize, she burst out laughing and in a distinctly male voice announced that *she* was really a *he* named Nigel Harwood (a college student, of course). Then Nigel/Nancy ran off the stage, "shaking with laughter." Under the circumstances, judges awarded second prize to someone else.

1963—Six-year-old Christine Anne Morgan won the title of Little Miss America at Palisades Amusement Park in New Jersey, over seventy-six other beauties between the ages of four through eight years of age. She had blond hair, blue eyes, stood four feet tall and weighed fifty-five pounds. Contestants were judged on the basis of "beauty of face, figure *(FIGURE!??),* charm, poise, and personality."

1966—Debora Bryant   Kansas

1967—Jayne Jaroe   Oklahoma

1968—Debra Barnes   Kansas

1969—Judi Ford   Illinois

2 Glued

UNBELIEVABLE TV SHOWS # 1 AND 2

"The Patty Duke Show"

Now here's something you don't see every day—identical cousins. ("They laugh alike, they walk alike, at times they even talk alike.") Sure it's a genetic miracle, but what the hell . . . it's just for laughs.

"My Mother the Car"

Your mother the what? Dave Crabtree, a small-town lawyer in search of a second-hand family car, stumbled on a 1928 Porter. But this was no ordinary 1928 Porter. It was his mother reincarnated (and her voice came through the radio). This has to be the most ridiculous premise for a TV show ever.

to the Tube

TV Facts

The Saga of Arnold Zenker. On March 29, 1967, when Walter Cronkite went on strike with the rest of the television actors, CBS was forced to fill his anchor spot with one of their executives. They auditioned seven men for the spot, but all of them seemed too tense. Finally in desperation, they picked their twenty-eight-year-old manager of programming, Arnold Zenker, without an audition, because he had looked calm on a local newscast that morning. For no apparent reason, he was an overnight smash. He received three thousand fan letters. He was so popular that when Cronkite returned in April he opened his first show with: "Good evening. This is Walter Cronkite, sitting in for Arnold Zenker." "Bring back Zenker" buttons could be seen in TV studios for a while, but the novelty gradually wore off. Zenker, however, was still in shock. "There's nothing like breaking in on the Cronkite show," he said.

"Hazel"

In this show, based on the cartoon by Ted Key, Dorothy Baxter couldn't imagine what she would do without her housekeeper/maid, Hazel. But her husband, Mr. B., a wealthy corporate lawyer who had to relinquish control of his home to Hazel, had plenty of ideas. ("I warn you, Dorothy, I'm the head of this house and if that woman doesn't bring me six pancakes she'll be fired!")

"Now a Word from Our Sponsor"

Excedrin Headache No. 45, The Family Car (on the way home from the beach).

HARRIED FATHER: "Listen, could you get the kids to deflate that dolphin? It's sticking right in my neck."

MOTHER: "Pull the thing out of the fish, will you, darling?"

FATHER: "It must be six feet long, just pull the pluggy out, that's all."

MOTHER: "Pull the plug . . . there it goes, all around the . . . oh . . . it's gone."

FATHER: "Will you please keep the kids quiet?"

MOTHER: "Mildred threw your glasses out."

FATHER: "My sunglasses?!!"

MOTHER: "Yes, and Georgie has to go to the bathroom. . . ."

A 60S! CLASSIC

"Bonanza"

In the sixties, the old shoot-em-up westerns became stories about ranchers. "Bonanza," the best example, was the saga of an unbelievably rich, unbelievably down-to-earth family—the Cartwrights: Ben Cartwright, known as Pa, who followed his dreams to the Ponderosa, where he raised his three boys alone (and raised them straight and true); Little Joe, the youngest brother, peppy and playful, but tougher than he looked, always came through in a pinch; Hoss, the giant with a heart of gold; and Adam, the oldest, trying to follow in his father's footsteps.

"Bonanza" and the Cartwrights were an American dream. They played fair and they worked hard. They were humble, they went to church, and yet, they had a sense of humor (except Pa, who liked a good laugh, but never got into any mischief). They were kind to strangers. They stood up for the underdog, they cared about people. And they were filthy rich.

Strangely enough, there were hardly ever any women around the Ponderosa, and never on a permanent basis. Maybe that was part of this American dream too. But somebody had to do the housework; so there was Hop Sing, the Chinese houseboy and cook. And in case you're wondering what happened to Ma Cartwright, she died a long time ago. She was killed by Indians, or a plague, or something. She must have been a wonderful woman.

60s selects

Twelve Forgettable Westerns

1. "Frontier Circus"

2. "The Westerner"

3. "The Outlaws"

4. "Wide Country"

5. "Redigo"

6. "The Legend of Jesse James"

7. "The Loner"

8. "Cowboy in Africa"

9. "The Legend of Custer"

10. "The Guns of Will Sonnet"

11. "Hondo"

12. "Outcasts"

James Drury played the mysterious cowboy known as "The Virginian."

A 60S! CLASSIC

"Wagon Train"

Each season, Major Seth Adams, wagon master (later replaced by Chris Hale, wagon master), Bill Hawks (lead wagon driver), Flint McCullough (frontier scout), and Charlie Wooster (cook) led the California-bound wagon train and its passengers across the open desert, Indian-ravaged Great Plains, and treacherous Rocky Mountains to the promise of the West. You'd figure that in eight years on the air they would have made it to California at least once. Oh well.

TV Facts

Westerns, which once dominated television, were headed for Boot Hill in the sixties. In the 1959–60 season, thirteen westerns were introduced, but only four made it to the next year. There were five westerns introduced the following season (for a total of twenty-two on the air), but one had been "shot daid" by December. Only long-established series like "Gunsmoke" and "Wagon Train" did well. In 1961–62 there was not a single new prime-time western. And the number on the air dropped to thirteen. By 1969, there were only five westerns on television, two of them ("Bonanza" and "Gunsmoke") left over from the fifties.

"Bonanza" was so popular that people often refused to believe that the Ponderosa was fictional. To accommodate them, a special tour was set up near Lake Tahoe, where outdoor scenes for "Bonanza" were filmed. Guides brought tourists to an anonymous old shack in the Lake Tahoe area and told them that this was the "real" Ponderosa.

A 60S! CLASSIC   "Gunsmoke"

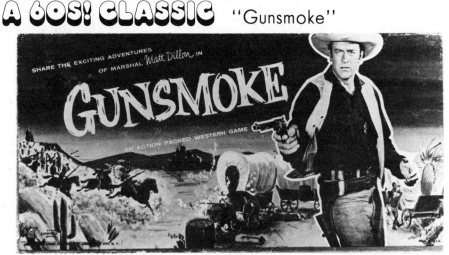

The last of a dying breed. Matt Dillon, marshal of Dodge City, was the strong silent type—a symbol of virtue and justice, with a warm spot in his heart for Miss Kitty. (But that's the only spot that ever got warm —no sex in *this* show.) "Gunsmoke" had all the elements of the standard western: wacky sidekicks (Chester and Festus); a kindly village doctor (named Doc, of course); and a weekly gunfight. This show was so popular that in 1962 it was the year's number-three show in its regular time slot, and the number-eighteen show as a rerun called "Matt Dillon, U.S. Marshal."

Good Guys Don't Always Wear White

Richard Boone played Paladin on "Have Gun, Will Travel."

Hey! That's Fess Parker in the coonskin cap—isn't he Davy Crockett? Nope, this is the sixties, so he must be Daniel Boone.

TV Facts

• The "Laugh-In" line "Look that up in your Funk and Wagnall's" was responsible for raising Funk and Wagnall's dictionary sales by 20 percent. They used it as an advertising slogan.

• The first national TV ad for a product directed exclusively at blacks was, in 1968, for Raveen Au Naturelle and Duke Natural, hair products.

• A lady came on "Let's Make a Deal" dressed as a little girl holding a baby bottle. Monty Hall took away her bottle and said, "All right, for two hundred dollars, show me another nipple."

UNBELIEVABLE TV SHOW #3
"F Troop"

Captain Wilton Parmenter was the perfect leader for the bunch of incompetents who made up F Troop. Parmenter had accidentally won a major victory for the Union army (by sneezing—which sounded like CHARGE!) in the last months of the Civil War. He was rewarded with a job as commanding officer of Fort Courage. He tried to be a model soldier, but Parmenter was so preoccupied with trying not to stab his own foot and escaping his aggressive girl friend, Wrangler Jane, that he never noticed that wheeler-dealer Sergeant O'Rourke and his assistant, Corporal Agarn, had secretly negotiated a private treaty with Chief Wild Eagle and the Hekawi ("where the heck-ah-we") Indians for an exclusive franchise selling souvenirs to tourists.

SITCOM OF THE CENTURY

"The Beverly Hillbillies"

Jed Clampett, a hillbilly from the Ozark Mountains, was hunting one day and accidentally discovered oil on his land . . . $25 million worth. So the Clampetts—Jed, Elly May, Granny, and Cousin Jethro Bodine—packed up their truck and they moved to Beverly . . . Hills, that is (swimmin' pools, movie stars). They became the Beverly Hillbillies, stars of one of the most popular shows in TV history. Why was it so popular? One critic suggested that "newly affluent Americans, bewildered by the technological sixties, see themselves as bumbling hillbillies lost in the suburbs. Just as dirty jokes relieve their anxieties about sex, hillbilly jokes release tensions about class, education, and status."

And besides, everyone likes corny jokes. For example, Granny called the billiard room the "fancy eatin' room." On special occasions, they ate at the pool table and passed dishes around with pool cues. Jed called the swimming pool the "see-ment pond" and longed to plant crops in the front lawn. "But," gasped Mr. Drysdale, the Clampetts' neighbor and banker, "this is Beverly Hills." Jed replied, "Dirt is dirt." Most critics were embarrassed by the show, but the public loved it.

UNBELIEVABLE TV SHOW #4

"Mr. Ed"

Carol and Wilbur Post bought a house in the country where they soon discovered from their neighbors, the Adisons, that the previous owners had left them a horse named Mr. Ed. And Mr. Ed had a hidden talent—he could talk. OK, a talking horse. But can he tap-dance?

UNBELIEVABLE TV SHOW #5

"I Dream of Jeannie"

Combine magic and space science and what do you get? An astronaut with his own personal genie. Astronaut Tony Nelson (a clean Boy Scout–type) seemed out of luck when his space mission aborted and he parachuted to a desert island. But he found a strange green bottle with a genie in it, and he was saved.

To make things a little more interesting, the genie was a beautiful, sexy girl who fell in love with him. Against Tony's wishes, she followed him to Florida,

A 60s! CLASSIC

"The Andy Griffith Show" and "Gomer Pyle, U.S.M.C."

Sheriff Andy Taylor, an easygoing widower with a young son, Opie, and his deputy, Barney Fife, shared the responsibility of keeping law and order in the small town of Mayberry, North Carolina. Mayberry was practically crime-free (except for Otis, the town drunk), so Andy and Barney spent their time at Floyd's Barbershop, settin' and jawin' with Goober, Floyd, and Howard, waitin' till Aunt Bea called them for dinner.

In 1964 Goober's cousin, Gomer, got his own TV show, "Gomer Pyle, U.S.M.C.," and the Marine Corps got a new image. Shazam! Betcha Gomer's gonna get in trouble with Sergeant Carter again! ("Pyle, you knucklehead . . . you lame-brain . . . do you realize how many regulations you've broken here?") Gollly! We was right!

moved in with him—strictly as a genie—and innocently turned his once-normal life into utter chaos with her powers.

It was a clever idea that managed to get a single man and a beautiful, unmarried woman who were living together onto prime-time TV—and a woman who would do anything the man asked her to, at that (she even called him master).

It lasted four years. Then, in 1969, they were married.

TV Trivia Questions

1. What show did Richard Nixon appear in on September 16, 1968, and what did he do on it?

2. In 1968, NBC canceled this show and received more complaining letters than ever before in its history. Name the show.

3. Where did Fred Flintstone work? What did he do there, and who was his boss?

4. What was the Farmer's Daughter's name? Who was her employer, and what did he do? How did she get the job?

5. Chuck Connors left baseball and starred in four different sixties TV series. What were they? Name them in chronological order.

Answers

1. "Rowan and Martin's Laugh-In." He said, "Sock it to me."

2. "The Monkees."

3. Slaterock Gravel Company. He ran a crane (dinosaur-powered). His boss was Mr. Slate.

4. Katy Holstrum. Congressman Glen Morley. While waiting for a government approval to work in the Congo, Katy stayed with the Morley family and was offered the job as governess.

5. "The Rifleman," "Arrest and Trial," "Branded," "Cowboy in Africa."

49

"Car 54, Where Are You?"

Officers Toody and Muldoon hand puppets

"Car 54" was the first situation comedy about cops. Officers Gunther ("Oo! Oo!") Toody and Francis Muldoon were lovable bumblers who patrolled one of New York City's toughest areas but never seemed to run into any serious crime.

A fascinating sidelight: The show was filmed on location in New York, and city officials were afraid that Car 54 might be mistaken for a real patrol car during the show's filming. So they painted the car red instead of green; on a black-and-white TV screen, viewers couldn't tell the difference.

"The FBI"

These adventures were based on real FBI cases. Each week Inspector Lew Erskine (Efrem Zimbalist, Jr.) and his G-men chased extortionists, counterfeiters, Communist spies, and radicals, keeping the world safe for democracy. The FBI was always portrayed in a favorable light.

At a time when cops were frequently under fire in the press, it's interesting that a show about the FBI could become so popular. It probably helped that J. Edgar Hoover gave his complete cooperation and personal endorsement to it.

"Dragnet"

In the sixties "Dragnet" (dum de dum dum), a popular show of the fifties, returned to TV as "Dragnet '67." Like the original show, episodes were based on cases taken from real police files in Los Angeles and presented with an air of realism ("just the facts, ma'am"). For the most part, stories used current issues, such as student dissidents and drug abuse, portraying young people as essentially good but misguided by some weird antiestablishment creeps. "Dragnet '67" was very popular among young people.

Relevant TV Show No. 1

"The Mod Squad"

"The Mod Squad" was proof that television knew how to "tell it like it is." Three hip disillusioned young people, "one white, one black, one blonde," who had bumped heads with the law, were recruited to form an especially unbelievable detail of undercover agents called the Mod Squad. Pete Cochran, the black sheep of a wealthy family, had been caught stealing a car; Linc Hayes had been arrested for looting during the Watts riots; and Julie Barnes had been picked up as a vagrant. Captain Adam Greer was their boss and the only one who knew these social dropouts were really cops.

50

"The Wild, Wild West"

"The Wild, Wild West" had a quality reminiscent of Jules Verne stories. It was set in frontier days, but was really a sophisticated spy show, like "The Man from U.N.C.L.E." In it, Macho man James T. West and his assistant, Artemus Gordon, a master of disguise and dialect, were intelligence agents on assignment from President Ulysses S. Grant. The two agents traveled in a unique private railroad car containing unusual weapons and advanced scientific devices, which they used to thwart revolutionaries, weirdos, midgets, and crazies who were trying to overthrow the government.

One year after "Perry Mason" went off the air, Raymond Burr returned as Robert T. Ironside, who had been the chief of detectives for the San Francisco Police Department until a would-be assassin's bullet left him paralyzed from the waist down. In his new role as a special police consultant, he continued to wage war against crime from the confines of a wheelchair. Nothing stopped Ironside.

Kookie, Kookie, lend me your comb . . .

Trivia Question

Name five shows in which the main character was either a widow or a widower.

Answer: "Bonanza," "Courtship of Eddie's Father," "The Andy Griffith Show," "The Governor and J.J.," "The Beverly Hillbillies," "Petticoat Junction," "The Ghost and Mrs. Muir," "My Three Sons," "The Big Valley," and many others.

"The Untouchables"

Good against evil. Week after week, Eliot Ness, played by Robert Stack, and his band of incorruptible treasury agents did battle with the villains of the Prohibition days to prove crime never pays.

Excedrin Headache No. 1040, the Tax Audit.

HARRIED TAXPAYER: "Well, that's a legitimate business expense. I buy a mink coat for my . . ."

AUDITOR: "For a client?"

TAXPAYER: "For my model. I'm in the dress line, and she was cold. I'm a giver, is that so wrong?"

AUDITOR: "Then you won't mind giving the government four thousand five hundred dollars."

"Burke's Law"

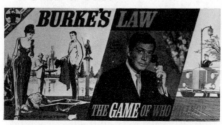

In one of television's most farfetched detective series, Gene Barry played the role of Los Angeles police chief, Amos Burke, an independently wealthy law enforcer. His police car was a chauffeur-driven Rolls-Royce, he lived in an elegant mansion, and he attracted young ladies à la Cary Grant. Was all that regulation?

"The Fugitive"

1. Name the train that ran through Hooterville. Who ran the Hooterville general store?

2. In 1968 the Beatles were in New York to announce the formation of Apple Corps., Ltd. They agreed to make an appearance on "The Tonight Show," but when they came onstage they seemed surprised and a little dismayed. Why, and what was the first thing John Lennon said?

3. Who was TV's first female private detective? What year? Who played the role?

Answers

3. "Honey West" premiered in 1965, starring Anne Francis as Honey.

2. They saw that Johnny Carson was on vacation, replaced by Joe Garagiola, of all people. Lennon's first words were "Where's Johnny," echoing the sentiments of every Beatle fan who had hoped for a good interview.

1. The Hooterville Cannonball. Sam Drucker.

Dr. Richard Kimble was wrongly convicted and sentenced to die for the murder of his wife. But the train that was taking him to prison derailed, and Kimble escaped his captor, Lt. Phillip Girard. Kimble spent the next four years simultaneously looking for the one-armed man who killed his wife and eluding Lieutenant Girard, who pursued him relentlessly.

Of course, realistically, it's incredible that Kimble could have been able to track the one-armed man, whose face he never even saw. And who was this lieutenant who could travel all over the country obsessively in pursuit of a single man? But the show was convincing largely because of its powerful image of an honest man,

banished from society and forced to be a loner, trying to vindicate himself. It was easy to identify with.

Unlike other shows, "The Fugitive" had a definite ending. In the final episode—watched by more people than any other episode of any other series in the entire decade—the one-armed man was apprehended, and so Kimble surrendered. But the one-armed man escaped. Kimble chased him to a deserted amusement park, trapped him, and got him to confess to the murder. Just as Kimble was about to be murdered, Lieutenant Girard, who had heard the confession, shot the one-armed man, and the series was over. Whew! A close one.

Relevant TV Show No. 2 "Daktari"

This program was inspired by the 1965 movie, *Clarence the Cross-Eyed Lion.* Set in Africa (but shot near Los Angeles), "Daktari" reflected the changing values of the late sixties. In a world where blacks were becoming part of mainstream America and Africa was full of emerging "democracies," Great White Hunters like Jungle Jim were no longer acceptable. But Great

White Doctors were fine; and of course, Dr. Tracy Marsh wasn't just any old doctor—he was a veterinarian concerned with conservation (at a time when environmental issues were just starting to receive serious media coverage). Clarence the lion and Judy the chimp provided just as much of the attraction as the people.

Relevant TV Show No. 3

"Mr. Novak"

In 1963, there were more kids in school than ever before, so this show was bound to be a hit. Mr. Novak was the dedicated, idealistic young English teacher everybody wished they had, but never did. Dreamy-looking James Franciscus (who looked like Dr. Kildare) became a national heart throb and his picture appeared in all the fan magazines.

A 60S! CLASSIC

"Peyton Place"

Dorothy Malone as Constance MacKenzie

Johnny Carson called this "the first TV series delivered in a plain brown wrapper." Based on the novel by Grace Metalious, "Peyton Place" was the most popular soap opera in prime-time history. Peyton Place had a cast of over one hundred regulars, including Mia Farrow as Allison Mackenzie; Ryan O'Neal as Rodney Harrington; Dorothy Malone as Constance Mackenzie; Barbara Parkins as Betty Anderson; and Ed Nelson as Dr. Michael Rossi. The action centered around the secrets and sexual affairs of the residents of a small New England town. Everyone in Peyton Place had a skeleton in his closet and millions of viewers were waiting to peek into it: Would Constance Mackenzie marry her daughter Allison's real father, Elliot Carson, when he got out of prison? Why did Allison disappear just as she was about to marry wealthy Rodney Harrington, Betty Anderson's ex-husband? And who would Betty Anderson's fourth husband be? Would Dr. Nelson be convicted of murder? Would Rita Jacks, the tavern-keeper's daughter, marry Norman Harrington? Who killed old-man Peyton's fiancée? Tune in next week to find out.

Ryan O'Neal as Rodney Harrington

Barbara Parkins as Betty Anderson

Mia Farrow as Allison Mackenzie

Blood and Guts

In the middle of the flowering of the postwar baby boom, shows about World War II began to appear. The most successful were comedies like "McHale's Navy" and "Hogan's Heroes," but there were a half-dozen dramas as well. Of these, three—"Gallant Men," "Garrison's Gorillas," and "Jericho"—bombed.

"Combat" was the first successful World War II TV drama ever. Starring Vic Morrow and Rick Jason, it told the story of a U.S. Army platoon fighting in Europe during World War II. Actual battle footage was used to enhance the realistic feeling of this muddy-bloody war drama. It aired for five years.

"The Rat Patrol" was particularly popular among young people. It consisted of four commandos (American and British) fighting Rommel's Afrika Korps in North Africa early in World War II. They bounced across the desert in jeeps with machine guns on the back blowing up Germans and, occasionally, Arabs.

In 1968, the assassinations of Martin Luther King, Jr., and Robert Kennedy made America critically aware of the level of violence around us, and television renounced its violent programs. The war shows disappeared.

A 60S! CLASSIC

"The Twilight Zone"

"There is a fifth dimension beyond that which is known to man. It is a dimension as vast as space and as timeless as infinity. It is the middle ground between light and shadow, between science and superstition, and it lies between the pit of man's fears and the summit of his knowledge. This is the dimension of imagination. It is an area we call The Twilight Zone." This eerie introduction opened each episode of the most popular science-fiction anthology series on television. It was narrated and hosted by playwright Rod Serling, who also wrote 89 of the 151 shows.

With its robots, devils, creatures from other planets, and everyday-objects-become-sinister (an ordinary-looking electric razor once chased its owner out of his house, where his car started automatically and attacked him), "The Twilight Zone"

was the kind of show that could give you nightmares for weeks.

In one episode, called "To Serve Man," beings called Kanamits arrived from space and announced at the UN that they were here to bring peace to our planet. They helped us to eliminate war and hunger, and even set up a travel program between their planet and ours. Earthlings loved to visit their planet. However, the Kanamits left a book and two UN cryptographers decided to decipher it. Halfway through the show, they figured out the title —"To Serve Man," which sounded promising. But at the very end, as one of them was boarding a ship to the Kanamits' planet, the other cryptographer ran up screaming "Don't go, don't go. I deciphered the rest of the book—it's a cookbook!" Too late.

A 60S! CLASSIC

"Gud eeevening . . ."

"The Prisoner"

This Kafkaesque TV series was considered by many critics to be the best of the decade. Said one: "If the 1968 television season is remembered for having contributed anything constructive to the medium, it will be for the seventeen-episode run of Patrick McGoohan's British-made metaphoric and frightening series." In it, a British secret agent who had resigned was drugged, kidnapped, and taken to a place called The Village. There, his captors tried to probe his mind for top-secret information, which he refused to divulge.

The agent—played by McGoohan—was called number six. When he wasn't trying to escape from The Village or being questioned by number two, he was looking for number one, who was finally seen in the last program. This series appeared to be a spin-off of "Secret Agent Man."

TV Facts

On March 9, 1961, Anthony (Tough Tony) Anastasia, the boss of the Brooklyn waterfront, backed by the Federation of Italian-American Democratic Organizations, launched a boycott of Liggett & Meyers' products, "The Untouchables" biggest sponsor, protesting that the show stereotyped Italian-Americans as criminals. Shortly afterward, L&M announced they would not renew sponsorship of the series. To make peace, Desilu, producer of the show, agreed: (1) there would be no more fictionalized hoods with Italian names in the show; (2) more stress would be put on the law-enforcement role of Nick Rossi, Ness' right-hand man; and (3) more emphasis would be given to the positive influence Italian-American officials have on reducing crime. The show was back next season, fully sponsored.

UNBELIEVABLE TV SHOW #7

"My Favorite Martian"

Tim O'Hara, a reporter for *The Los Angeles Sun*, witnesses a crash landing. It's a space ship from Mars! What kind of hideous creature will emerge from the rubble? Some slimy green thing with three eyes and tentacles? No, it's lovable Uncle Martin. Will Tim report the news story of the century? No, he will invite Uncle Martin to live with him. Won't somebody notice that Martin's not from this planet? Of course not. Except for their retractable antennae, Martians look exactly like earthlings.

You may remember this show for Uncle Martin's ability to levitate objects by pointing his finger at them, or for his ability to speak with dogs, or perhaps for Tim's dingbat landlady Mrs. Brown. But what really made it memorable was the acting of Ray Walston (Martin) and Bill Bixby (Tim). They brought this ridiculous premise down to earth and helped the show last for three years.

TV Trivia Questions

1. In what year did Johnny Carson take over "The Tonight Show," and who were his first four guests?

2. On welcoming her son back from his successful space mission in 1962, John Glenn's mother wanted to meet only one of the many TV celebrities who were on hand to greet the astronaut. Who was he?

3. "The Defenders" won thirteen Emmys in its four-year run, three times for Outstanding Dramatic Series. Its star won two Emmys. Who were the show's stars, what were the names of their characters, and what shows did they go on to star in later in the decade?

In an episode called "The Zanti Misfits," antlike visitors from outer space turn out to be criminals sent here by their home planet, using earth as a penal colony.

A 60s! CLASSIC

"The Outer Limits"

"There is nothing wrong with your TV set. We are controlling transmission. We can control the vertical. We can control the horizontal. For the next hour sit quietly and we will control all that you see and hear. You are about to participate in a great adventure, you are about to experience the awe and mystery which reaches from the inner mind to . . . the Outer Limits."

Answers

Reed to "The Brady Bunch."

3. E. G. Marshall as Laurence Preston, Robert Reed as Kenneth Preston. Marshall went to "The Bold Ones" in 1969,

2. Walter Cronkite.

1. October 2, 1962. Rudy Vallee, Joan Crawford, Tony Bennett, Mel Brooks.

55

Great, Mom. Just what I wanted—
a TV dinner.

TV Trivia Questions

1. Name five shows that featured black actors.

2. Pam Austin, Gunilla Knutsen, and Barbara Feldon caught the public's attention on TV commercials in which they said one memorable line apiece. What commercials, and what was the line?

Answers

Tiger." Top Brass.
Cream. BARBARA FELDON: "Sic 'em,
off. Take it all off." Noxema Shaving
lion." Dodge. GUNILLA KNUTSEN: "Take it
2. PAM AUSTIN: "Join the Dodge Rebel-
Trek."
Cosby Show," "Land of the Giants," "Star
"The Leslie Uggams Show," "The Bill
"Mission Impossible," "Room 222,"
1. "Julia," "The Mod Squad," "I Spy,"

TV Facts

Today color television is common; but in 1960 it was an expensive novelty. The only network advocate was NBC (remember the peacock?), whose parent company, RCA, had spent countless millions developing it and was trying to sell color sets.

• 1961: color TV turning point—"The Walt Disney Show" switched to NBC and became "Disney's Wonderful World of Color."

• 1963: a million and a half color sets were in use, compared with 60 million back-and-white sets.

• 1964: Sunday, December 20, between 9 P.M. and 10 P.M., all three networks were broadcasting in color simultaneously for the first time.

• 1968: color TV sets topped black-and-white for the first time. Six million color sets were sold, 5.5 million black-and-white sets.

"Hogan's Heroes"

Although it was funny, this had to be the most tasteless comedy presented in the decade. The laughs took place in Stalag 13, a Nazi POW camp where those bumbling examples of Aryan supremacy, Colonel Klink and Sergeant Schultz (who could barely tie his own shoelaces), allowed Colonel Hogan and his scrappy band of prisoners to run the Allied war effort right under their noses.

For six years (longer than the United States was actually in World War II) Hogan smuggled resistance fighters in and out of Germany, transmitted top-secret information to Allied headquarters, passed phony intelligence information on to Hitler, and never lost a single man. Sure the Gestapo—a bunch of real meanies—would stop by every once in a while, but you could count on Hogan to outsmart them. It's hard to believe those silly Germans ever thought they could win the war.

UNBELIEVABLE TV SHOW # 8

"Gilligan's Island"

No one told the folks on Gilligan's Island about the sexual revolution. It took a lot of skill to maroon three single men (Gilligan, The Skipper, and The Professor) and two beautiful women (Mary Ann and Ginger) on a tropical island for three years and still make an innocent family sitcom out of it.

A 60S! CLASSIC

"The Smothers Brothers Comedy Hour"

• In 1959, the Smothers Brothers made their TV debut on Jack Paar's "The Tonight Show."

• In 1965, Tom and Dick Smothers had their own series on CBS called "The Smothers Brothers Show," a half-hour situation comedy. It flopped.

• In 1967, CBS approached the Smothers to do a variety show with the intention of jolting "Bonanza" from its number-one spot in the TV ratings. Although the Smothers brothers ranked only eighteen in the 1967–68 season, the show managed to bring "Bonanza" down from number one that year.

• The show appealed mainly to the under-thirty generation because the "Comedy Hour" addressed the Smothers' concern with contemporary issues like the Vietnam War. To the dismay of the network, Tom Smothers was determined to use the show to express political viewpoints, speak for the young and minorities, and openly criticize the Johnson administration. The Smothers brothers also wanted to use the show to introduce little-known performers (like Mac Davis, Glen Campbell, Kris Kristofferson, John Hartford, and Pat Paulsen), and to bring back performers like Pete Seeger and Joan Baez who had been unofficially blacklisted. They succeeded in both cases. It took open war with CBS to do it, however.

• The Smothers' battles with CBS censors were well known. For example, censors cut a skit on film censorship with Elaine May and Tom Smothers; Harry Belafonte singing a calypso song in front of a collage of events at the Democratic convention in Chicago; and an interview with Dr. Benjamin Spock (the baby doctor) because, Tom Smothers said, "they [CBS] tell us he's a convicted felon."

• After the telecast of David Steinberg's "blasphemous" sermonette during Easter week in 1969, CBS demanded that the complete tapes of each program be flown to New York where network affiliates could preview the shows. It was the only show on the network required to do this. Obviously, CBS did not approve of the material being presented on the show. A telegram sent to Tom Smothers by the president of CBS said: "Please be advised that you are not free to use 'The Smothers Brothers Comedy Hour' as a device to push for new standards. If you cannot comply with our standards—whether or not you approve of them—'The Smothers Brothers Comedy Hour' cannot appear on CBS."

• On April 3, 1969, "The Smothers Brothers Comedy Hour" was canceled. Its replacement was "The Leslie Uggams Show" described by the vice-president of programs at CBS as a program that "would accent youthful entertainment and music with light and contemporary comedy."

TV Facts

• In 1965, a Penn State professor suggested that the "general unrest among young people" was caused by TV's "unseen radio, radar, and TV waves."

• The only time Walter Cronkite was ever left speechless by one of the news events he was covering was the moment when Buzz Aldrin and Neil Armstrong landed on the moon. Said Cronkite: "I just went blank."

• On January 13, 1965, Soupy Sales was suspended from his children's program "because he told young viewers to reach in their fathers' billfolds and send him 'those little green pieces of paper.'" The station was afraid the joke might be "misinterpreted" by viewers.

• One of the most-watched television events of the decade (and certainly one of the most talked-about) was the marriage of Tiny Tim to Miss Vicky Budinger on "The Tonight Show."

Tiny Tim had mentioned that he was getting married within earshot of a "Tonight Show" publicist. The PR man suggested to Johnny Carson that he offer to let Tim get married right on the program. Tim's response: "Oh, could we?"

NBC went all out. For the man who sang "Tiptoe Through the Tulips" they ordered ten thousand tulips directly from Holland and filled the stage with them. Miss Vicky wore a twenty-five-hundred-dollar Victorian gown, Tim a black silk frock coat with a top hat. They passed up Carson's champagne toast in favor of a milk-and-honey drink that Tim concocted, and when they were pronounced man and wife, they kissed. "The fifth kiss we ever had," said Tiny.

Then they flew off to their honeymoon and at least three days of celibacy. ("S-E-X is the least important part of marriage," explained Mr. Tim.)

Relevant TV Show No. 4

"Julia"

"Julia" was a sixties phenomenon. Until then, it would have been unthinkable to portray a black as part of mainstream American culture. Julia, played by Diahann Carroll, was a nurse in a totally integrated middle-class environment. This was the first time a black woman had been given a lead role —other than as a servant—in prime-time television history. That, in fact, may have been the whole point of the show. To the relief of network executives who felt they had taken a great risk, "Julia" was extremely popular.

Here Come De Judge

Rowan and Martin and Ruth Buzzi

"ROWAN AND MARTIN'S

Gordon's Interview with Dick Martin

Q: How did you come up with the actual format for "Laugh-In," Dick?

A: Well, Dan and I had wanted to do something like it for a long time. We'd been around television, doing Ed Sullivan, Perry Como, and all the variety shows. But after awhile they all seemed alike to us. We did the Dean Martin summer show in 1966, and it was very highly rated. So NBC came to us and said, "We would like you to do a variety show." But we didn't want to do another variety show—we wanted to do our own show. We hassled back and forth and finally they signed us to do a special. That was the fall of 1967. That show didn't get high numbers, but all the critics loved it. So NBC reluctantly decided to let us do thirteen shows as a mid-season replacement for the "Man from U.N.C.L.E." They threw us to the wolves, putting us opposite the number-one and number-three shows in the country, "Lucy" and "Guns-moke." By the next year, *we* were the number-one show. NBC never understood what we were doing. After every show they said, "Gee that was funny, but what are you going to do next week?" We said, "We're going to speed it up." The secret was that Dan and I always felt that television could be more than just televised radio. We wanted to exploit it as a *visual* medium. I've often said that one of the real stars of our show was Art Schneider, our editor, because there were sometimes as many as three hundred and fifty edits in that show. You couldn't walk out of the room because you would miss a lot in thirty seconds.

Q: I know "Laugh-In" was pretty controversial, but I guess being the number-one show, you could get away with a lot.

A: Yes, we broke a lot of barriers. For instance, people didn't realize you couldn't do pregnancy jokes when we did them. We had Joanne Worley standing, obviously pregnant, at the crook of the piano singing, "I should have danced all night." We did a lot of them. We broke the marijuana ban. In one show, Judy Carne said, "my boyfriend's so dumb he thinks a little pot is Tupper-ware for midgets." Then we had one of those streamers going across the screen that said, "For the first time in the history of the United States, everyone has agreed on everything and they walked out with their arms around each other. The officials are still looking to find out who put the grass in the air-conditioner." The censor didn't know what it meant. He came and asked, "What's so funny about putting grass in the air-conditioner?" We said, "Trust us, it's funny." About eight weeks later he came and said, "I knew what that was."

Q: You mean there was actually a person who was a censor?

A: Just for us. Up until "Laugh-In," you just submitted your script and they said yes or no to everything. But we had one on the set. They assigned a man to us. He was in editing and he was in on the script because he knew we ad-libbed so many of the things.

Q: You mentioned those streamers going across the screen. I remember one that said, "Little Orphan Annie call the eye bank." They were hilarious.

A: You know, they stopped us after the first season from doing it. We had one that said, "Help, I'm being held prisoner in the newsroom," and we gave the call letters of a TV station. The cops went there with guns drawn. They said, "What if some national emergency comes along and these nuts are flashing these things . . . nobody would believe it." So they stopped us from doing it.

LAUGH-IN''

Q: I wanted to ask you about having Nixon on the show.

A: Well, because of the equal-time thing, we offered Hubert Humphrey and Nixon a chance to come on. Nixon took it and Humphrey didn't. That was a surprise. Nixon came on and said, "Sock it to me," and made people think, "Well, maybe he really does have a sense of humor." Humphrey regretted his decision. He came back five weeks later and wanted to come on, but then it was too late. We would have loved to have Humphrey come out and say, "Sock it to him, not me."

Q: Were there any other political people you invited to be on the show?

A: Yes. The one who was the funniest was Bill Buckley. When we wired him to do cameos, he sent a telegram saying, "Not only will I not appear on the show, but I am insulted by being asked." So we sent him another telegram and another and finally we sent him one saying, "We would like you to be on the show, and if you come we'll send you an airplane with two right wings." He turned out to be one hell of a nice guy and he said, "I can't resist anyone with a sense of humor like that." He came on and did the show, and, incidentally, with brilliance. We did a mock news conference with Dan and I as the moderators and we gave the cast questions, and Buckley said he didn't want to know what they were. He just winged it, and he was funny.

Q: This may seem like a big jump from Buckley and Nixon, but how did you find Tiny Tim?

A: He came into our office up in Burbank. We thought our executive producer, George Schlatter, was putting us on and George thought we were putting him on. No one had ever seen this guy. He sang "Tiptoe Through the Tulips" and I was hysterical. Still, we didn't let him sing alone. We had a "New Talent Department." Dan would stick him with me and say, "Now I have something really good for you." And so, it was funny by my standing there, and I couldn't leave the stage, and this guy sang the whole song.

Q: You let Tiny Tim sing, but you never let Sammy Davis, Jr., sing.

A: That's right. Every time he would start to sing, we would drop him through a trapdoor. But we never would have had "Here come the judge" if it weren't for Sammy. We were doing judge skits, and Sammy remembered Pigmeat Markham. He did that as a gag in the rehearsal hall. We said, "Oh, hell! Leave that in." That became one of the big things of the sixties, "Here come the judge."

Q: What, in general, stands out in your mind about the sixties?

A: There was a lot of unrest and some violence, but there was something about the sixties that still lent itself to humor. It stands out as a very progressive time.

Dan and Dick with guess who? John Wayne.

The "Laugh-In" Cast

A 6OS! CLASSIC

"Star Trek"

"Space, the final frontier." Representing the United Federation of Planets, the starship USS *Enterprise* set out in the twenty-second century to explore new life and new civilizations. Led by Captain James T. Kirk, the *Enterprise* had weekly encounters with hostile aliens, such as the Romulans and the Klingons, strange forms of life from gaseous creatures to beings made of silicone, and of course humanoids from all corners of the universe.

This well-written science-fiction series revolved around eight principle characters: Kirk; Spock, a brilliant but emotionless creature ("Highly illogical, Captain") who was the son of a Vulcan father and Earthling mother; Dr. Leonard "Bones" McCoy, the ship's medic; Scotty, the chief engineer ("It can't be done, captain. The matter-antimatter pods will blow us all up"); Lieutenant Uhura, the communications officer; Sulu and Chekov, the navigators; and Nurse Chapel, chief nurse (secretly in love with Spock). The stories were action-packed, suspenseful, and, for the most part, intelligently conceived. At the end of every episode, Captain Kirk reaffirmed the nobility of the human spirit.

The *Enterprise* was on a five-year mission, but "Star Trek" lasted only three. Despite protests from millions of fans, NBC canceled the show. Sponsors were after adult viewers and "Star Trek" appealed primarily to teenagers. The show remains, however, one of the most popular shows of the sixties.

UNBELIEVABLE TV SHOW # 9

"The Invaders"

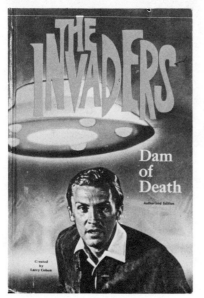

An architect witnessed the landing of aliens who planned to take over the earth because their home planet was dying. He learned of the only flaw in their human form, a crooked little finger on the right hand. Shows depicted him trying to warn and convince other people that the danger was here, and scrutinizing the hands of everyone he met.

TELEVISION LUNCHBOXES   Take Your Favorite Show to School with You.

New TV Cartoon Characters of the Sixties

1. The Flintstones
2. George of the Jungle
3. Quick-Draw McGraw (alias El Ka-Bong)
4. Road Runner
5. Tom Terrific
6. Professor Ludwig Von Drake
7. Super Chicken
8. King Leonardo (and Odie)
9. Beany and Cecil
10. The Jetsons

A 60S! CLASSIC

"Bullwinkle" was adult satire in cartoon clothing. Here are all the characters from the show. Can you name them? No answers from us—they're right there in the photo. By the way, in case you wondered where the name "Bullwinkle" came from . . . it was the name of a car dealer in California.

TV Facts

• The shortest running TV show in the sixties—or any time—was called "Turn-On," a "Laugh-In" imitation that was on once (February 5, 1969). It was canceled the next day.

• ABC's first color program was "The Jetsons" in 1962.

• November 10, 1969, the first "Sesame Street" program was aired.

• The last "Howdy Doody" show was on September 30, 1960.

Nine Popular Shows from the Fifties That Returned as Saturday Morning Reruns in the Sixties

"Jungle Jim"

"Sky King"

"Roy Rogers"

"Fury"

"Rin Tin Tin"

"Crusader Rabbit"

"Rama of the Jungle"

"Annie Oakley"

"Captain Gallant of the Foreign Legion"

TOP TEN

The Most Popular TV Shows in America, 1959–1969

1959–60

1. "Gunsmoke"
2. "Wagon Train"
3. "Have Gun, Will Travel"
4. "The Danny Thomas Show"
5. "The Red Skelton Show"
6. "Father Knows Best"
7. "77 Sunset Strip"
8. "The Price Is Right"
9. "Wanted: Dead or Alive"
10. "Perry Mason"

1960–61

1. "Gunsmoke"
2. "Wagon Train"
3. "Have Gun, Will Travel"
4. "The Andy Griffith Show"
5. "The Real McCoys"
6. "Rawhide"
7. "Candid Camera"
8. "The Untouchables"
9. "The Price Is Right"
10. "The Jack Benny Program"

1961–62

1. "Wagon Train"
2. "Bonanza"
3. "Gunsmoke"
4. "Hazel"
5. "Perry Mason"
6. "The Red Skelton Show"
7. "The Andy Griffith Show"
8. "The Danny Thomas Show"
9. "Dr. Kildare"
10. "Candid Camera"

1962–63

1. "The Beverly Hillbillies"
2. "Candid Camera"
3. "The Red Skelton Show"
4. "Bonanza"
5. "The Lucy Show"
6. "The Andy Griffith Show"
7. "Ben Casey"
8. "The Danny Thomas Show"
9. "The Dick Van Dyke Show"
10. "Gunsmoke"

1963–64

1. "The Beverly Hillbillies"
2. "Bonanza"
3. "The Dick Van Dyke Show"
4. "Petticoat Junction"
5. "The Andy Griffith Show"
6. "The Lucy Show"
7. "Candid Camera"
8. "The Ed Sullivan Show"
9. "The Danny Thomas Show"
10. "My Favorite Martian"

1964–65

1. "Bonanza"
2. "Bewitched"
3. "Gomer Pyle, U.S.M.C."
4. "The Andy Griffith Show"
5. "The Fugitive"
6. "The Red Skelton Hour"
7. "The Dick Van Dyke Show"
8. "The Lucy Show"
9. "Peyton Place"
10. "Combat"

1965–66

1. "Bonanza"
2. "Gomer Pyle, U.S.M.C."
3. "The Lucy Show"
4. "The Red Skelton Hour"
5. "Batman (II)"
6. "The Andy Griffith Show"
7. "Bewitched"
8. "The Beverly Hillbillies"
9. "Hogan's Heroes"
10. "Batman (I)"

1966–67

1. "Bonanza"
2. "The Red Skelton Hour"
3. "The Andy Griffith Show"
4. "The Lucy Show"
5. "The Jackie Gleason Show"
6. "Green Acres"
7. "Daktari"
8. "Bewitched"
9. "The Beverly Hillbillies"
10. "Gomer Pyle, U.S.M.C."

1967–68

1. "The Andy Griffith Show"
2. "The Lucy Show"
3. "Gomer Pyle, U.S.M.C."
4. "Gunsmoke"
5. "Family Affair"
6. "Bonanza"
7. "The Red Skelton Hour"
8. "The Dean Martin Show"
9. "The Jackie Gleason Show"
10. "Saturday Night at the Movies"

1968–69

1. "Rowan and Martin's Laugh-In"
2. "Gomer Pyle, U.S.M.C."
3. "Bonanza"
4. "Mayberry R.F.D."
5. "Family Affair"
6. "Gunsmoke"
7. "Julia"
8. "The Dean Martin Show"
9. "Here's Lucy"
10. "The Beverly Hillbillies"

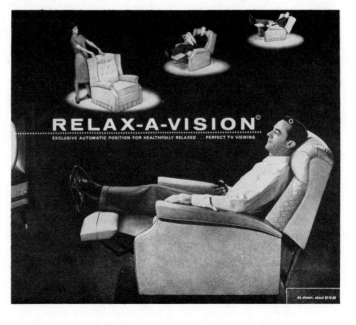

A DAY IN THE LIFE OF PRESIDENT KENNEDY
BY JIM BISHOP

Kennedy was the first politician/superstar of the electronic era. He had charisma and a "star quality" that came through on television; during his presidency he capitalized on it whenever possible. He held the first televised presidential press conferences, and when they seemed to go well, he held them frequently. He created a new qualification for running for political office: looking good. This paved the way for ex-movie actors like Ronald Reagan to enter politics.

C-238
35¢
A CARDINAL EDITION

Profiles IN Courage

In this remarkable book, the Junior Senator from Massachusetts writes brilliantly about a handful of American statesmen who, at crucial times in our history, risked their personal and public lives to do the one thing that seemed in itself right.

Senator John F. Kennedy

THE COMPLETE BOOK

Foreword by ALLAN NEVINS

The Kennedys were the closest thing we had to a royal family in the sixties. They were rich, aristocratic, handsome, intelligent. Jack was a war hero and a Pulitzer Prize–winning author. Jackie was the well-bred fashion queen who charmed foreign leaders *and* was a good mother. And Bobby and Teddy were princes, sure to get their chance at the throne—not that everyone loved them, but they *were* the center of attention; you couldn't pick up a newspaper or magazine or watch television news without seeing some reference to the Kennedy family, even after the assassination. Wherever the Kennedys led, America followed.

The Kennedy In-fluence

• Reading—Kennedy was a speed reader and an author. Reading was "in."

• Physical Fitness—The Kennedys were into sports. They played touch football on the White House lawn and went for well-publicized fifty-mile hikes. They started the "physical fitness movement." Getting in shape was "in."

• Idealism—Kennedy's inspiring speeches gave us a sense that America was a force for good in the world. Proof: the Peace Corps. Idealism was "in."

• Intellectualism—The Kennedy combination of glamour and intellectualism was a new style. It was "in" to be smart.

• Sex—Kennedy was a sexy politician. Sexy was "in" for politics.

• Youth—Kennedy was young, and he encouraged young people to get involved in government. "Ask not what your country can do for you," he said. "Ask what you can do for your country." Getting involved was "in."

The Kennedy Wit

The Kennedy Style

Kennedy was known for his sense of humor. He appreciated a good joke, even at his own expense. His refusal to take things seriously all the time lent a welcome air of informality to the climate of the country during tense times. Comedy flourished while he was president. Stand-up comics from Lenny Bruce to Bob Newhart were in demand.

PRESENT
THE FIRST FAMILY
FEATURING
VAUGHN MEADER
WITH
EARLE DOUD ~ NAOMI BROSSART ~ BOB BOOKER ~ NORMA MACMILLAN

The Kennedys were trend-setters in fashion. JFK made the one-button suit popular, but angered hatmakers by seldom wearing a hat. Jackie was the clothing industry's favorite American. She made it fashionable to be fashionable, popularizing the pillbox hat, the A-line dress, the bouffant hairdo. She is even credited with saving the mini-skirt. When she shortened her skirt in 1965, clothing manufacturers supposedly decided that the mini was here to stay, and committed themselves to manufacturing them.

JFK had a back problem, and his physician, Dr. Janet Travell, recommended he use a rocking chair whenever possible for therapy. He brought it to his office in the White House and was photographed sitting in it in early 1961. Suddenly all America wanted to sit in rocking chairs. Dr. Travell announced that it was a "Carolina Rocker" made by P & P Chair Co., in Asheville, North Carolina. Guess whose phones started ringing off the hook? The P & P Co. found themselves with a backlog of orders overnight; other manufacturers successfully promoted their chairs in conjunction with Kennedy's, too.

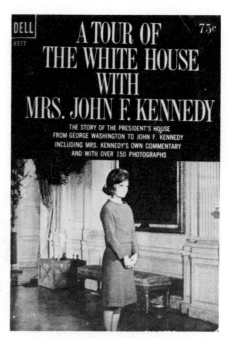

DELL
8977
75¢
A TOUR OF THE WHITE HOUSE WITH MRS. JOHN F. KENNEDY
THE STORY OF THE PRESIDENT'S HOUSE FROM GEORGE WASHINGTON TO JOHN F. KENNEDY INCLUDING MRS. KENNEDY'S OWN COMMENTARY AND WITH OVER 150 PHOTOGRAPHS

When Jackie displayed how valuable she considered antiques during her television tour of the White House, many people recognized their value for the first time. Up until then, anything old was embarrassing to the masses. You could get Victorian furniture for free if you would haul it away. People painted oak tables. But if Jackie was proud to have antiques in her house, then they had to be good.

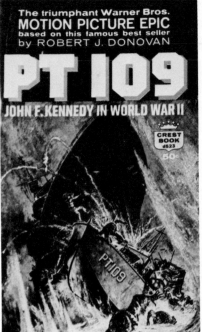

The triumphant Warner Bros.
MOTION PICTURE EPIC
based on this famous best seller
by ROBERT J. DONOVAN

PT 109

JOHN F. KENNEDY IN WORLD WAR II

CREST BOOK d523 50¢

JFK wanted Warren Beatty to star in the movie made from PT-109, but the director considered Beatty too unstable, and got Cliff Robertson instead. "Don't tell *me* how to make an exploitation movie," he told Kennedy's press secretary, Pierre Salinger, when Salinger protested.

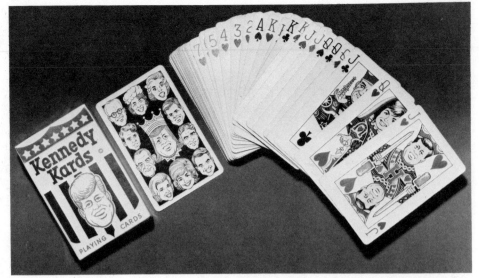

Playing cards with the Kennedy clan's faces on the picture cards. Guess who the joker is—Barry Goldwater.

A "Joke" Book

JFK cologne

A Halloween mask of JFK

The Kennedys Game

CAROLINE'S DOLL BOOK

by JOYCE HABER • drawings by R. TAYLOR

Caroline's doll book—Windup doll jokes with a Kennedy theme.

The Kennedy Image—
The Way We Remember JFK

Rich and Glamorous

Loving Father

Family Man

World Leader

Brothers

War Hero

The Enemy

Close Call of the Decade

The Cuban Missile Crisis

In October, 1962, the climax to the sixties end-of-the-world hysteria took place. It was JFK's finest hour, and the closest we ever came to World War III.

• After Cuba went Communist, Americans became apprehensive about the ramifications of having a Communist satellite only ninety miles from our shores. What if Russia used it as a missile base?

• In the fall of 1962, our worst fears were realized. Reconnaissance planes showed that Russia was placing nuclear missiles in Cuba, aimed directly at us.

• Discovery of the missiles (not yet operational) set off a crisis in the White House. A team of expert advisers was set up to study this top-secret information and recommend a course of action to the president. What should we do? Should we bomb Cuba immediately (which might spark WW III); or just deliver an ultimatum? Fortunately, Kennedy chose not to attack.

• October 22, 1962, Kennedy announced

Actual spy photo of Soviet ship carrying nuclear missles to Cuba

the situation publicly, including the decision to impose a "quarantine" until the missles were removed. Two days later, we set up a naval blockade.

• International tension was at a peak. All over the world people waited for World War III. In America, children were taught how to "protect themselves" if a nuclear bomb was dropped. Fallout shelter sales boomed.

• But four days later—October 28, 1962 —the world breathed a sigh of relief. The Russians backed down. Khrushchev agreed to stop building missile bases and to remove missiles from Cuba.

In the fall of 1961 the Soviet Union scared the pants off the American public when they exploded their largest nuclear bomb ever. The Russians had signed a 1958 test ban treaty, but obviously, they never meant it; they had just used the treaty as a smokescreen while they built bigger bombs. Now that they had the Big Bomb, what were they going to do with it? Millions assumed it was just a matter of time until they tried to use it on us.

This letter was written by President Kennedy as an introduction to an issue of Life Magazine which dealt exclusively with surviving a nuclear explosion.

A 60s! CLASSIC

Dr. Strangelove, or How I Learned to Stop Worrying and Love the Bomb

There's nothing funny about the end of the world—but you can only take so much before you have to laugh. Stanley Kubrick's movie masterpiece of black humor was released in 1964, two years after the missile crisis. The plot: General Jack D. Ripper, believing that the Communists are trying to take over the world by fluoridating the water supply, sends a fleet of B-52's armed with nuclear weapons to attack Russia. President Merkin Muffley

contacts Soviet Premier Alexei Kissoff with the news. He is informed that a nuclear explosion will set off a "Doomsday" device and destroy all life on earth. General Ripper commits suicide rather than cancel the mission; but his aide figures out the recall code in time. Unfortunately, one plane, piloted by Major "King" Kong, makes it through. The bomb is dropped and the world self-destructs.

> The White House
> September 7, 1961
>
> My Fellow Americans:
>
> Nuclear weapons and the possibility of nuclear war are facts of life we cannot ignore today. I do not believe that war can solve any of the problems facing the world today. But the decision is not ours alone.
>
> The government is moving to improve the protection afforded you in your communities through civil defense. We have begun, and will be continuing throughout the next year and a half, a survey of all public buildings with fallout shelter potential, and the marking of those with adequate shelter for 50 persons or more. We are providing fallout shelter in new and in some existing federal buildings. We are stocking these shelters with one week's food and medical supplies and two weeks' water supply for the shelter occupants. In addition, I have recommended to the Congress the establishment of food reserves in centers around the country where they might be needed following an attack. Finally, we are developing improved warning systems which will make it possible to sound attack warning on buzzers right in your homes and places of business.
>
> More comprehensive measures than these lie ahead, but they cannot be brought to completion in the immediate future. In the meantime there is much that you can do to protect yourself—and in doing so strengthen your nation.
>
> I urge you to read and consider seriously the contents of this issue of LIFE. The security of our country and the peace of the world are the objectives of our policy. But in these dangerous days when both these objectives are threatened we must prepare for all eventualities. The ability to survive coupled with the will to do so therefore are essential to our country.
>
> *John F. Kennedy*
>
> John F. Kennedy

The End of the World

The Fallout Shelter Years

In 1961, the Kennedy administration urged Americans to build fallout shelters to guarantee themselves protection from radioactive particles that would shower the earth if a nuclear attack occurred. America went fallout crazy. Some people took advantage of the free government plans for do-it-yourself shelters, and others bought them ready-made. One company reported in late 1961 that they were selling a thousand a week. "My best salesmen," said the company's owner, "are Kennedy and Khrushchev." Another commented: "Khrushchev sells shelters like crazy every time he opens his mouth." A strange attitude, considering the very real possibility of total destruction.

But it was a strange time. Fly-by-night salesmen laughed that if their shelters didn't work, the customers certainly couldn't complain. For panic-stricken homeowners it turned into a sort of mad competition: otherwise-sane families told reporters that they wouldn't hesitate to gun down their neighbors if they had to protect their shelters in war; people who wanted to keep their shelters secret told their neighbors that plumbing was being repaired; one man, apparently unconcerned about the end of the human race, had a sign over his shelter that read: "He who lasts, laughs."

Inside view of a fallout shelter

$ A Fast Buck $ Shelter Merchandise

• A woman's dress shop sold "bright, warm, comfortable things" for shelter-wear. Recommended: "gay slacks and a dress with a cape that could double as a blanket."

• In Jacksonville, Florida, supermarkets, Surviv-All, Inc. marketed "survival kits" to be used in case of nuclear attack. They included food, canned water, vitamin C, can opener, and hardware. Price: $4.98. Now there's something you can count on.

• A decorator offered a specially designed shelter interior. She said: "Be comfortable . . . why be drab about your shelter when it costs no more to survive in style?" Good question.

Recorded instructions for survival

Don't Forget Your Toothbrush

An actual 1961 list of what to bring with you to your fallout shelter:

Food and cooking equipment: water (a two-week supply, minimum seven gallons per person); two-week supply of food; eating utensils; paper plates, cups, and napkins (two-week supply); openers for cans and bottles; pocket knife; special foods for babies and the sick.

Supplies and equipment for sanitation: garbage pail; covered pail for toilet purposes; can for human wastes (ten-gallon); toilet paper, paper towels, sanitary napkins, disposable diapers, ordinary and waterless soap.

Household chlorine and DDT (one quart)

Waterproof gloves

Shelter equipment: battery radio with CONELRAD frequencies marked, and spare batteries; clothing; bedding (rubber sheets and special equipment for the sick); a first aid kit; reading and writing material; screwdriver, pliers, and other household tools; games and amusement for children.

Items outside the shelter, but within reach: cooking equipment (canned heat or camp stove), matches; home fire-fighting equipment; rescue tools.

Before

After

The sixties changed popular dancing forever. It was the first time that dances didn't necessarily involve touching your partner. It was unstructured and easy to do—you just did whatever you wanted to. It didn't matter. In fact, after a while dancing got so wild and unstructured that it became a symbol of freedom. Anyone who wanted to "let it all hang out" in public for a few hours did so on the dance floors.

Top 20 Dances of the Sixties

★ ★ ★ ★ ★ ★ ★ ★ ★ ★ ★ ★ ★

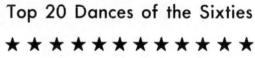

The Bird	The Limbo
The Boogaloo	The Locomotion
The Bristol Stomp	The Mashed Potato
The Freddie	The Monkey
The Frug	The Pony
The Funky Chicken	The Shing-a-ling
The Hitchhike	The Slop
The Hucklebuck	The Swim
The Hully Gully	The Twist
The Jerk	The Watusi

The Inside Story:

The Origin of the Twist

Chubby Checker's mother had a dream that he was going to have a hit record with someone else's song, a song that he would create a dance for. So he was on the look-out for one.

The Twist was already a fairly popular song among blacks (written and performed by Hank Ballard), but it had no dance. Chubby wanted to come up with a dance, and he was having a hard time figuring one out. So he asked his seven-year-old brother, Spencer, what he thought a dance called the Twist would look like. Spencer got up and just swiveled his body around, the way a seven-year-old might—and the Twist was born.

Scandals of the Sixties

To Twist or Not to Twist?

1962: Tampa, Florida, banned the Twist in its community centers.

1962: The United Arab Republic banned the Twist.

1962: Red Chinese newspapers castigated "ugly displays" of young people doing the Twist in Maoming Cultural Park in southern China.

1962: The Twist was banned by the Buffalo, New York, diocese in parish, school, and CYO events.

1962: The South African foreign minister deplored the fact that South African youth were doing the Twist, calling it a "strange god from the United States."

1963: The Twist was East Germany's most popular dance, despite the fact that the Communist party had denounced it.

1963: The South Vietnamese government said the Twist "was not compatible with its anti-Communist struggle," and banned the dance, the records, and even *singing* Twist songs.

Even the president was involved: In 1961, Pierre Salinger, JFK's press secretary, was forced by probing reporters to deny allegations that anyone was doing the Twist at a White House party (good heavens!). "I was there until three A.M., and nobody did the Twist," he said.

A month later, AP reported a scandalous scoop. "Under a secret service guard," AP claimed, "Mrs. Jacqueline Kennedy slipped out of Palm Beach last night and for an hour and a half danced the 'Twist' in a Fort Lauderdale nightclub." Whoops! Mistaken identity . . . Jackie was home all night. AP had to publish a public apology—its first since it announced the end of World War II prematurely.

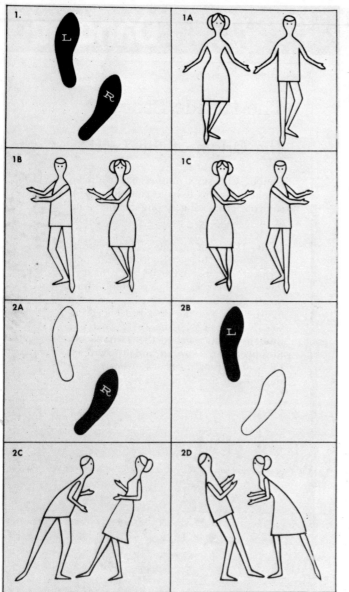

How to do the Twist? Here is a 1962 diagram with step-by-step instructions.

Chubby Checker Tells You How to Do the Twist

"It's like putting out a cigarette with both feet and coming out of a shower and wiping your bottom with a towel to the beat of the music. And it's just that simple."

$ A Fast Buck $

Twist Merchandise

While the Twist was *the* popular dance, Twist merchandise sold like hot cakes. You could get "twist" anything. Clothes became "twist clothes" if you put fringes on them (fringes would fly out when you twisted); a "twister chair" was so twisted that you couldn't sit on it; you could even eat a misshapen hot dog called a "twist-furter" ("the twist has now danced its way onto the dinner table," announced its manufacturer). The fad lasted a few years, and then most twist merchandise got thrown away. If you still have any, save it. It's a collector's item.

A few relics of the era when the Twist was king: Nat Sherman's "twist cigar," a twister hat from Arlington, a novel about a con man who gave "benefit" twist parties, and a Barbie doll all dressed up to shake those fringes

60S! HALL OF FAME

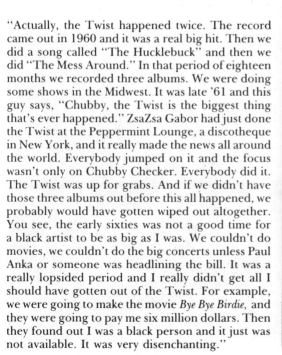

Chubby Checker, Mister Twister

"Before the Twist came, everyone danced together. I'm the guy that started people dancing apart. You know, I taught the world how to dance as they know it today. I'm almost like Einstein creating atomic power. Whatever dances came after the Twist, it all started here."

The Meaning of the Twist

"It's sex. It really is. You go on the floor and you dance with someone and she's shaking her body at you, that's pretty powerful. Today it's no big deal, but back in 1960, you never heard of such a thing. It was shocking."

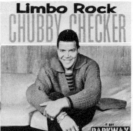

Trivia Question:

What is Chubby Checker's real name?

Answer: Ernest Evans

"Actually, the Twist happened twice. The record came out in 1960 and it was a real big hit. Then we did a song called "The Hucklebuck" and then we did "The Mess Around." In that period of eighteen months we recorded three albums. We were doing some shows in the Midwest. It was late '61 and this guy says, "Chubby, the Twist is the biggest thing that's ever happened." ZsaZsa Gabor had just done the Twist at the Peppermint Lounge, a discotheque in New York, and it really made the news all around the world. Everybody jumped on it and the focus wasn't only on Chubby Checker. Everybody did it. The Twist was up for grabs. And if we didn't have those three albums out before this all happened, we probably would have gotten wiped out altogether. You see, the early sixties was not a good time for a black artist to be as big as I was. We couldn't do movies, we couldn't do the big concerts unless Paul Anka or someone was headlining the bill. It was a really lopsided period and I really didn't get all I should have gotten out of the Twist. For example, we were going to make the movie *Bye Bye Birdie,* and they were going to pay me six million dollars. Then they found out I was a black person and it just was not available. It was very disenchanting."

Swing with Hi-Fi while you dry

It's Groovy!

Swing in hi-fi while you dry.
Turn it on . . . Tune it in.
The Oster Combination Radio/Hairdryer.

"Dances" out deep-down dirt !

Nice slicing Nice carving, too

in the Sixties

1960 Predictions

It's raining hard and she's busy. So she presses a button and talks to the store over a two-way TV-telephone. She sees her merchandise in color and makes her choice. Already they're working on this.

All kinds of new appliances are just around the corner, the inventors say. One of these days you may shop by TV . . . have an appliance that takes food from the freezer to the range, then cooks and serves it, all electrically . . . and a scrubber that cleans the kitchen floor automatically and scurries back to its wall-cupboard.

Two Frigidaire refrigerator ads.

1960: Queen of the house

1966: Queen of outer space

A History Lesson: The Teflon Age

Anthropologists have told us about the Stone Age and the Iron Age. But what about the Teflon Age? Let's take a look at a few of the things we know about Middle American Man (Middle Americanus Plasticus) way back in the Teflon Age, ca. 1960:

• He believed in plastic and filled his home with objects made of it. His spiritual goal was called "convenience," and his spiritual leader was called "Television," which spoke to him through parables called "commercials."

• When Middle Americans achieved "true convenience," they were said to be in a state of "easy living."

• One ritual that Middle Americans performed to try to achieve "true convenience" was called "shopping." In it, females would dress up and trudge down the aisles of department stores—sometimes parched for lack of a Coke because there was no snack bar—looking for items they referred to as "the latest."

• When they returned home with "the latest," they usually placed them on an altar called the "kitchen counter," where family and guests could admire them.

Spiritual leader

Middle Americanus Plasticus, ca. 1966

Great Moments of the 60s

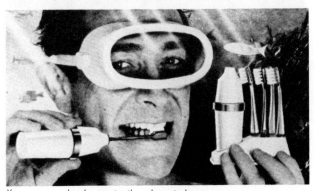

Electric toothbrush

Refrigerator Racing

Imagine this: You're at a football game in 1965. It's the New York Jets at home vs. the Oakland Raiders. It's half time. You settle back with a beer and wait for the marching band to come out and entertain you.

Not today. Today you're going to see the finals of the Hotpoint Roll-It Derby, which means you'll be watching a dozen or more women push refrigerators across a football field. The one who goes halfway, stops and fills her refrigerator full of groceries, and then goes the rest of the way first, wins. This is the kind of event for which they invented the word "incredible".

You can even brush your teeth underwater!

Outdoor barbeque 1960s style—all electric—with a General Electric "Partio Cart"

Town and Country

Maverick

You'll never guess what these lovely ladies are demonstrating . . . Designer refrigerators from Kelvinator! Over twenty different designs were available. Many, like the one on the right, were covered in leather. Their only problem: They cost too much for the average homeowner.

Great Moments of the 60s

Brand X Strikes Back

For years, Americans watched as manufacturers compared their products to the mysterious "Brand X" in television demonstrations. It was pathetic—Brand X towels didn't absorb enough water; Brand X laundry detergent never quite got clothes clean enough; Brand X cleanser left ugly rings in sinks. But everyone knew there was no real Brand X.

Then, in 1960, an independent inventor came up with a window cleaner he believed was the best ever created. But with no money to advertise, how could he tell people about it? He had a brainstorm. He copyrighted the name "Brand X" and, capitalizing on all the publicity other companies had given it, offered "Brand X Window Cleaner" to the public. He called it "the best-known product in the world."

AMAZING
BRAND "X"

TRADE MARK   PAT. PEND.

NEW SCIENTIFIC MIRACLE

ONE TIME WINDOW CLEANER for WINDOWS, MIRRORS AND CHROME

Some bugs fly. Ours dry.

Beautybug is really a professional hair dryer in disguise. It works just like the ones used in the finest salons. Except that Beautybug is portable.

There's a big hood large enough for any hair style or setting. Inside the hood are dozens of small openings that direct tiny jets of filtered air over, around and through your hair without disturbing the set.

The Beautybug is so quiet that you can dry your hair and talk on the phone, gossip with friends or watch old monster flicks on TV. It's quick too!

When you're finished, Beautybug scrunches down to hatbox size for easy carrying and storage.

Or you can keep it out in the open and make a pet out of it.

beautybug

Hey, Kids—Soap Just fer You!!!

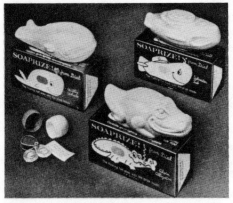

Soaprize. Someone figured out a way to get kids to use soap—put a prize in the middle of the bar. That way, they have to use up the soap to get at the prize. Pretty sneaky. Plus, Soaprize came in the shape of three different characters—Willie Whale, Alvin Alligator, and the ever-popular Sylvester Submarine.

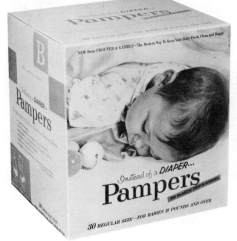

Hands-Up. Kiddie soap in an aerosol can, introduced in 1962. Instead of a nozzle there was a plastic gun mounted on top. You got soap out of the can by squeezing the trigger! The "Hands-Up" slogan: "Gets kids clean and makes them like it."

IT'S A CORDLESS ROTISSERIE...   TILT   IT'S A CHARCOAL GRILL   FOLDS UP, GOES PLACES!

Miles from the nearest Peeping Tom, you and your date can enjoy a very special outdoor meal with the portable electric rotisserie.

Americans Did It Twenty-five Billion Times a Year and Hated It Every Time

What is it? Changing diapers. There were only two ways of handling used diapers in the early sixties—wash them yourself or send them to a diaper service. But either way entailed handling and saving soggy, smelly diapers. Very unpleasant. And in the affluence of America in the 1960s, why should anyone have to deal with that kind of nuisance?

Anyone who could make a disposable diaper could make millions. In 1961, Procter & Gamble did it with Pampers, the first affordable, fully disposable diaper. And they were well rewarded, selling $30 million worth in the first three years. That's not just making wee-wee in the wind.

Manners the Butler was only as tall as your lap
—the perfect height to make sure you were
wearing a Kleenex napkin.

60S!
HALL OF FAME

''Mr. Clean gets rid of dirt and grime and grease in
just a minute. Mr. Clean will clean your whole
house and everything that's in it. Mr. Clean, Mr.
Clean, Mr. Clean.''

Madge the Manicurist advises her clients to use
Palmolive dishwashing liquid to soften their
hands. She first appeared in 1965, with the
immortal words: ''You're soaking in it.''

Jane Withers played Josephine the Plumber, who
helped people remove ugly stains from their kitchen
sinks with Comet (''Bleaches out tough food stains
better than any other leading cleanser'').

''Calling Man from Glad. Calling Man from Glad.
Woman with child who refuses to eat stale
sandwich.'' Solution: Glad sandwich bags with the
fold-lock top. ''Thank you, Man from Glad.''

1967: This lovely homemaker demonstrates the world's first countertop microwave oven for the home, the Amana Radarange.

What Is It?

Obviously it's a chair . . . but what's special about it? Give up? It has a fluorescent light under the seat that shoots a beam of light through the plastic, all the way to the top. The Laverne Luminous Chair, with the perfect built-in reading lamp.

February 28, 1963: Just when people thought taking snapshots was as easy as it could possibly be, Kodak came out with a new camera, the Instamatic. No more accidentally unrolling the film as you tried to thread it into the camera. No more changing film in a closet. Just plunk in a plastic cartridge, and it's ready to shoot.

60s Selects

The Ten Most Ridiculous New Products of the Sixties

1. A battery-powered electric spaghetti fork (winds spaghetti on fork for you)

2. Slippers equipped with tiny flashlights so people won't trip over things walking around in the dark

3. A combination desk lamp and sun lamp that makes it possible to get a suntan on the job.

4. Edible machine lubricant

5. An alarm cap for drivers. It looks like a baseball cap—if a driver starts to nod off, a buzzer contained in the hatband sounds.

6. Sleep machine: Why not use "television" to induce sleep (so many people fall asleep in front of it anyway)? This machine was designed to produce blue haloes emanating from a TV-like screen, creating a hypnotic, monotonous effect and lulling the watcher to sleep.

7. An ashtray with a built-in radio

8. His and Hers submarines from Nieman Marcus, offered in 1963. Cost: $18,700.

9. A toothbrush that loads toothpaste from an aerosol container in the handle.

10. Any takers? A solid-gold percolator, with 250 diamonds and 150 rubies. Cost: $50,000.

Telephones

1954: before

By 1960, almost everyone had a telephone. It was one of those household objects considered a "necessity." So Ma Bell mounted a massive ad campaign to convince Americans to put a second or even a third phone in their houses. They pushed wall phones for kitchen use, and new "Princess" phones for bedrooms. The petite "Princess" had a light-up dial, presumably to make answering surprise late-night calls easier (you could dial under the covers now, too). And phones came in decorator colors—they didn't have to be eyesores in the color-coordinated suburban home.

1966: after

Phone Phacts

1962: Telephone with a memory introduced. It automatically rings any one of fifty selected numbers.

1963: Bell introduces a wireless paging system with mobile "beepers" for doctors.

1963: Push-button telephones came calling. They cut dialing time from nine seconds to two seconds.

1965: Picture-phone rates: three minutes from Washington, D.C., to New York City, $8.00; New York to Chicago, $13.50; Chicago to Washington, $10.50!

1969: Most expensive phone offered, adorned with pearls, rubies, and diamonds. Cost: $1,000.

IBM Selectric Typewriter

In 1961 IBM introduced the revolutionary typewriter, which set the standard for all typewriters of the future. Its main feature, the interchangeable type element, could make the dullest letter look like an important document.

DIED IN THE SIXTIES:

Austin DeFlaun, our milkman

Milk Bottles

"Now milk comes in modern, disposable cartons! No more bottle-washing! No more broken bottles! No more spilled milk!"

A True Story: Every Tuesday and Thursday, while we were eating breakfast before school, we could hear Mr. DeFlaun come clattering up the side steps with his case of milk bottles. He'd open the door a crack, stick his head in the door, yell "Hello," and then come marching into the kitchen with four or five bottles of milk. He scooped up the empty milk bottles Mom had waiting for him and headed back to his Welsh Farms milk truck.

Mr. DeFlaun was a fixture in our lives in the sixties, and so were milk bottles. Yet today, kids can hardly believe they even existed. Looking back, we wonder whether milkmen could see that bottles didn't stand a chance against the wonders of modern packaging.

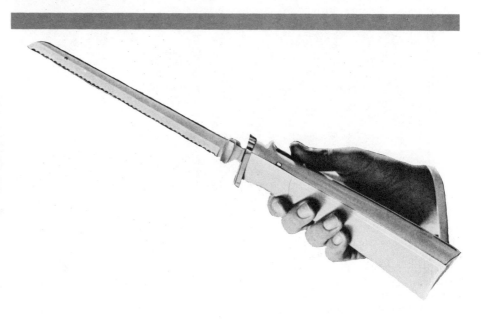

JFK's death was a national experience—something the whole country went through together. Every American who was old enough to know what was going on remembers exactly where he or she was and what they were doing when they heard the news. Ask anyone.

60s Salutes...

TV's Finest Hour

• One hundred seventy-five million Americans watched TV accounts of events in the four days after the assassination.

• UPI was the first to report, at 1:34 P.M., that JFK had been shot.

• The earliest bulletin on TV came at 1:40 P.M. when Walter Cronkite broke into "As the World Turns" to announce that the president had been "seriously wounded."

• The three major networks suspended all commercials and regular programming (triggering less than fifty complaints from the whole country) on the Friday of the assassination.

• At 10 A.M. (Dallas time) on Sunday, November 24, Oswald was shot in the basement of the Dallas police station. NBC was the only network that carried the first live killing in TV history. (CBS and ABC were set up at different areas, so they didn't get the killing on camera.)

• By November 26, when regular programming resumed, the three networks had been telecasting for two hundred hours over a four-day period with a total loss of $40 million in commercials.

• Twenty-three countries were able to watch what was going on via satellite.

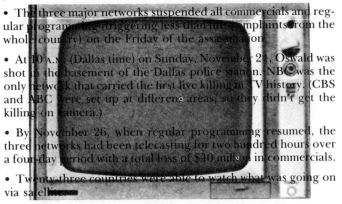

• A study by Social Research Inc., showed: (1) many people believed that media coverage of the shooting, and particularly the handling of Lee Harvey Oswald, had contributed to Oswald's assassination; (2) TV appeared to have helped prevent panic among the public; and (3) the decision to return to regular broadcasting after four days had "set an orderly limit on the period of mourning" and told the public, "now we should all get back to the task of living."

The American JFK memorial stamp was issued on May 29, 1964, his forty-seventh birthday. The design was selected by Mrs. Kennedy.

1964—The Kennedy half-dollar was the last silver coin minted in the United States.

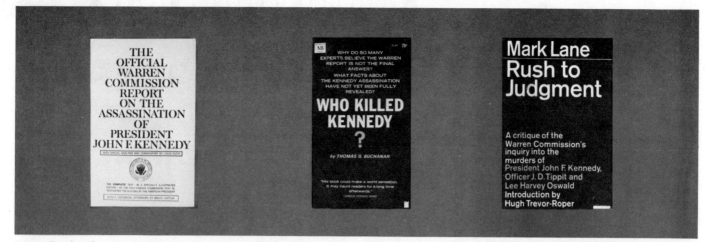

Immediately after Kennedy's death, Lyndon Johnson appointed a blue-ribbon commission to delve into the details of the assassination so that Americans could learn the truth about it. The commission consisted of seven respected men: Chief Justice Earl Warren, Senator Richard Russell of Georgia, Senator John Sherman Cooper of Kentucky, Representative Hale Boggs of Louisiana, Representative Gerald Ford of Michigan, Allen Dulles (former head of the CIA), and John McCloy, a Kennedy adviser.

The commission came up with a 469-page volume, called the Warren Report, with a 408-page appendix. Their conclusion: Lee Harvey Oswald assassinated John Kennedy all by himself. Rarely mentioned, though, is the fact that Boggs, Cooper, and Russell publicly stated doubts about the accuracy of the conclusions. And they weren't the only ones with doubts. Other books documented the oversights and contradictions of the Warren Report, arriving at the opposite conclusion—that there was more than one assassin, and that Oswald might even have been framed. *Who Killed Kennedy?*, the first book to raise serious doubts about Kennedy's death, was a best seller in Europe before it was ever published in America. *Rush to Judgment* brought the controversy into the headlines of America.

The public's verdict: In polls, over 50 percent always said "Conspiracy!"

$ A Fast Buck $

"Commemorative" items available a month after Kennedy's death included:

• Lapel pins that said "In Memory of our beloved President"

• A salt-and-pepper shaker set that featured a rocking chair for pepper and a figure of JFK for salt

• A night-light with a portrait of JFK, guaranteed to burn for fifty thousand hours and marketed as the "Eternal Flame of Light to Remember."

• Ballpoint pens, tie clips, plastic encased photos, tapestries, and plaques.

The assassinations hit the top forty: Dion DiMucci, singing star of the early sixties (Dion and the Belmonts), revived his career with this emotional song about losing our leaders. It was a number-one hit in 1968.

Among the best-selling "memorials" to JFK were record albums of his speeches. One manufacturer—Premier Records—claimed sales of 4 million in one month. This one was issued by the *New York Times*.

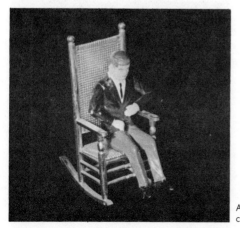

A plastic likeness of JFK on his favorite rocking chair.

Plaster busts of Kennedy like this one sold for $12.50 (larger ones could be had for $25.00).

60s! HALL OF FAME

Sean Connery, a.k.a. James Bond. His double-oh-seven designation meant he had a license to kill.

Robert Vaughn, a.k.a. Napoleon Solo

David McCallum, a.k.a. Illya Kuriakin

Bill Cosby and Robert Culp, a.k.a. Alexander Scott and Kelly Robinson.

James Coburn, a.k.a. Derek Flint. The suave star of the spy parodies "In Like Flint" and "Our Man Flint."

Barbara Feldon, a.k.a. 99—Agent 99
Don Adams, a.k.a. Maxwell Smart, Agent 86

Why Spy?

Kennedy's death—and the nagging belief that he was the victim of a conspiracy—suggested that there was more going on in this country than we had ever imagined. We suddenly awoke to the fact that much of the real action was behind the scenes where we couldn't see it and never would.

From there, the spy fantasy was an easy one. In fact, it probably helped to relieve tension. It was reassuring to think that if there was all this undercover stuff, then the best agents were on *our* side. Secret agents were the cowboys of the post-Kennedy years. They rode white horses (fancy sports cars), they fought the good fight and won, and they always got the girls. America loves a winner.

James Bond started it all, of course. *Dr. No* came out in 1963, the year that Kennedy was shot, and introduced Sean Connery to the world. It was a box-office smash, and spawned dozens of imitations. In 1966 alone, there were twenty-three spy movies, along with ten regular TV shows that featured spies.

Spies

Scandals of the Sixties

The big spy story of the sixties was the U-2 incident, starring Francis Gary Powers as the spy who got nabbed. Unfortunately, it showed that the U.S. government isn't nearly as cool as James Bond. We were flying spy missions in a secret plane called the U-2, and the Russians finally shot one down in 1960. This didn't worry the CIA, though. The pilot was supposed to activate a switch that would destroy the plane, so all the evidence would be gone. They made up a story about a weather-observation plane that accidentally went off-course. But then Khrushchev, Russia's

The U-2 Incident

premier, appeared before the world with the information that the pilot of the plane was caught, the plane was intact, and they had proof that the United States was spying on them. The U.S. government had LIED!! Oops. Well, the government had to admit that that was true, but at least the president didn't know about it. Oops, soon it came out that President Eisenhower *did* know about it, and it created an international controversy that resulted in Khrushchev's canceling a summit meeting. Stay tuned for Watergate.

The Inside Story: The Man from U.N.C.L.E.

The most popular TV spy show, "The Man from U.N.C.L.E.," starred Robert Vaughn as Napoleon Solo and David McCallum as Illya Kuriakin, his Russian sidekick (wasn't he cute, girls?) They were the good guys—agents of U.N.C.L.E.—and each week they battled the bad guys—agents of THRUSH, a criminal organization bent on world domination. If it seemed a little like James Bond, that could be because the show's creator was Ian Fleming, the man responsible for James Bond. He and U.N.C.L.E.'s producer, Sam Rolfe, got together to do a tongue-in-cheek version of the spy thriller. Fleming wanted to call it "Solo," after a character in one of his James Bond books (*Goldfinger*), but when Fleming had to withdraw from the project because of a heart attack, the owners of the Bond films told Rolfe *they* owned the name. The show was changed to U.N.C.L.E., and the main character became Napoleon Solo.

No one knew what U.N.C.L.E. stood for, including the show's producer. Viewers assumed it implied Uncle Sam or that it was a UN organization—in fact, official visitors to the UN occasionally asked to see the second basement (U.N.C.L.E. headquarters in the show) to the puzzlement of their guides (it was a parking lot in real life). Finally, three months *after* the show began, the show's producers gave in to public pressure and came up with a meaning for the initials, United Network Command for Law Enforcement.

Trivia question

How did U.N.C.L.E.'s agents enter their headquarters?

Answer: U.N.C.L.E. agents entered headquarters through a dry cleaner's.

"Mission Impossible"

Each week Jim Phelps could be found in some telephone booth or a men's room in a deserted gas station or some other unsuspecting place looking for a hidden tape recorder and a batch of photographs. "Your mission, Jim, should you decide to accept it . . ." usually was to intervene (covertly, of course) in a crucial power struggle somewhere in the world. Oh, by the way, Jim, 'the' secretary (whose secretary?) will disavow any knowledge of your actions should you be captured or 'killed.' Then the moment we'd been waiting for—the tape self-destructed.

In seven years on TV, the IMF (Impossible Missions' Force) saved enough banana republics and eastern European almost-Communist countries to start their own branch of the United Nations.

TOP TEN
Spy Gadgets

1. James Bond's Aston Martin, equipped with: tire-slashers, oil-slick squirter, smoke-screen device, concealed machine gun, bulletproof windshield, and the ever-popular ejector seat.

2. Our Man Flint's special cigarette lighter. Performed eighty-three different functions and was the only weapon he needed.

3. Maxwell Smart's shoe-phone (and a watch-phone for when the shoe was being resoled).

4. James Bond's black attaché case containing a folding telescopic rifle, fifty gold sovereigns hidden in the lining, flat throwing knives that popped out at the touch of a button, and a tear-gas cartridge that exploded when the case was opened in the "normal" way.

5. The Cone of Silence, which kept anyone on "Get Smart" from overhearing a secret conversation. It also kept the people who were *having* the conversation from hearing it ("Oh no, Max—not the Cone of Silence").

6. Self-destructing tape recorder from "Mission Impossible."

7. James Bond's scuba tank from *Thunderball*. Equipped with CO_2 guns, a smoke screen, and a jet-propulsion engine.

8. "Little Nellie" one-man helicopter, used in *You Only Live Twice* by James Bond. Has an arsenal similar to the Aston Martin's.

9. Hymie, the robot, from *Get Smart*.

10. A watch, with a retractable wire for strangling someone. Bond almost got it with this.

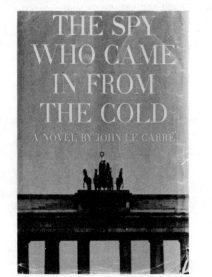

The first spy thriller ever to be the top bestseller of the year.

Seven Women Who Made It with James Bond

Honeychile Rider. A "nature girl" innocently collecting seashells on Crab Key, Dr. No's island, who unwittingly becomes involved with Bond and falls in love with him.

Tatiana Romanova. An innocent Russian girl working in the Soviet consulate in Istanbul (*From Russia with Love*). She is singled out by Rosa Kleb (villain) to seduce Bond and lure him into SPECTRE's trap. She thinks she's working for the Russians, unaware that SPECTRE plans to kill both her and Bond. How naïve. She falls in love with Bond.

Pussy Galore. Goldfinger's personal pilot and a real tough cookie, until, of course, she is kissed by Bond. After one kiss (and who knows what else), she switches sides and warns Washington of Goldfinger's plan to crack Fort Knox.

Jill Masterson. Goldfinger's girl until she is charmed by Bond.

Goldfinger takes his revenge on her by having her painted entirely with gold paint, which suffocates her. A ghastly fate.

Domino. Largo's mistress in *Thunderball*. She is befriended (and bedded) by Bond and eventually saves his life by killing Largo in the nick of time.

Fiona Volpe. It won't work this time, James Bond. Fiona is a SPECTRE agent (in *Thunderball*) who allows Bond to seduce her, but will not switch sides. She tries to kill Bond but only succeeds in getting herself killed. She should have switched.

Kissy Suzuki. A beautiful girl whom Bond "marries" for cover's sake in *You Only Live Twice*. Her great line: "It will be a pleasure serving under you."

Three Famous Sayings of Maxwell Smart

1. "Sorry about that, chief."

2. "Would you believe . . ."

3. "Missed it by *that* much."

The smashing success of "The Man from U.N.C.L.E." inspired a spin-off—"The Girl from U.N.C.L.E." (April Dancer, played by Stephanie Powers). About the only difference was a little less violence in "Girl" (it wasn't ladylike). Otherwise, not even the producer could tell the difference. "The plots are basically the same," he said. "Evil wins every battle and loses every war. Frankly, I can't tell one from the other."

James Bond

James Bond was the creation of British novelist Ian Fleming, himself a former spy, who had been writing spy thrillers since 1953. Fleming's successful mixture included beautiful girls, international intrigue, a plethora of special weapons used by and against Bond, high living on martinis and Beluga caviar, bad guys bent on world domination, high-stakes gambling in world-reknowned casinos, and a specially equipped car with concealed machine guns, ejector seats, and other unique weapons.

In the 1960s the movie versions of *Dr. No, From Russia with Love, Thunderball,* and *Goldfinger,* with Sean Connery starring as James Bond, made Fleming's hero even more popular. Millions of people around the world flocked to theaters to see them. (In Italy, Bond was known as Mr. Kiss-kiss Bang-bang.) Bond-age became an international passion.

Naturally, along with the success of Bondism came commercialism. Merchandisers went wild with items like 007 sweat shirts and quilts, 007 cologne and aftershave ("makes any man dangerous"), 007 pajamas (with secret pocket), a lace nightgown with 007 sewn into the hem ("go to bed dressed to kill"), 007 shoes and ladies' underwear, and numerous toy spy gadgets, including a toy exploding briefcase by Milton Bradley.

The spy angle was even worked into TV commercials. Bond Bread featured James Bread ("I'm Bread from Bond.") who foiled a plot to put phony Bond Bread on supermarket shelves. And Prince Macaroni featured a bad guy called "Goldnoodle" who get caught infiltrating stores with inferior noodles.

What was the appeal of the moral-less, shoot-'em-in-the-back Bond? As a fifteen-year-old boy put it, "That Bond's got guts. I wish my life was that exciting. A gorgeous dame on each arm and one in every bedroom."

NOTE: One James Bond product that they refused to license was a "Pussy Galore Nutcracker."

The Inside Story:

James Bond: Who Dunnit?

Ever stop to think how James Bond got popular in America? Fleming's books were already selling pretty well when *Dr. No* came out as a film in 1963. We'll give you a hint: In the early sixties, a well-known intellectual who reputedly read one book every day was asked by a reporter from *Life* magazine what his favorite books were. The list he gave them was filled with scholarly works, except for one —*From Russia with Love,* a James Bond thriller. This was the only book on the list that most of the American public could wade through or understand. The man had so much influence in America that James Bond became an overnight sensation in bookstores. Guess who.
Answer: John F. Kennedy.

U-2 Can Be a Spy

AFTER SHAVE

Colgate-Palmolive thought they had a winner with 007 after-shave. After all, doesn't every man want to smell like a secret agent?

Ric-Tic RECORDS

Myto Music BMI
Time: 2:45

RT-103
ZTSC-104309
Arranged By:
Sonny Sanders

AGENT DOUBLE-O-SOUL
(C. Hatcher, B. Sharpley)

EDWIN STARR
A Hitbound Production

Edwin Starr had this top-ten soul hit in 1965.

A battery-operated Secret Agent Double-O Seventy helicopter

This is Secret Agent Herb Regan. Well, actually, he's not a secret agent. He's an avid collector of James Bond memorabilia. But he'd make a great-looking secret agent, wouldn't he?

Gold plastic model of James Bond's famous Aston Martin. Today's price: $150–$200.

This Odd Job doll throws its hat when you pull the arm back, just like the real thing in *Goldfinger*. In the box, this guy is worth about $75.

007 Bond-O-Matic water pistol. Today's price: $25.

007 Goldfinger game

An ordinary dollar bill, right? Wait a minute! Some Bond-O-Maniac switched Sean Connery's face for George Washington's.

Your very own U.N.C.L.E. badge and credentials

Toy version of 007's gadget-filled briefcase. Today's price: $75–$100.

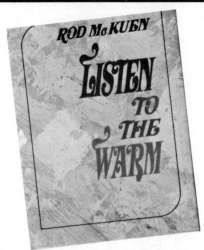

It's hard to believe that anyone ever thought Rod McKuen was profound. But lots of people did. He was the first author ever to have three books on "the best-seller of the year" lists, in 1968.

One of dozens of books of predictions by America's "Sleeping Prophet." Atlantis was supposed to rise in 1969. Oh well.

Maybe you've noticed we haven't said "Age of Aquarius" once in this book. Whoops! There goes our perfect record. Oh well, we might as well get the rest of it out too. What's your sign?

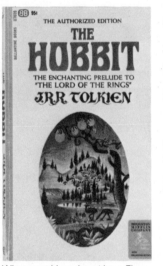

An autobiography by one of the founders of the Black Panther party

This 1937 book of poetry was rediscovered in the sixties when a New York disc jockey named Rosko began reading it to a background of sitar music late at night. Very heavy.

Where would we be without *The Lord of the Rings?* Think of all the hours you spent with J.R.R. Tolkien in Middle-earth. Frodo lives.

A classic by Malcolm X, who was later assassinated, another victim of the violence of the sixties.

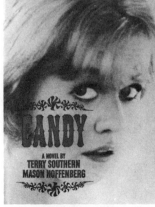

A TV dinner, Eastern mystic-style. This one and *Steppenwolf* were read by every self-respecting middle-class counterculture kid.

Soft-core porn for the masses. The *Chicago Tribune* stopped calling its best-seller list "best sellers" so that it wouldn't have to list *Candy.*

The author who understands postwar America better than anyone. A special "well-done hamburger" award to one of America's treasures.

The Academy Awards

Best Picture	Year
The Apartment	1960
West Side Story	1961
Lawrence of Arabia	1962
Tom Jones	1963
My Fair Lady	1964
The Sound of Music	1965
A Man for All Seasons	1966
In the Heat of the Night	1967
Oliver!	1968
Midnight Cowboy	1969

Julie Andrews   John Wayne   Sidney Poitier

Best Actor	Movie	Year
Burt Lancaster	*Elmer Gantry*	1960
Maximilian Schell	*Judgment at Nuremberg*	1961
Gregory Peck	*To Kill a Mockingbird*	1962
Sidney Poitier	*Lilies of the Field*	1963
Rex Harrison	*My Fair Lady*	1964
Lee Marvin	*Cat Ballou*	1965
Paul Scofield	*A Man for All Seasons*	1966
Rod Steiger	*In the Heat of the Night*	1967
Cliff Robertson	*Charly*	1968
John Wayne	*True Grit*	1969

Best Actress	Movie	Year
Elizabeth Taylor	*Butterfield 8*	1960
Sophia Loren	*Two Women*	1961
Anne Bancroft	*The Miracle Worker*	1962
Patricia Neal	*Hud*	1963
Julie Andrews	*Mary Poppins*	1964
Julie Christie	*Darling*	1965
Elizabeth Taylor	*Who's Afraid of Virginia Woolf?*	1966
Katharine Hepburn	*Guess Who's Coming to Dinner?*	1967
Katharine Hepburn	*The Lion in Winter*	1968
Maggie Smith	*The Prime of Miss Jean Brodie*	1969

$ Top Movies of the Decade $

1960

1. *Ben-Hur*
2. *Psycho*
3. *Operation Petticoat*
4. *Suddenly Last Summer*
5. *On the Beach*
6. *Solomon and Sheba*
7. *The Apartment*
8. *From the Terrace*
9. *Please Don't Eat the Daises*
10. *Oceans 11*

1961

1. *The Guns of Navarone*
2. *The Absent-Minded Professor*
3. *The Parent Trap*
4. *Swiss Family Robinson*
5. *Exodus*
6. *The World of Suzie Wong*
7. *The Alamo*
8. *Gone With the Wind* (reissue)
9. *101 Dalmations*
10. *Splendor in the Grass*

1962

1. *Spartacus*
2. *West Side Story*
3. *Lover Come Back*
4. *That Touch of Mink*
5. *El Cid*
6. *The Music Man*
7. *King of Kings*
8. *Hatari*
9. *Flower Drum Song*
10. *The Interns*

1963

1. *Cleopatra*
2. *The Longest Day*
3. *Irma La Douce*
4. *Lawrence of Arabia*
5. *How the West Was Won*
6. *Mutiny on the Bounty*
7. *Son of Flubber*
8. *To Kill a Mockingbird*
9. *Bye Bye Birdie*
10. *Come Blow Your Horn*

Top Box-Office Stars of the Decade

1960
1. Doris Day
2. Rock Hudson
3. Cary Grant
4. Elizabeth Taylor
5. Debbie Reynolds
6. Tony Curtis
7. Sandra Dee
8. Frank Sinatra
9. Jack Lemmon
10. John Wayne

1961
1. Elizabeth Taylor
2. Rock Hudson
3. Doris Day
4. John Wayne
5. Cary Grant
6. Sandra Dee
7. Jerry Lewis
8. William Holden
9. Tony Curtis
10. Elvis Presley

1962
1. Doris Day
2. Rock Hudson
3. Cary Grant
4. John Wayne
5. Elvis Presley
6. Elizabeth Taylor
7. Jerry Lewis
8. Frank Sinatra
9. Sandra Dee
10. Burt Lancaster

1963
1. Doris Day
2. John Wayne
3. Rock Hudson
4. Jack Lemmon
5. Cary Grant
6. Elizabeth Taylor
7. Elvis Presley
8. Sandra Dee
9. Paul Newman
10. Jerry Lewis

1964
1. Doris Day
2. Jack Lemmon
3. Rock Hudson
4. John Wayne
5. Cary Grant
6. Elvis Presley
7. Shirley MacLaine
8. Ann-Margret
9. Paul Newman
10. Richard Burton

Rock Hudson

1965
1. Sean Connery
2. John Wayne
3. Doris Day
4. Julie Andrews
5. Jack Lemmon
6. Elvis Presley
7. Cary Grant
8. James Stewart
9. Elizabeth Taylor
10. Richard Burton

1966
1. Julie Andrews
2. Sean Connery
3. Elizabeth Taylor
4. Jack Lemmon
5. Richard Burton
6. Cary Grant
7. John Wayne
8. Doris Day
9. Paul Newman
10. Elvis Presley

1967
1. Julie Andrews
2. Lee Marvin
3. Paul Newman
4. Dean Martin
5. Sean Connery
6. Elizabeth Taylor
7. Sidney Poitier
8. John Wayne
9. Richard Burton
10. Steve McQueen

1968
1. Sidney Poitier
2. Paul Newman
3. Julie Andrews
4. John Wayne
5. Clint Eastwood
6. Dean Martin
7. Steve McQueen
8. Jack Lemmon
9. Lee Marvin
10. Elizabeth Taylor

1969
1. Paul Newman
2. John Wayne
3. Steve McQueen
4. Dustin Hoffman
5. Clint Eastwood
6. Sidney Poitier
7. Lee Marvin
8. Jack Lemmon
9. Katharine Hepburn
10. Barbra Streisand

Doris Day

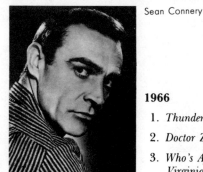

Sean Connery

1964
1. The Carpet-baggers
2. It's a Mad, Mad, Mad, Mad World
3. The Unsinkable Molly Brown
4. Charade
5. The Cardinal
6. Move Over Darling
7. My Fair Lady
8. What a Way to Go
9. Good Neighbor Sam
10. The Pink Panther

1965
1. Mary Poppins
2. The Sound of Music
3. Goldfinger
4. My Fair Lady
5. What's New Pussycat?
6. Shenandoah
7. The Sandpiper
8. Father Goose
9. Von Ryan's Express
10. The Yellow Rolls-Royce

1966
1. Thunderball
2. Doctor Zhivago
3. Who's Afraid of Virginia Woolf?
4. That Darn Cat
5. The Russians Are Coming, The Russians Are Coming
6. Lt. Robin Crusoe USN
7. The Silencers
8. Torn Curtain
9. Our Man Flint
10. A Patch of Blue

1967
1. The Dirty Dozen
2. You Only Live Twice
3. Casino Royale
4. A Man for All Seasons
5. Thoroughly Modern Millie
6. Barefoot in the Park
7. Georgy Girl
8. To Sir with Love
9. Grand Prix
10. Hombre

1968
1. The Graduate
2. Guess Who's Coming to Dinner?
3. Gone With the Wind (reissue)
4. The Valley of the Dolls
5. The Odd Couple
6. Planet of the Apes
7. Rosemary's Baby
8. The Jungle Book
9. Yours, Mine, and Ours
10. The Green Berets

1969
1. The Love Bug
2. Funny Girl
3. Bullitt
4. Butch Cassidy and the Sundance Kid
5. Romeo and Juliet
6. True Grit
7. Midnight Cowboy
8. Oliver!
9. Goodbye Columbus
10. Chitty Chitty Bang Bang

Dustin Hoffman

The young lady's dress is made from stainless steel. It weighs two pounds and won't rust in the rain.

Before the sixties, only nurses wore white stockings and only waitresses in sleazy nightclubs wore fishnet stockings. There goes one more taboo out the window. These leg fashions are by Hanes.

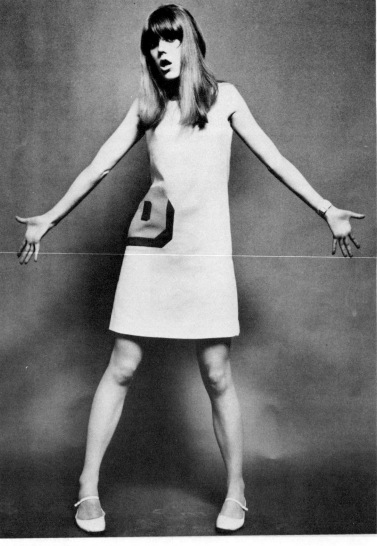

92

4 Fashion

1962

1968

Design by Pauline Trigère

Design by Rudi Gernreich

SHOES ON PARADE

Creative Capitalism Award to...

Thom McAn

No one knew how to latch on to teenage fads like Thom McAn Shoes did. Here are a few examples:

• Chubby Checker Twister Shoe. Cherry red, lacquered boots with a zipper on the side. Endorsed by Chubby himself in the early sixties as *the* shoe to twist in.

• Bombay Buckles. Inspired by the Indian music fad in 1968. Ads featured Ravi Shankar playing the sitar and a contest to win a "magical mystery tour."

• Monkee Boots. Half-boots with a buckle, tied in to the groovy TV show. When the show was canceled, the boots were dropped.

• GTO Shoes. The world's first "high-performance shoes." Promoted in conjunction with the popular Pontiac muscle car. They had "pointed toes, beveled accelerator heel, and double-beam eyelets." The cars were donated for a contest by Pontiac, and the shoes were donated to charity by Thom McAn when they flopped.

BOOTS-A-GO-GO

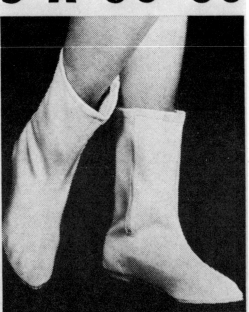

ALL THOSE IN THE KNOW — SWING WITH BOOTS-A-GO-GO. Cause a hullabaloo at your next shindig—wear the famous white Corrèges boots that are sweeping the discothèques. Here is a way-out style at a near-by price—now in a supple, lined vinyl that is cleaned in a wink and waterproof. Sizes 5 to 10 **$3.95**

For winter weather, order Knitted Orlon Bootliners. Red, White, or Black. **$1.00**

Flop of the Decade

Paper Dresses

From a 1966 press release: *Now every girl can have a paper dress to call her own.*

For the first time ever, paper is being made into dresses for real dolls—teenage girls. These "Paper Capers" are brightly printed skimps for beach and play. Made from specially prepared paper with a crisp, waffly textured surface, they are treated for fire resistance and sell for $1.25 each.

A girl might wear a Caper to her next patio party, then for a few outings at the beach, and then get to work with her scissors! She can cut it down to a tunic, then a shell, then to unusual place mats.

The paper dresses were developed by the Scott Paper Company, which sold them as a special offer by mail. When they received orders for five hundred thousand of them in six months, the fashion industry—and paper companies—got very excited. Disposable clothes *had* to be the wave of the future. Experts predicted that by 1980, 25 percent of the clothes that Americans wore would be made of paper, and from there, who knows? But how many paper dresses do you have in your closet?

Paper shoes from Herbert Levine

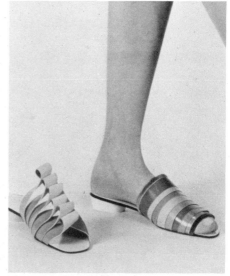

TOP TEN

Strange New Personal Care Products

1. *Dear Ear.* Ear makeup to wear with or without earrings, in "pink pearl" or "iridescent silver"

2. Mentholated tissue for "the sneeze that refreshes"

3. *Body Paint* from Coty. It came in lime, blue, and mauve, so a wearer could coordinate her skin with her mini-skirt. Included were a paint roller; paint pan; and miniature paint can.

4. Bosom makeup from Kenneth, a New York hairdresser. It came with a "cleavage delineator" and a "tip blush," which is "drawn across tips in a circular motion to achieve glistening rosy hue."

5. *Tatu.* Resembled a tattoo, but could be rubbed off with nail-polish remover. Designs included butterflies, hearts, and dollar signs.

6. *Leg Colour* leg makeup from Givenchy came in "shocking pink," violet mauve," turquoise blue," and sea green."

7. A nylon stocking with an automatic beauty treatment: stockings treated with a mixture of mink oil, turtle oil, sesame oil, and lanolin

8. *Knee Glo,* powder rouge for knees

9. Vinyl winking eyes to go on the knees, after applying knee makeup

10. Toothbrushes impregnated with strawberry, chocolate, lemon, lime, vanilla, and orange ice-cream odors.

60S! HALL OF FAME

Jean Shrimpton: The Shrimp

Until the sixties, modeling was considered to be a less-than-respectable profession. But that changed when Jean Shrimpton hit the scene. As put in *Beyond the Looking Glass,* "Riding the wave of 'swinging London' with the Beatles and the mod revolution, [she] was the first genuine model star to be imitated and adored for her own look, to become a model for her generation the way that Brigitte Bardot or Marlene Dietrich were models for theirs."

What People Said about the Shrimp

TWIGGY: "At school we were all mad about Jean Shrimpton . . . she was my idol. I always had a picture of her with me."

THE SHRIMP: "I have long arms, a long neck, long hands, long everything. If you take off the makeup, I'm ugly." Sure.

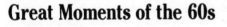

THE MINI-SKIRT— AN INTERNATIONAL CONTROVERSY

The Vatican. Women in mini-skirts were not allowed to enter Vatican City.

Malagassy Republic. An anti-mini-skirt law went into effect in 1967. Violators were subject to ten days in jail.

The Congo. In 1967 police arrested three hundred women wearing mini-skirts, which were banned.

Venezuela. Churches in Caracas put up signs telling people to give up their minis or "be condemned to hell."

Egypt. Women in minis were subject to a charge of indecent behavior. This law was passed because two women wore mini-skirts in the center of the city and caused a two-hour traffic jam.

Zambia. Gangs of youths roamed the streets assaulting girls in mini-skirts and forcibly lowering their hemlines. After a week, the war against mini-skirts was declared officially over when women went on television and said they "realized their mistake."

Greece. Anyone wearing them was jailed.

The Philippines. A congressman proposed that mini-skirts be banned. But the proposal was withdrawn when a congresswoman threatened to retaliate by outlawing elevator shoes.

Swaziland. Mini-skirts were considered immoral, but going topless was OK—that was the traditional form of dress.

Great Moments of the 60s

In Rio De Janeiro, in 1966, a sixty-three-year-old man on a bus was overcome when a young woman wearing a mini-skirt crossed her legs in the seat next to him. What did he do? What does *any* hot-blooded sixty-three-year-old do? He bit her on the thigh. He was sentenced to three days in jail.

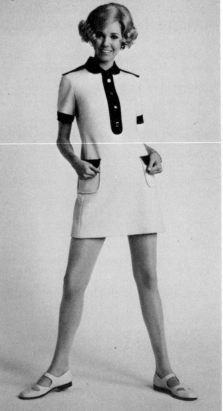

WHAT'S NEW

Pantyhose

At the beginning of the sixties, every woman wore stockings, but as the mini-skirt caught on, stockings and a garter belt became impossible to wear. Whenever a woman sat down, the tops of her stockings showed. It was embarrassing. But what could she do instead?

Hosiery manufacturers looked desperately for a solution to the problem. They tried all kinds of strange things—stocking glue (roll it onto the top of your leg, and the stocking will stick there—no garters needed), decorating the tops of the stockings (so it looked like they were meant to be seen), even girdles with stockings already attached. The only alternative that really made sense was a new kind of sheer tights called pantyhose, but they were much more expensive than stockings. Would women want to pay for them?

Where there's a buck, there's a way. Enter Mary Quant, with the "Total Look." She made tights fashionable, adding patterns to them to complement the rest of an outfit. Now a woman *had* to wear pantyhose with mini-skirts—it was part of the style. The convenience of pantyhose and gradually lower prices made them the only thing to wear. By the early seventies, only 5 percent of all hosiery sold was stockings.

The Meaning of the Mini-Skirt, Part I

Mary Quant, creator of the mini-skirt, reveals the meaning of the mini-skirt: "Sex."

TIME CAPSULE

The Kneel Test: In most schools during the sixties, if the hem of a dress didn't touch the floor when a girl was kneeling, it was considered a mini, and the guilty party was sent home. "And don't come back until you look respectable, young lady."

The Meaning of the Mini-Skirt, Part II

"Without a doubt, the pill bred the mini, just as it bred the topless bathing suit by Rudi Gernreich in 1964. They were intended to prove that women were in control of their destiny and would choose whom they wished to mate with . . ."—*In Fashion*, by Prudence Glynn

Fashion Photo of the Decade

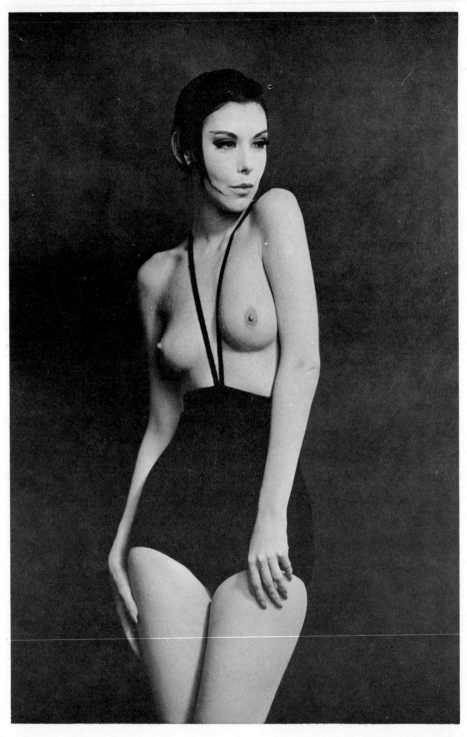

This photo of Rudi Gernreich's topless bathing suit made fashion history. The model is the extraordinary Peggy Moffitt. The photographer is William Claxton (who is also Ms. Moffitt's husband).

Scandals of the Sixties

Topless Bathing

• June 1964—New York City Commissioner of Parks Newbold Morris said women wearing topless bathing suits on NYC beaches would be issued summonses by police for indecent exposure. L.A. police issued the same warning.

• July 1964—The Vatican newspaper *L'Osservatore Romano* headlined an article on topless bathing suits "The Ultimate Shame," and said it "negates moral sense."

• June 1964—In an article entitled "Back to Barbarism," the Soviet newspaper *Isvestia* called the topless suits a sign of America's moral decay. "So the decay of the moneybags society continues," it said.

• July 1964—The topless suit was modeled in the *San Francisco Chronicle*—by a four-year-old girl.

60s Salutes

The Reverend Ed Watt

In Dallas, the Reverend Ed Watt and a group of protesters from the Carroll Avenue Baptist Mission picketed a department store that was displaying a topless bathing suit in its window. Their placards read: "We Protest these Suits in the Name of Christ." Watt said that church action was long overdue—topless shorts would be next.

The picketing continued until the department store removed the one topless suit it had from its display.

Were the protesters successful? Not exactly. They attracted so much attention to the suit that someone went in and bought it. Congratulations on a job well done, Ed.

The Inside Story: The Origin of the Topless Bathing Suit

The topless suit began simply as a prediction. One day in 1963, in an interview, fashion designer Rudi Gernreich commented that "in five years every American woman will be wearing a bathing suit that is bare above the waist." After saying that, he realized that if *he* didn't make that topless suit immediately, someone else would. But should he?

Before he could decide, Hess Brothers department store in Allentown, Pennsylvania, ordered some. Then other stores across the United States did too. Gernreich put the suit into production.

One of the things that focused national attention on the topless suit was that 1964 was an election year, and the Republican party seized on it as a symbol of the "deca-

dence" in America.

This produced millions of dollars worth of publicity for Gernreich, who said in amazement: "I never dreamed it would go beyond the fashion business into sociology."

By the way, the topless suit was never popular to wear—only three thousand were sold.

Great Moments of the 60s

Nude-Look Funnies, Part I

From the *New York Times*, Las Vegas, April 16, 1966: *State's Attorney Harvel Dickerson announced plans to initiate action to block the Silver Nugget Casino in North Las Vegas from using women blackjack dealers "clad in see-through chiffon costumes." He said it would increase the casino's chance of winning because "no one is going to be able to pay attention to his cards when the girls are standing across the table attired like that."*

Nude-Look Funnies, Part II

From the *New York Times*, London, June 24, 1964: *There were some second thoughts today on bare-bosom cocktail dresses. The company making the black crepe sheaths on sale here for about $15 each said it would like to stop production, but could not right now because it had so many orders to fill.*

Carnegie Models, Ltd., the manufacturer, said it had no idea there would be such interest in the topless models, which it made as a "giggle," and supplied to West End stores.

"A joke's a joke," a spokesman for the company said, "but this is promiscuous."

What's New

The "No-Bra" Bra

Bra manufacturers were a little scared. What happened if the burn-your-bra fad caught on?

But Rudi Gernreich came to the rescue with the "No-Bra Bra"! Suddenly there was no need to toss away your bra to look "with it," because the no-bra made the wearer look bra-less. The sheer "No-Bra" did so well that soon there were others, like "Dare" ("let a girl control what you see through a see-through"), "Bare Minimum," "Never-the-Less," and "Sweet Nothings."

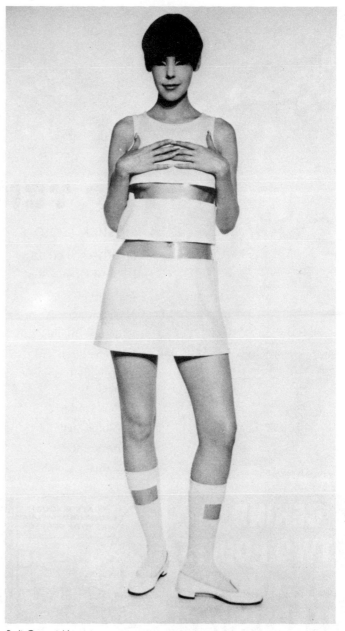

Rudi Gernreich's mini-dress with vinyl inserts

See-through cowboy boots from Herbert Levine's 1966 fall collection

Here's looking at you, kid

The bird is the word

TOP TEN

Lipstick Colors of the Sixties

1. Great Granny Red
2. Apricola
3. Nectaringo
4. Orange Jujube
5. In the Flesh
6. Naughty Iridescent Violette
7. Pink Paisley
8. Glitter Mellon
9. Bronze Rage
10. Carnaby Coral

The Cleopatra look

Cut up, cut out, cut loose with Max Factor's

CALIFORNIA
PINK·A·PADES

**Two pink escapades for lips and fingertips.
Two sheer…two shimmering…too tempting!**

It's the great new color adventure for summer.
Say it Pink-A-Pale (soft, feminine, fragile)
or Pink-A-Fling (lively, zingy, daring).
Wear it either super-sheer or super-frosted.
Any way you play it, have a wild
pink Pink-A-Pade!

California Pink-A-Pades by Max Factor

SUNGLASSES

"Sunglasses now sell faster than lipstick and makeup"—
Sea and Ski president, William Randall, 1968

Who's That Behind the Foster Grants?

Woody Allen

Jane Fonda

Hey, transistor sister! Dig this pair of sunglasses—its got a radio built into the frame, so you can really stay cool in the sunshine! Except it doesn't work too well. Every time you turn your head, the antenna gets blocked off and the groovy sounds fade away. And you can't go around with your head facing in one direction all the time. Nice idea, though.

Julie Christie

Robert Goulet

Five Stars Who Got America into Sunglasses

1. Jackie Kennedy. Popularized wraparound sunglasses

2. Audrey Hepburn. Wore big "lollipop" sunglasses in *Breakfast at Tiffany's*

3. Marcello Mastroianni, star of *La Dolce Vita*

4. Barry Goldwater, Republican candidate for president, 1964

5. Jim McGuinn, leader of the Byrds. Bought a pair of old "granny glasses" at a secondhand store, had them turned into sunglasses to shield his eyes from spotlights during performances, and started a fad.

BATHING SUITS

1961

The Inside Story: The Origin of the Bikini

The atomic bomb is responsible for many terrible things and at least one attractive thing—the bikini.

In July 1946, the American government announced that it would be exploding an atomic bomb as a test. This was the first *announced* atomic bomb blast, and rumors spread that it was going to be a "super-bomb" that could easily get out of control, start a massive chain reaction, and blow up the world. Rumors were especially prevalent in Paris, which had just come out of World War II, but Parisians simply couldn't take any more pressure. Hostesses used the bomb threat as an excuse to hold "end-of-the-world" parties. Young men used it as an excuse to convince reluctant girl friends to go "all the way"—if the world was going to end, why not break *all* the rules. When it was revealed that the test would take place in the then-unheard-of Bikini Atoll, the parties became "bikini" parties.

Meanwhile, a fashion show was being planned for the Piscine Molitor in Paris on July 5, 1946 (*piscine* is French for swimming pool), and they wanted something special in the way of publicity. Since people seemed to be throwing modesty to the winds, PR men came up with the idea of a "bikini" costume that would go as far as anyone dared to go with a bathing suit. So in the middle of the fashion show, Paris model Micheline Bernardini shocked the crowd when she appeared in the world's first bikini, and of course the scandalous suit got international attention.

Fifteen years later, the A-bomb was in the news again, and so were bikinis. But this time it was because the suits were popular and magazines applauded the number of women who were letting it all hang out.

1964

Creative Capitalism Award

The "Scandal Suit"

For "nice girls" who wanted to show a little skin, too, Cole of California introduced the Scandal Suit in 1965. They planned to make only forty thousand, but before the season was out, they had sold over two hundred thousand of them. It was the largest selling suit in the history of the bathing suit industry. What made it so popular? It had mesh in places that more daring suits left bare, so it was suggestive, but not blatant ("new but not nude," the company said). The name probably helped too. In fact, they came up with the name "Scandal Suit" before they had any idea what the suit would look like. And then there was the ad, which featured a girl on a beach—lying in a big brass double bed. Hmmm. Wonder what they meant by that.

1969

Scandals of the Sixties

Long Hair, 1965

• At Tremper High School in Kenosha, Wisconsin, Principal Harold Brushton kicked out one hundred fifty boys until they got their hair cut, despite one parent's protest that "God put hair on the head and there should be hair on the head."

• Students at Thomas Jefferson High in Springfield, Virginia, picketed when twenty boys were ordered to get haircuts, with signs such as "Do you have to be bald for an education?"

• Samuel Bell, fifteen, was expelled from Cleveland Heights High until he shaved off his neatly trimmed goatee. His mother said, "It's a case of one more American freedom down the drain."

• At Haverhill, Massachusetts, High, forty-seven football players had their hair cut after Coach Paul Ryan told them, "Either get haircuts or don't play ball. I'm not coaching a girls' team."

1963

1968

In 1963 this was considered outrageously long hair

Hey—all you guys with straight jobs and straight hair cuts —all these hairy new fashions got you down? Feel left out? Wanna look hip but you can't because your boss is square? Well, you don't have to *be* hip to *look* hip—all you need are fake moustaches, beards, or sideburns. Here's a 1968 testimonial from a satisfied customer: "Say tonight you've got a date with a swinging fashion model. You go home and change into your dinner clothes, but instead of putting on a shirt and tie, you put on a turtleneck. Then you put on your sideburns, moustache, and beard. You're as swinging as she is. Tomorrow you go back to Wall Street looking like a broker again."

Overreaction of the Decade

From the *New York Times*, February 12, 1966: *On February 11, 1966, in Lansing, England, a fifteen-year-old Rolling Stones fan committed suicide by throwing himself in front of an oncoming train. He was upset because his guardian had made him get a "short back and sides" haircut.* Now it'll never grow back.

60s! HALL OF FAME

Andre Courréges
Father of the Mini-Skirt

In 1965, Andre Courréges brought the mini-skirt and go-go boots to the world of high fashion. This made it a "style" instead of a fad and inspired the women whom the world watched— including Jackie Kennedy—to shorten their skirts. "They don't have to be worn that short," said the man who started a fashion revolution; "one exaggerates to establish an idea, to put across a point."

Mary Quant
Mother of the Mini-Skirt

Mary always hated the straight clothes that grown-ups wore. So in 1955 when she opened the world's first boutique, the clothes she designed for it were wild and "kinky." They used bright colors, lots of plastic, and her dresses had shorter hemlines than the normal. In 1965, taking a cue from the young girls in London, she manufactured skirts that were outrageously short for the time—mini-skirts. Though she is not considered a designer by fans of haute couture, she had more influence on fashions of the decade than most of the premier fashion designers.

Rudi Gernreich

Master of the "outrageous gesture" in clothes, creator of the topless swimsuit. "The generation feels defeated; nothing seems to make any difference. The look in clothes expresses an antiattitude, the result of being bored—bored by being told what to do, bored by the hopelessness of the bomb, and the abstractions of government, bored by sexual discovery in high school. And so if you're bored, you go for the outrageous gestures. Everything else seems to have lost any meaning."

HAIR

Five Hairstyles
by Vidal Sassoon

Great Moments of the 60s

In L.A., June 1962, fifteen stewardesses from American, United, Western, and Trans World Airlines called a press conference demanding the right to color their hair. The airlines didn't allow stewardesses to color their hair because, according to one official, "If you let those girls run wild there's no telling what would happen. They might end up with green hair to match the seat coverings."

TIME CAPSULE

1965—A new fad for girls: ironing your hair to make it straight like folk-singer Joan Baez's. Handy hint: instead of regular rollers, use beer cans.

1963—EXTRA! EXTRA! Mobsters stealing human hair wigs! (Human hair costs $228/oz., gold costs $36/oz.)

STOP OVERSPRAYING YOUR HAIR!

NEW EXCLUSIVE HAIRSPRAY DEVELOPMENT

Breck Shampoo takes care of your hair the way beauty soap takes care of your skin. Because of all leading shampoos only Breck doesn't have a synthetic detergent base. So it helps leave in natural oils that keep hair soft and manageable.

The beauty soap for your hair.

BRECK

DADDY GOES WILD!

1. Daddy says "clothes make the man," but he's tired of looking like all the other stockbrokers.

2. Johnny Carson wore a Nehru suit and a turtleneck on TV, so Daddy tried one, too.

3. Edwardian styles were in, so Daddy bought a double-breasted jacket.

4. "Why should I hide my mod shirt and tie under a dull jacket," he said, when they wouldn't let him into the country club.

5. "Why should I wear a tie *at all?*" Look at Daddy's bell-bottoms and sandals; isn't he hip?

6. He liked his new threads so much that he and his friend (they're just friends) went to Carnaby Street (that's in London, England) and bought these far-out suits.

7. Daddy got tired of dressing in suits—too formal—so he decided to wear nothing but jeans (embroidered, of course).

8. Oh, no! Daddy! What's going on here? Daddy said, "Clothes hide the inner man," and left to join a commune in Oregon. What will the other stockbrokers think?

WOMEN IN PANTS

Quant

It wasn't considered "ladylike" for a woman to wear pants in the sixties. In 1968, for example, *Women's Wear Daily* polled several employers about it. Some of the comments: Macy's, New York: "We don't allow it"; First National Bank of Boston: "We would allow our women employees to wear pants if they continue to act like women"; Chase Manhattan Bank: "We don't hire women wearing pants"; Citizens and Southern National Bank, Atlanta: "We would not want to be among the first . . ." Today this seems ridiculous.

Pucci

Great Moments of the 60s

In 1969, Judy Carne, a star of "Laugh-In," visited the posh "21" Club wearing a "tunic-topped pants-suit." When the management refused to let her in because of its policy against women in pants, she took off her pants, checked them in the checkroom, and sailed off into the dining room wearing only her tunic—barely long enough to be called a micro-mini-skirt. The club changed its policy on pants the next day. Sock it to 'em, Judy.

TIME CAPSULE

Until around 1969—or even later—girls were not allowed to wear pants to school.

Courrèges

JUNIORS
& PETITES

Turtleneck pullover
sold on p. 72.

J. C. Penney

110

Three Forgotten Dresses of the Sixties

1. The Canned Dress, or "Le Canned Dress," as it was called. Created by Wippette Sportswear in 1966, because the company's owner was "being driven crazy by cans . . . every time I turned around I bumped into a can. . . . First I saw canned candles, then canned air, and then—I wondered why dresses couldn't be packed the same way."

2. The do-it-yourself dress. In 1966, innovative American designer Betsy Johnson created a thirty-dollar "clear vinyl, halter-necked shift," which came, for five dollars extra, with a do-it-yourself kit of "copper coin dots, silver stars, and metallic blue rays" to paste onto the dress however you wanted.

3. The Electric Dress. In 1967, Diana Dew, a New York designer, came up with a "bright idea"—a dress with plastic lamps sewn into it and attached to a rechargeable battery pack. There were as many as fifty lights in a dress, and a dial on the battery pack controlled them—they flashed from one to twelve times per second, depending on how flashy a girl wanted to be.

Rock stars were trend-setters. They could get away with wearing anything—and did. Pictured here is Procol Harum.

Designed by Donald Brooks

Great Moments of the 60s
The Brigitte Bardot Bra

In 1960, Lovable Brassiere Company introduced the bra they hoped everyone had been waiting for—the Brigitte Bardot Bra. "Now the secret of the 'Bardot Look' is yours," they said. With such an alluring female supporting the project, could sales possibly droop? Sales stacked up to the well-rounded figure of thirty-six thousand a week.

111

"That'll be $15.76 for your week's worth of groceries, ma'am."

Unprecedented affluence made shopping more popular than ever in the sixties.

To accommodate all the eager shoppers, developers built huge commercial areas with scores of stores. At first shopping centers were just for shopping. But more and more they became a place to go, a place to be. They had a parklike atmosphere, with trees and benches. Soon they began to include movie theaters, fancy restaurants, nightclubs. Community events like fashion shows, local proms, fund-raising activities were held there. Teenagers hung out there, too.

Most Bizarre Shopping Center Idea of the Decade

In 1962, a developer announced plans to build a shopping center in Roswell, New Mexico, that would double as a fallout shelter, accommodating eight thousand people underground for two weeks. People could reserve space for two hundred fifty dollars per person, which would guarantee "organized school, movies, games, and survival." Education "would serve to minimize panic and depression." Great. But would stores stay open late?

Now the store comes to you—The McCrory Shopmobile!

Great Moments of the 60s

In 1968, Richard Nixon scheduled seventeen of his one hundred major campaign speeches in shopping centers. His workers were delighted to discover that *everyone* knew where the centers were—as opposed to his downtown speeches, when they had to give out maps to make sure he had an audience. But not every center was willing to let him appear. The Garden State Plaza in Paramus, New Jersey, for example, denied his request: "He would have interfered with shopping," plaza officials said. First things first, we always say.

He loved shopping centers in 1968.

Three Fascinating Statistics about Shopping Centers

1. In 1952 there were only about 100 small shopping centers in the whole country. By 1969, there were 12,500. Of these, 8,500 were built during the sixties.

2. Shopping centers in the fifties were just a few local stores, built in the same lot as a supermarket. By 1962, the average shopping center had 40 stores in it. By 1968, the average shopping center had 125 to 150 stores. They had virtually become shopping *cities!*

3. Nine hundred million square feet of shopping center space opened up in the sixties.

But not this one—Garden State Plaza, Paramus, New Jersey.

From out of nowhere, a new art form appeared in 1961—Pop Art. It consisted of comic strips, cigarette packs, enormous hamburgers, and everyday objects.

You call *that* art? How could anyone take a critic seriously when he raved about a giant Brillo box? Even some gallery owners were appalled. When Andy Warhol's first Campbell's Soup Can paintings went on display in an L.A. art gallery for one hundred dollars apiece, another gallery down the street contemptuously stacked soup cans in its windows with the sign: "The real thing, 29¢."

But whatever it was, Pop Art seemed to take hold. Newspapers and magazines covered it. Museums exhibited it and gave it respectability. And galleries found they could make money selling it. The result: a handful of artists whom most Americans considered charlatans changed the way we looked at ourselves.

Manufacturers picked up on the self-conscious humor of Pop and made products that appealed to it: Pop Art posters, inflatable Seven-Up cans, pillows in the shape of Alka Seltzer packages, towels with Heinz Ketchup bottle pictures on them. Soon, it was a worldwide fad.

Andy Warhol.
Campbell's Soup Can. 1964.

Taking a cue from Warhol: The Campbell's Souper Dress. Available from Campbell's Soup Company in 1968.

Scandals of the Sixties

Andy Warhol and the Brillo Boxes

For a show at a gallery in Toronto in 1965, Andy Warhol moved eighty of his Pop Art sculptures of Brillo boxes, cornflakes boxes, and the like across the Canadian border, only to discover that they were classified as "merchandise" instead of "art" by the Canadian government. That meant that the gallery owner had to pay an import duty, which he refused to do. He told newsmen that Canada had embarrassed itself and was now the "laughing-stock of the art world."

A government spokesman countered that the boxes looked too much like their commercial counterparts, and "the only thing the artist adds is his signature."

But, said Warhol, "I don't sign them."

Roy Lichtenstein. *Popeye.* 1961.

Tom Wesselmann. *The Great American Nude #53.* 1964.

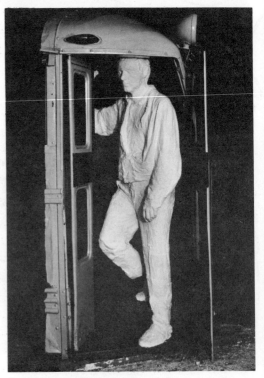

George Segal. *Man Leaving Bus.* 1967.

Wow! These are about the grooviest pens anywhere. 1967.

What's Op, doc? Nothin' much. Except my eyeballs are falling out looking at these cra-a-azy patterns! And they're everywhere. They're puttin' 'em on clothes, wallpaper—even pens. This world's freakin' out, I tell ya!

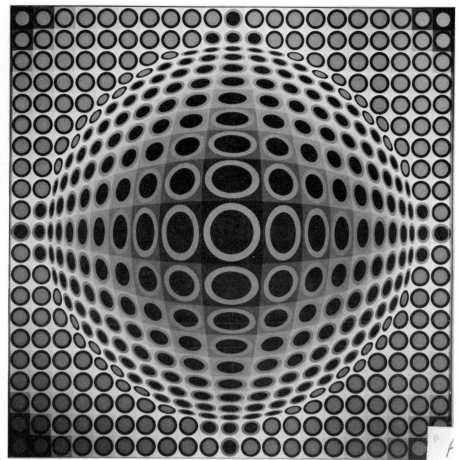

Victor Vasarely. *Vega 222.* 1969.

Bridget Riley. *Current.* 1964.

An inflatable plastic Coca-Cola bottle

"What's black and yellow and read all over? The Yellow Pages dress! It's wacky, wild, wonderful. A flashy paper put-on that's just plain fun to wear." 1967.

Outer Space

Inner Space

Launch Vehicle

Blast-off

Space Suit

Space Travel

Inner Space

Outer Space

In Orbit

View from Space

COPS EAT FLOWERS

Floating in Space

Outer Space   Inner Space

America's First Spaceman

Space Travelers

Space Rendezvous

120

121

KENNEDY FOR PRESIDENT

JOHNSON FOR VICE PRESIDENT

1960

NIXON·AGNEW
MAKE MARYLAND'S VOTE COUNT FOR AMERICA

VOTE **NIXON LODGE** Experience counts!

1960

Posters

Bobby

1968

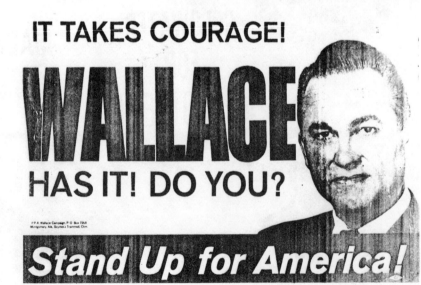

IT TAKES COURAGE!
WALLACE
HAS IT! DO YOU?
Stand Up for America!

1968

A 1968 banner announcing that the Republicans were the honest party. Pre-Watergate, of course.

Prelude to disaster. While the Democrats were nominating Hubert Humphrey for president, the Chicago police were beating demonstraters to a pulp outside the convention hall. The entire spectacle was shown on national TV and cost the Democrats the election.

We Knew Them When

George Bush's first run for office was in 1964, when he was nominated for Senate by the Republicans. Though he lost in the Johnson landslide, he did well enough to be considered a hot prospect. In 1966, he was the first Republican ever sent to Congress from Houston, the only office he was ever elected to until 1980, when he was elected vice-president.

This is one of the rarest buttons of the sixties. There are only two in existence, to our knowledge. But if you've got one, put it in your safe-deposit box. It's worth about one thousand dollars.

Believe it or not, Spiro Agnew was elected governor of Maryland as a liberal/moderate in 1966. His opponent was a perennial loser whose slogan "A man's home is his castle" was a code word for racism, and Agnew (who later, as vice-presidential candidate, told white audiences that there *was* no "black vote") played it for all it was worth.

Jimmy Carter won his first bid for elective office in 1962, when he was elected to the Georgia State Senate. In 1966, he came in third in the Democratic primary for governor. He spent the next four years traveling around the state, giving over eighteen hundred speeches, preparing to run for governor in 1970. He won that race. Hmmm . . . maybe it would work for a higher office too.

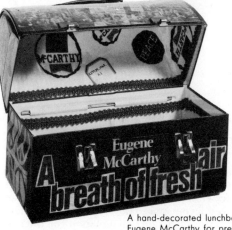

A hand-decorated lunchbox advocating Eugene McCarthy for president

125

ACTORS IN POLITICS

★ ★ ★ ★ ★ ★ ★ ★ ★ ★ ★ ★

Starring Ronald Reagan as "The Governor" (1966)

Now Ronald Reagan fulfills his acting potential with a dramatic role suited to his acting skills—Republican candidate for governor! You'll laugh with delight as this tall, ruggedly handsome Good Guy makes the toughest choice of his life—should he sign on for another season as host of "Death Valley Days" or run for governor? Thrill to his campaign rhetoric as he ignores his opponent and attacks welfare bums, dirty hippies, and leftist college students. Watch in amazement as his popularity grows!

George Murphy as "The Senator" (1964)

Who says vaudeville is dead? Remember George Murphy, the master of the Old Sof' Shoe, tap-dancing with Shirley Temple in *Little Miss Broadway* (1938)? Remember when he starred with Judy Garland in *Little Nellie Kelly* (1940)? How about when he adopted Margaret O'Brien, a homeless waif, in *Big City* (1948)? Well, now he's got a new starring role—watch in 1964 as he tap-dances into the United States Senate.

Shirley Temple as "The Losing Candidate"

Golly! Is that Shirley Temple? Little Shirley won the hearts of the nation in the thirties, but she couldn't win a California Congressional primary election. She ran as a Vietnam hawk and lost to Paul McCloskey, an outspoken dove. Maybe voters thought she'd break into a chorus of "Good Ship Lollipop" on the House floor.

Dick Gregory as "The Comedian" (1968)

For a comedian, Dick Gregory sure takes things seriously. Imagine—a black man running for president! "A lot of people ask me what is the first thing I would do if I became president of the United States. I thought everyone knew the first thing I would do is paint the White House black . . . But when I get to be president, I'll be fair. I'll have one white cat in my cabinet . . . and since LBJ gave us our first colored cabinet member, I'd make him my white cabinet member . . . I'll make LBJ Commissioner of Barbecued Ribs."

Goldwater Trading Stamps. "Trade in Johnson for Goldwater."

A President Lyndon Baines Johnson doll from Remco. But what would you possibly want one for? Well, to doll collectors, it is worth about forty dollars.

Great Moments of the 60s
Pat Paulsen for President (1968)

Pat Paulsen threw his hat into the presidential ring on "The Smothers Brothers Comedy Hour." Running on the STAG (Straight Talkin' American Government) party ticket, Pat Paulsen made more sense than most of the other candidates. And *they* were taking it seriously. Some of his pearls of wisdom:

• "This is the richest nation in the world, and we'd be even richer if it weren't for all the poor people."

• "I know what the average American wants. In fact, I'd like to get a little of it myself."

• "I will always be aware of my humble station in life as a common, ordinary, simple savior of America's destiny."

• "I hear there's a lot of talk in California for Governor Reagan. Well, there's a lot of talk in California for Donald Duck, too."

Not everybody thought Paulsen was funny. "Hubert Humphrey once told me I cost him the election," Paulsen told us, "and he wasn't smiling when he said it."

For all you effete snobs and pusilanimous pussyfooters, here's your very own Spiro Agnew watch.

"I'm the only president you've got."

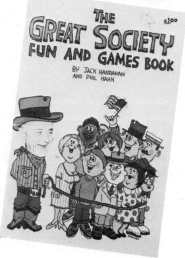

"Happiness is . . ."

The catalyst that created the "Peanuts" boom was a small, square volume called *Happiness Is a Warm Puppy*—a collection of phrases gathered from "Peanuts" comic-strips and combined with Charles Schultz illustrations into a book of simple truths about emotion.

What the public didn't know was that although Schultz had written the text, the entire project was actually assembled by Connie Boucher, a businesswoman (and "Peanuts" lover) who had proved her business acumen by forming her own company, Determined Productions, to successfully publish a *Winnie-the-Pooh Coloring Book* when no New York publisher would touch it.

In 1962, Ms. Boucher's entrepeneurial sixth sense was right on target again. *Happiness Is a Warm Puppy* was exactly what America wanted to read. It was on the best-seller list for two years, sold over half a million copies in its first six months, spawned at least two imitators and two sequels (Imitators: *Happiness Is a Rat Fink* and Johnny Carson's best seller, *Misery Is a Blind Date*. Sequels: *Security Is a Thumb and a Blanket* and *A Friend Is Someone Who Likes You*), and actually created a whole genre of American expression—"Happiness is . . ." (even used in a Kent cigarette ad campaign), "Love is . . . ," "A Friend is . . ."

This was just the beginning for "Peanuts" and Determined Productions. Ms. Boucher turned her success into a lasting one by turning the world on to "Peanuts"—particularly Snoopy—with sweat shirts, stuffed Snoopys, "Peanuts" dolls, and much more.

Snoopy Dogfood. "Our own dog thinks it's great," said Charles Schultz.

Creative Capitalism Award

To the Ford Motor Company, the First to Use "Peanuts" Characters in an Advertisement

"Peanuts" characters were first used in advertising by Ford to help promote its 1960 compact car, the Falcon. Ford thought the "Peanuts" gang would be perfect because "they were just like the Falcon: compact in size, fun, and they had adult appeal." Luckily for Ford, Schultz was a satisfied Ford owner, which made it easy for him to go along with the idea. The ads—a big success—were given credit for helping Falcon become the top-selling American small car. They also proved to businessmen that "Peanuts" characters sold merchandise. The ads ran until 1962, when Ford decided that the rights to use the characters were too expensive.

Look at it this way, Snoopy—happy people make the very best masters, and Falcon knows many ways to make people happy! Falcon's improved engine gives them great gas economy—takes them 6,000 miles between oil changes, too. Falcon also offers comfortable room for 6 people—luggage and all. And it's still America's lowest priced 6-passenger car! Today, with over one million happy owners, Falcon is America's favorite compact. For happiness—and a Falcon—see your Ford Dealer.

FORD Falcon '62
AMERICA'S BEST SELLING COMPACT CAR

"Peanuts"

The "Peanuts" Story

Today, Snoopy, Charlie Brown, and the rest of the "Peanuts" gang are recognized worldwide as symbols of American culture. But it was during the sixties that they first began to assume that identity. What made them folk heroes? Here's what Charles Schultz said in 1969: "The strip is very introspective and there are a lot of losers in it, and maybe we're going through a phase like that. Practically everyone can identify with a loser. There are very few club champions."

Whatever the reason, their popularity is amazing:

As a Comic Strip. From humble beginnings in 1950, when about a dozen newspapers carried it, "Peanuts" grew to 650 papers in 1961, 700 papers in 1966, and *1,000* in 1969!

On TV. Schultz turned down a regular TV series in favor of specials so that he could prepare them properly. "A Charlie Brown Christmas," "Charlie Brown's All-Stars," and the rest drew huge audiences. For example, in 1969, his Christmas special drew more than 55 percent of the TV audience even though it was the *fifth* time it had been broadcast.

Books. In 1963, *Happiness Is a Warm Puppy* (which made Snoopy a star) became a number-one best seller, selling over 500,000 copies in its first year. It was followed by two more, *A Friend Is Someone Who Likes You* and *Security Is a Thumb and a Blanket.*

Products. The most incredible indicator of "Peanuts" popularity was (and is) in the marketplace. It was estimated by *Business Week* that in 1969, $50 million worth of "Peanuts" merchandise was sold. "We once thought about putting out a Charlie Brown baseball glove," Schultz commented, "but what kid would want one? He couldn't catch a thing with it."

The Royal Guardsmen's tale of Snoopy in the skies sold millions of records, soaring to number one in early 1967.

"Peanuts" in Space

Snoopy and Charlie Brown even got official recognition from NASA. In 1967, NASA initiated a program that would honor contractors with good safety records. The award they settled on was a silver pin in the image of . . . Snoopy! It was commonly referred to as the "Silver Snoopy Award." A NASA spokesman explained that Snoopy was chosen as a mascot because he was "the only dog with flight experience." *Curse you, Red Baron!*

Then, in 1969, the command and lunar modules for *Apollo 10* were designated with the code names "Snoopy" and "Charlie Brown." "We thought Snoopy as an astronaut would be perfect," said a spokesman for NASA. "We took it to the astronauts and they liked it."

Schultz was quite flattered. "It was a great thrill, especially for an old Buck Rogers fan, to know your characters would be the first in outer space." But Schultz added a practical note as well: "Using Charlie Brown on a space flight is almost like tempting fate, isn't it?"

PEANUTS characters: © 1950, 1952, 1958 United Feature Syndicate, Inc.

131

> *. . . I believe that this nation should commit itself to achieving the goal, before this decade is out, of landing a man on the moon and returning him safely to the earth. No single space project in this period will be more impressive to mankind, or more important for the long-range exploration of space; and none will be so difficult or expensive to accomplish.* —President John F. Kennedy, May 25, 1961

$ A Fast Buck $

1. Helms Bakery in L.A., which sold NASA sixteen loaves of bread for $6.72, called itself "the first bread selected by NASA to go to the moon."

2. The Hilton Hotel Corp. placed an ad with the headline: "If someone had to beat the Hiltons to the moon, we're glad it was *Apollo 11.*"

3. Cramer Gum Corp. made gumballs with moonlike craters. They called them "moon landing specials."

4. Bristol Myers offered a moon globe for $5.75 and a Bufferin boxtop.

5. A book about the moon landing was on sale at bookstores before the *Apollo 11* astronauts were even out of quarantine.

Destination: Moon

Hand-blown glass Christmas-tree ornament, made in Italy

The Inside Story:

Why We Don't Own the Moon

The United States waived any claim to the moon when it signed the Treaty on Exploration and Use of Outer Space in 1967. This established the lunar surface as the property of all mankind.

Mike

Buzz

Neil

Apollo 11 Collector

George Wahlert has what he believes to be the world's largest collection of *Apollo 11* memorabilia. No moon rocks or lunar module yet, but he has stamps, plates, mugs, cups, plaques, medals, flags, towels, curtains, T-shirts, hats, pencils, spoons, watches, clocks, and even a bedspread—all commemorating the *Apollo 11* flight to the moon. When *Apollo* landed on the moon on his birthday, George became hooked on collecting. Now he has enough stuff to fill a museum. Would he like to go to the moon someday? He already has his Pan Am ticket. He even bought two acres of moon land and has a moon deed to prove it. "There's probably a lunar rover parked on my property right now," he says.

Five Reactions to the Moon Landing

1. *Ghana.* Nagai Kassa VII, a tribal chief, listened to the *Apollo 11* saga on his shortwave radio through the Voice of America. Reportedly, he was worried that the astronauts would fall off the moon, and was amazed that they were able to fit on it at all. "The moon is so small as I see it that I didn't think there would be enough room," he said.

2. *India.* Astrologers wondered if the moon was "too tainted for use in soothsaying, now that a man had walked on it."

3. *Alaska.* Unimpressed with the scientific aspects of the lunar landing, an Eskimo interpreted the moon landing for a reporter as a way to predict the weather. He said it was a sure sign of a "hard winter next year."

4. *Somewhere in the Arab World.* Al Fatah, the terrorist organization, objected that Arab newspapers were giving more attention to the moon landing than "terrorist missions against Israel."

5. *N.Y.C..* The lunar landing was celebrated with a "moon bash" in Central Park. The Department of Parks invited the millions of New Yorkers to enjoy huge screens with live TV coverage, searchlights, a film collage, synthetic Northern Lights, dancing to "moon music," inflatable sculpture, and a blue-cheese picnic.

The World's Most Expensive Rock

The first lunar rocks cost $400,000,000 per pound.

133

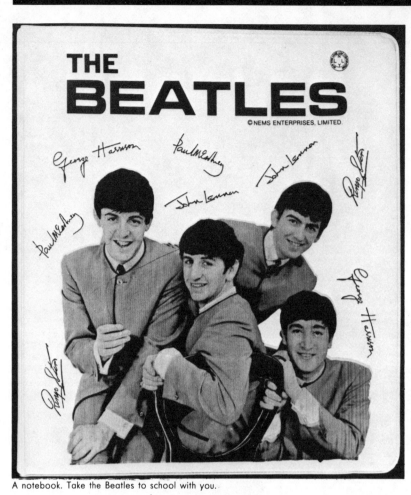

A notebook. Take the Beatles to school with you.

Looks like a Ringo doll, but it's a bubble bath (the head unscrews).

60s Selects... Five Acts of Beatlemania

1. On February 17, 1964, windows were broken, autos damaged, youngsters hit by flying glass when the Beatles landed at Miami International Airport.

2. In Seattle a fan trying to get as close as possible fell from an overhead beam and landed at Ringo's feet.

3. In Cleveland the Beatles were dragged offstage by fans while mounted police lassoed two hundred fans together in a giant net.

4. In Toronto they arrived at the airport at 3 A.M. and passed seventeen miles of parked cars of fans waiting to see them.

5. In Denver the bed linen they had used at two hotels during stopovers was purchased by a business consortium, placed in a maximum-security bank vault, and later cut into three-inch squares and sold for ten dollars apiece.

The Beatles

A REMCO TOY COMPANY SPOKESMAN: "They are the most promotional item since the flapper era."

PRINCE PHILLIP: "It seems to me that these blokes are helping people to enjoy themselves, and that is far better than the other [fighting and stealing]."

ISVESTIA (SOVIET) ARTICLE: "The reason for the immediate cult of the Beatles is youth looking for idols to replace those worshiped by their parents."

THIRTEEN-YEAR-OLD FAN: "The Beatles are just so funny and nice and, well, cool."

INDONESIA'S PRESIDENT SUKARNO: "Beatlemania is a mental disease."

HARVARD UNIVERSITY PROFESSOR: "It's a form of protest against the adult world."

THE NATION: "Beatlemania as a phenomenon is food for dull minds."

AN AMERICAN TEENAGER: "I suppose the Beatles were outlets for love and hate. When absolutely nothing else was good, I'd go to my room and have the Beatles, especially my darling, John. They gave me something to live for when everything was black and depressing."

THE SUNDAY TIMES (London): "The Beatles are the greatest composer since Beethoven."

GEORGE HARRISON: "We're rather crummy musicians."

JOHN'S AUNT MIMI: "The guitar is fine, John, but you'll never make a living at it."

TOP TEN
Beatles Firsts

• First U.S. TV appearance: tape of them singing "She Loves You" on Jack Paar, January 3, 1964.

• First live TV appearance in United States: The Ed Sullivan Show," 2/9/64; sang "All My Lovin'," "She Loves You," and "This Boy."

• First U.S. tour: 8/19/64–9/20/64. Toured twenty-five cities. Opening show at Cow Palace, San Francisco. Supporting acts: Jackie DeShannon, Righteous Brothers, Bill Black Combo, The Exciters.

• First U.S. Beatles single: "My Bonnie," April 23, 1962. Released as Tony Sheridan and the Beat Brothers. They were backing Sheridan.

• First U.S. single to hit the charts: "I Want to Hold Your Hand," January 1964.

• First tour ever: Early 1960. Two-week tour of Scotland backing a singer named Johnny Gentle. At that time, called themselves the Silver Beatles and used phony names—John: Johnny Silver; Paul: Paul Ramon; George: Carl Harrison.

• First U.S. concert: February 11, 1964, Washington D.C., at the Coliseum. Other acts: The Caravelles, Tommy Roe, the Chiffons.

• First Beatles recording ever: Hamburg, Germany, December 1960. Backed a singer with the song "Fever." It wasn't released; only four 78 rpm records were made from it. The rarest record of the sixties.

• First audition for a recording contract: January 1, 1962, with Decca. They were refused.

• First Beatle single in England: "Love Me Do." Recorded September 11, 1962.

Beetle Comb™

COMB THE BEETLES OUT OF YOUR HAIR!

©PAPCO Roslyn, L.I., N.Y.

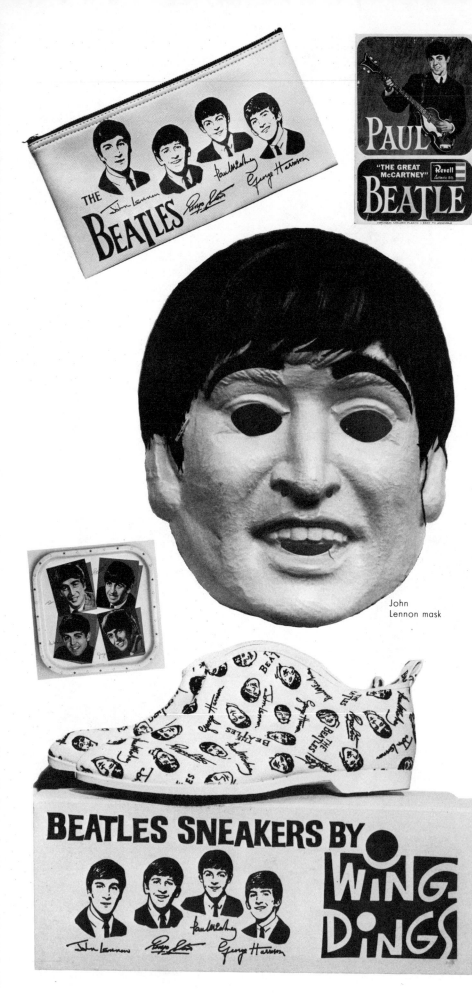

John Lennon mask

BEATLES SNEAKERS BY WING DINGS

PAUL "THE GREAT McCARTNEY" BEATLE Revell Authentic Kits

TOP TEN

Fab Facts about the Fab Four

1. How they got their name (one story): "I was thinking about what a good name the Crickets would be for an English group. The idea of Beetles came into my head. I decided to spell it 'Beatles' to make it look like beat music, just a joke." John Lennon.

2. The Beatles used seven other names before the Beatles: the Beat Makers; Johnny and the Moondogs; the Nurk Twins (just John and Paul); the Quarrymen; the Rainbows; Ricky and the Red Streaks; and the Silver Beatles.

3. Their number-one U.S. songs, in chronological order include: "I Wanna Hold Your Hand"; "She Loves You"; "Can't Buy Me Love"; "Love Me Do"; "A Hard Day's Night"; "I Feel Fine"; "Eight Days a Week"; "Ticket to Ride"; "Help"; "Yesterday"; "We Can Work It Out"; "Paperback Writer"; "Penny Lane"; "All You Need Is Love"; "Hello Goodbye"; "Hey Jude"; and "Get Back."

4. In less than a decade, they sold over 125 million singles and 85 million LPs.

5. They had the most number-one records during the sixties—seventeen—compared to the Supremes, who were second with twelve.

6. They had the most top-ten hits during the sixties—twenty-nine.

7. They were in second place for most records to make the charts in the sixties. They had sixty-two to Elvis's sixty-three.

8. In 1964, they had thirty-one songs that hit the charts. Elvis was averaging around six per year at that time.

9. On April 4, 1964, they had the top five songs on the *Billboard* charts—1. "Can't Buy Me Love"; 2. "Twist and Shout"; 3. "She Loves You"; 4. "I Wanna Hold Your Hand"; 5. "Please Please Me."

10. The last live concert the Beatles ever gave was at Candlestick Park in San Francisco on August 29, 1966.

Sleep with the Beatles.
A Beatles pillow.

Superman's pal goes back in time
and becomes the redheaded
Beatle of 1000 B.C.

Do you still have your Beatle cards? Sharon does.
She has most of the items shown here and more.
She was only eight years old when the Beatles
invaded this country, but she's a true fan. We love
you Beatles, oh yes we do.

True Beatlemania

"FROM ENGLAND THEY CAME"

A poem written in 1964 by Loretta Macy, age twelve, of Albany, New York.

Four British lads came here one day,
And stole my loving heart away.
I will name them one by one,
Starting with George Harrison.

George, George Harrison.
Tall and thin describes this one.
I love him very, very much.
I'd nearly faint to have one touch.

Paul McCartney, next in line
With the guitar he plays so fine.
He's going steady, but who cares,
I love him to his precious hairs.

John, John, the married one,
I love him too, he's got fun.
He and Paul write songs
Which raise the screaming, crying throngs.

Ringo, Ringo, he's the one
I love him more than anyone.
He's the dancer, he's so sweet;
With the drums he's got the beat.

Altogether they are one thing;
The Beatles, who have talent and sing.
There's something in common with every one of them
They're wonderful boys and to me they are a gem.

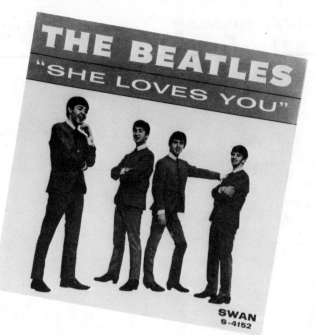

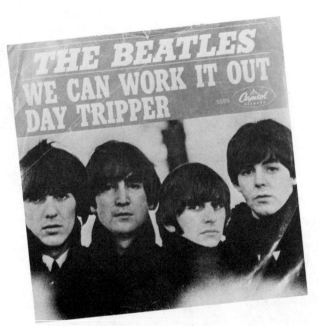

The Story of Beatle Wigs

In 1963, a friend of Julie Cooper, vice-president of Lowell Toys, returned from a visit to England with stories of a musical group that was taking Britain by storm. They were so popular, she said, that English kids were starting to wear wigs to imitate the group's long hair.

Julie sold the president of Lowell Toys on the idea of making Beatle wigs. "Fortunately for us, it was summer," he says, "because to make the wigs we needed the machines they use to sew fur." Cooper excitedly called up some friends who were department-store buyers to announce his "first": "Hey, I've got Beatle wigs!" His friends wanted to be nice, but they just didn't know what to say. "Julie," one finally said, "why do you want to put wigs on beetles?"

138

Someone figured out that part of "Revolution #9" played backward sounds like "turn me on, dead man." Instantly, every picture and record the Beatles made seemed to be full of clues proving Paul died in 1966. In case you're wondering, he didn't.

Their first U.S. album repackaged as a "battle of the bands" with The Four Seasons.

Another milestone for the Beatles. Who ever heard of a rock 'n' roll singer who could write?

The first "American" to go into space

Pets, of course, are not exclusively an obsession of the sixties. But it was in the sixties that the market for pampering pets was discovered to be universal; it wasn't just the "eccentric" upper classes who worried that Fido wasn't eating right—it was all pet owners.

The statistics are staggering: in the mid-fifties, Americans spent approximately $1½ billion on pets and pet-related merchandise. By 1963, it was $3 billion. And by 1968, we spent $5 billion to $6 billion *a year* on our pets. In 1969, there was almost a billion dollars spent on dog food alone. There were an estimated 60 million dogs and cats in America at the end of the decade.

Here are some reasons given by sociologists for the frightening growth of pet pampering in the sixties:

• With the dissipation of the nuclear family, neurotic adults sought child surrogates that could be counted on to respond with affection and to depend on them.

• Affluence made it acceptable to extend concern for the welfare of the family to the family pet.

• Modern society became so frightening and frustrated, so lonely and dehumanized, that people retreated to emotional relationships with pets instead of people.

• With common status symbols taken away (everyone could afford a car), exotic pets were a convenient new way to establish social status.

SOS! HALL OF FAME

You probably thought that animal actors never get more than a pat on the head for a job well done. But then you probably never heard of the Patsy Awards, the animal kingdom's version of the Oscars. Mr. Ed (1962 and 1963) and Arnold Ziffle (the "Green Acres" pig—1968 and 1969) are each two-time winners. Other stars honored in the sixties: Lassie, Flipper, Gentle Ben, Judy the Chimp, Tramp the sheep dog ("My Three Sons"), and dozens more.

Celebrity Pet Stories

1. Elizabeth Taylor, working on a film in England, was not allowed to bring her four Pekinese dogs into the country with her (they had to remain in quarantine). So she hired a $2,500-a-week 190-ton luxury yacht, *The Beatriz*, to anchor offshore and serve as a kennel for them.

2. Jayne Mansfield appeared in England in 1967 trying to smuggle in her two Chihuahuas (guess where she hid them . . . ?) to avoid quarantine.

3. The Beatles, in their recording of "A Day in the Life," ended it with an ultra-sonic whistle, audible only to dogs. "I planned it as a message to Martha and for all other dogs in the world. I wanted them to have something completely to themselves."—Paul McCartney (Martha was his English sheep dog)

4. Ronald Reagan took his dog to a Beverly Hills canine psychologist in which he had to participate in the "therapy."

Five Facts about Dogs That You're Better Off Not Knowing

1. By 1968 there was medical insurance for dogs, such as Canine Shield in New York City. No physical exam was required.

2. NOT a best seller: In 1963 a new cookbook was called *The Secret of Cooking for Dogs.*

3. In 1960, officials at dog shows began nose-printing dogs to avoid cases of mistaken identity. Like people's fingerprints, no two nose-prints are alike.

4. In 1966, R. T. French came out with "People Crackers for Dogs"—featuring "crunchy little milkmen, mailmen, policemen, dog catchers, and burglars."

5. *Touring with Towser,* a 1965 book, listed six thousand motels and hotels that would let you bring your dog with you on vacation.

TOP TEN

The Most Ridiculous Pet Products of the Decade

1. Petnix: panties for dogs in heat to prevent intercourse

2. Happy Breath: a spray dentifrice for dogs

3. Kitty Duplex: a two-story cat

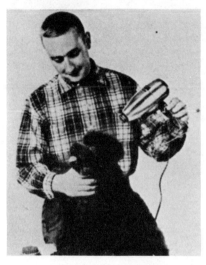

house with a cushioned downstairs and a bedroom upstairs

4. Fallout shelters for pets, "to give pets an equal chance for survival"

5. Rhinestone tiara for poodles (cost: $13.50)

6. Motoring goggles for dogs (cost: $7.50)

7. Gold and rhinestone cookie jars for dogs, with a picture of the owner's breed and the legend "My Favorite Yummy"

8. Upjohn introduced an oral contraceptive for dogs, for "Planned Puppyhood"

9. Don't like the way your dog smells? Try Parfumes de Poodle-oo in two scents—Le Chien No. 5 and Arf-peggio

10. Don't let your pet walk—try the Pampered Pet Taxi Service, Hollywood, California

Flop of the Decade

Creative Playthings introduced the "Animal of the Month Club" in the sixties. It entailed their sending out an exotic "pet" every month to subscribers. Animals included the Argentine toad, snails, musk turtles, newts, Mongolian gerbils, and more. In 1968, they had orders for four thousand Argentine toads and were having trouble finding enough of them in the Argentine swamps. But that wasn't the worst of their troubles. Some of the animals arrived dead, squashed, or dehydrated. Ultimately, Creative Playthings gave up.

LBJ had his troubles, even with pets. At one press conference he picked up his beagles, Him and Her, by their ears, sharing a chuckle with reporters at the way they yelped. He was inundated with complaints from pet-lovers who labeled him cruel to animals and inhumane. Johnson couldn't believe it. He said they liked it, and it didn't hurt the dogs. All this was going on while the war in Vietnam was escalating, and a lot of people couldn't believe that either.

It's hard to imagine Richard Nixon without a dog. Checkers died before Nixon got to the White House (a shame, considering all he did to help), and the Nixon family got a new pet—King Timahoe, an Irish Setter.

The Inside Story:
The Origin of McDonald's

In 1954 when Ray Kroc was fifty-two, he had his own company selling a milk-shake machine that could mix *five* milk shakes at once! It was called Multimixer. Ray thought everyone should have one.

Ray noticed that a lot of people who bought his mixer referred to it as "the one that the McDonald brothers have." He wondered what they meant by that, so he looked it up. He discovered that the Mc-Donald brothers owned a restaurant in San Bernardino, California, and that they had eight Multimixers, enough to make *forty* milk shakes at once! Ray could hardly believe it. So he flew to California to see how they did it.

Here's what he found: a clean little self-service drive-in with fifteen-cent hamburgers and a long line of loyal customers.

Ray watched the McDonald brothers in action for a while, and then he introduced himself. They were happy to meet him. They called him Mr. Multimixer and showed him plans for their new building with funny yellow arches that "went right through the roof." Ray was excited. "Why don't you open more places like this," he said. "You could make a fortune!" (Ray was thinking that he could make a fortune too—selling eight multimixers to each restaurant.)

But the McDonalds weren't interested. They were satisfied with their one little drive-in. "Too much trouble," they said. "Anyway, who would run it for us?" Ray heard opportunity knocking. "How about me?" he asked. "Why not," they replied.

So when Ray went home to Chicago, he was signed up to open all the restaurants called McDonald's that he wanted. He would make them exactly like the one in San Bernardino and would pay the McDonald brothers a percentage of whatever the restaurants made. Ray's friends thought he was crazy.

He opened his first McDonald's in Des Plaines, Illinois, selling hamburgers, french fries, and shakes. He worked very hard, but that didn't bother him. "Work is the meat in the hamburger of life," he said. Soon he opened more restaurants, and people rushed to buy his food. By the time he was fifty-eight years old —in 1960—he had sold more hamburgers than most people can even imagine. Millions. And that was just the beginning . . .

Big Mac. Born in 1968

TIME CAPSULE
McDonald's Menu

1964: hamburgers 15¢, french fries 12¢, shakes 20¢

1968: hamburgers 18¢, french fries 18¢, shakes 25¢

Fast food, Mexican-style, started in California and spread east in the sixties.

6 Let's Eat

Fast Food Flops

You Can Get Anything You Want. Catapulted into the national spotlight by Arlo Guthrie's best-selling album and a popular movie, Alice Brock announced the opening of a coast-to-coast restaurant chain in 1969 called Alice's Restaurants, of course.

Pat Boone Dine-O-Mats. Ninety-six were planned throughout the country in 1961. The gimmick: fast food from vending machines, heated with self-service microwave ovens. How clever. Too bad America didn't want fast food dispensed by vending machines.

And A-Waaay We Go. A Jackie Gleason fast-food restaurant in Miami was going to be the first in a chain, but the first restaurant had a unique problem: When they installed an exhaust system in their restaurant, owners neglected to include air *in*take as well. So every time someone opened the door, all the dust from the parking lot came swirling into the dining area.

Kentucky Fried Chicken was the largest fast-food chain in the sixties. Here Annette Funicello and Dwayne Hickman take a few minutes off from their latest beach movie to enjoy a few "finger-lickin' good" buckets of it.

An aquatic version of the drive-in . . . the Boat-In, complete with "boat-hops"

Burger King, ca. 1960

TOP TEN
Forgotten Celebrity Restaurants of the Sixties

1. Fats Domino New Orleans Style Fried Chicken
2. Tony Bennett Spaghetti House
3. "Here's Johnny" Restaurants (Johnny Carson)
4. Broadway Joe's Restaurants (Joe Namath)
5. Laugh-In Restaurants (featuring Fickle-Finger Franks)
6. Mickey Mantle's Country Cookin'
7. Willie Mays Say-Hey Restaurants
8. Mahalia Jackson's Glori-fried Chicken
9. Minnie Pearl's Chicken
10. Trini Lopez Mexican Restaurants

BREAKFAST

In the fifties, it was still popular to portray breakfast as a traditional family meal. But by the sixties there was a new head of the breakfast table . . . kids. Not that adults gave up breakfast altogether, but things were changing. More mothers were working than ever before. And the move to the suburbs meant more fathers rushing out in the morning as commuters. Teenagers gave up breakfast to stay thin, and because maybe they thought cereal wasn't "cool." So it was the kids and their cereal. But who needs grown-ups when you have Tony the Tiger, Cap'n Crunch, or the Trix Rabbit?

Three Rules for Eating Cereal

1. Go with Mom to the supermarket *only* if she promises that *you* can pick the cereal. When she reaches for the kind that isn't presweetened, tell her you won't eat it.

2. Check the cereal supply before you go to bed. If there is only a little of the good kind left, be sure to get up early so that you can beat your brothers and sisters to it.

3. Always put more milk in the bowl than you need so that when you finish the cereal, you'll still have some milk left at the bottom. Add more cereal. When you finish that batch, you'll probably still have milk left in the bowl. Add more cereal. Continue this process until the milk is all gone. (Froot Loops and Trix make multicolored milk.)

Blessings on thee, little man,
barefoot boy with cheeks
full of **Kellogg's** CORN FLAKES

In a decade that spawned dozens of sugar-coated, gimmicky cereals, the consistent best seller was *still* the granddaddy of them all. Kellogg's Corn Flakes.

144

Flop of the Decade

Corn Flakes with Freeze-Dried Fruit

America's love affair with the space age and modern technology led Post to believe they had a sure winner when, in 1964, they added freeze-dried strawberries to their cornflakes. Indeed, far more people bought "Corn Flakes with Strawberries" than they ever expected. Confident, they built a multi-million-dollar plant to produce the cereal, and added blueberries and peaches to their freeze-dried line.

Meanwhile, Kellogg's was testing their own version, Kellogg's "Corn Flakes with Instant Bananas." To support it, Kellogg's bought the world rights to the song "Yes, We Have No Bananas" and hired Jimmy Durante to sing it a new way on TV. "Yes, we now have bananas," he sang. It was a great commercial. The problem was that the product didn't work.

When you poured on the milk, the fruit was supposed to regain its original shape and flavor. It didn't. It got soft on the outside, but stayed crunchy on the inside. What's worse: By the time the fruit was soft, the cereal was soggy. And it certainly never looked like fruit again. Most consumers tried the cereal once, but never came back for a second helping.

What's New

In 1965 the Carnation Company introduced Instant Breakfast, a nutritious powder that dissolved in milk and tasted like a milk shake.

"Our research shows that approximately half the people in the country don't eat a home-cooked breakfast," a Carnation spokesman said. "What they want is a new and quick breakfast food." Carnation was right. Instant Breakfast was an instant success.

But it wasn't just an easy-to-prepare breakfast . . . it represented a step toward the meal of the future, the perfect food Americans always expected scientists to create. With a "meal-in-a-glass" here today, could "food pills" be far behind?

Five 1960s "Improvements" on Bacon and Eggs

1. *Bottled eggs.* Someone figured out how to get eggs into bottles without breaking the yolks. You *poured* them into the pan. These babies were sold by the pound.

2. *Toaster bacon.* If you're already having frozen waffles or pancakes, why dirty a pan for the bacon? Just pop these foil-wrapped slices of bacon into your toaster. A big flop.

3. *A foot-long hard-boiled egg.* Invented in Britain for restaurant use.

4. *Instant bacon.* Regular bacon, but precooked by radiation before it's packaged. Cooks to crispness in three minutes (for those who can't wait nine minutes for *normal* bacon).

5. *Low-cholesterol egg substitutes.* After medical research showed that cholesterol contributed to heart disease, several companies offered a nu-tech product that, mixed with water, "looked and tasted like eggs" but was 99 percent free of cholesterol.

Creative Capitalism Award

To Quaker Oats for Inventing Cap'n Crunch Cereal *After* They Invented the Commercials

In 1965 kids discovered an animated TV commercial for a brand-new cereal. It actually had a cast of characters the way cartoons did: lovable old Cap'n Crunch, his crew of kids, his faithful pet, Seadog, and the villains, archenemy Magnolia Bulkhead and Jean LaFoot, the barefoot pirate. The kiddie videophiles loved the commercials and, of course, made their parents buy the cereal.

Quaker made the cereal as good as the commercials. Sweet and crunchy, it didn't get soggy in milk. It quickly became the most popular new cereal of the decade, giving Quaker the sweet taste of success.

The fascinating thing is that it was carefully planned out as a TV promotion before the cereal even existed. TV was *that* important in selling cereal, and the manufacturers knew it. Quaker hired Jay Ward, creator of Bullwinkle, to create a cartoon character and produce one-minute commercials—cereal serials of Cap'n Crunch sailing the high seas, keeping the world safe for breakfast. *Then* they came up with the actual cereal.

Snap, Crackle and Pop dolls

145

Inspired by the Beatles' movie *Yellow Submarine*

If you laid all the Hostess Twinkies that were sold in the sixties end to end in a straight line, they would go completely around the earth ten times. That means Americans ate more than 26 *billion* Twinkies during the sixties. Think about that.

In 1969, Hershey raised the price of the nickel candy bar to ten cents.

The Most Ridiculous New Names for Snack Food in the Sixties

Munchos	Fiddle Faddle
Korkers	Fandangos
Diggers	Tang-O-Chips
Onyums	Onion Funions
Whistles	Potato Piffles
Hanky Panky	Dippy Canoes
Chipsters	Salty Surfers
Chipos	Sausage Scrambles
Bugles	Crispi-taters
Krunchy Nuggets	Chipniks
Daisys	Bokoo
Bows	Zooper Dooper
Buttons	Kanga-Moo
Funyons	B.L.T. Tickles
Snackadoos	Sesame Sillys
Doo Dads	Caraway Crazys

Great Moments of the 60s

Potato Chip Wars

At the end of the decade, a new type of potato chip appeared. Made from "reconstituted potato granules," it was packaged differently (it came in a canister instead of a bag), and it was made by a big corporation (like Procter & Gamble) instead of the usual local potato chip company. Would this mean the end of the potato chip as we knew it? Potato chip companies were scared it would—they actually *sued* General Mills for calling its Chipo's "new-fashioned potato chips," claiming that General Mills didn't have the right, since they weren't "authentic" chips.

Scandals of the Sixties

The Frito Bandito

Do you remember the Frito Bandito, the mustachioed cartoon character in Fritos commercials? He showed up on TV in 1967 wearing a sombrero and toting six-guns, ready to steal your Fritos Corn Chips.

In his prime, the Bandito devised some pretty sneaky ways of fleecing gringos. One commercial showed the *Apollo 11* astronauts landing on the moon. Who do you think they found waiting for them? The Frito Bandito, standing next to a parking meter with his burro. "I ham the moon parking lot attendant," he announced. "Now if you will kindly deposit one bag of cronchy Fritos corn cheeps for the first hour . . ."

But after Frito-Lay decided to use him in all its commercials, the Mexican-American Anti-Defamation Committee protested that the Frito Bandito was spreading the "racist message that Mexicans are sneaky thieves." Frito vehemently denied any racist intent or hidden meaning. But several California TV stations quickly banned the commercials and the Anti-Defamation Committee announced its intention of asking the FCC for equal time.

Although he was an effective TV salesman, the Frito Bandito was ultimately withdrawn from Fritos commercials. In fact, Frito-Lay wouldn't even let us show his picture here.

Great Moments of the 60s

Sugar Smack

What else could you call chocolate candy that comes in plastic containers resembling hypodermic needles and syringes but "junk food"? For junk-food junkies, presumably. It's hard to believe, but these nifty little items, bearing slogans like "Hippy Sippy says 'I'll try anything' " (get it?) and "Happiness Lives" showed up at neighborhood candy stores in 1968.

Sixties Survival Hint

If you ever run out of snacks, you can eat breakfast cereal right out of the box.

147

BEER

"We've got to find out why beer drinking has gone out of style and get it back before it's too late," moaned a brewer in 1963. Out of style? Believe it or not, brewers were worried because beer sales had gone flat. But time was on their side—a whole new generation of beer drinkers was aging. And to meet the challenge, beer companies were bubbling with new ideas: new advertising, new packaging, and new kinds of beer.

TOP TEN
Beer Slogans of the Sixties

1. Budweiser—"Pick a pair of six-packs, buy Bud"

2. Schlitz—"Real gusto in a great light beer"

3. Pabst—"Old-time flavor likes you best"

4. Falstaff—"The choicest product of the Brewer's art"

5. Carling Black Label—"Have a Black Label. You earned it"

6. Schaefer—"The one beer to have when you're having more than one"

7. Rheingold—"My beer is Rheingold the dry beer"

8. Ballantine—"Who is the ale man? (He could be you—the man with a thirst for a manlier brew.)"

9. Miller—"Champagne of bottle beer"

10. Coors—"Brewed with pure Rocky Mountain spring water"

Olde Frothingslosh

Olde Frothingslosh—"The pale, stale ale with the foam on the bottom"—started out as a radio joke and became a real tradition when the Pittsburgh Brewing Company decided to manufacture it. Each year, they offered a limited supply of the beer, with humorous new labels and ads. But few people have ever heard of it, so here's a sample of what you probably missed:

1960—Radio ads carried an endorsement by a baseball star. "I always shave with it," he said.

1962—Ads said the beer was "neurotically inspected." To prove it, it came in a "sick pack."

1964—Frothingslosh was promoted as "the only two-headed beer"; ads assured customers that the beer was "good for what ales you."

1966—Keeping up with the times, bottle labels were printed in red and green Dayglow ink, and the beer was sold as "Beer-Au-Glo-Glo." Ads said it was "the only beer you can find in the dark"; it was "sold only to people of volting age" through "electrical outlets."

Flop of the Decade
Low-Calorie Beer

Today, almost every brewery makes a low-calorie beer. But in the sixties it was a brand-new idea. "Light" beer raised its head three times, and all three times it flopped.

#1—1961—Trommer's Red Letter Beer, "the first low-calorie beer ever." Other brewers feared it would call attention to the high caloric content of regular beer, but they needn't have worried. No one paid any attention to Trommer's Red Letter Beer.

#2—1967—Meister Brau's Lite Beer called itself a "low-calorie" beer too. It was targeted at women and occasional beer drinkers who watched their weight. Ads featured "Miss Lite," a twenty-one-year-old California blonde in a leotard. The sexy approach didn't work either.

#3—1967—Gablinger's, the "Edsel of beers," probably got the most publicity—not all of it good. Rheingold Breweries tried to make a celebrity out of Hersch Gablinger, the Swiss chemist who formulated a "no-carbohydrate" beer, in 1964. They even put his picture on the cans and bottles. Gablinger's ad pitch was aimed at heavy beer drinkers; "It doesn't fill you up" was supposed to mean that they would have room for more beer. But drinkers privately panned the brew—it tasted watery and couldn't hold a head. If that weren't enough, the federal government seized a shipment of Gablinger's because of "misleading" statements on the label, and a Rheingold competitor promptly filed suit, charging that the product was "falsely promoted." Rheingold made the necessary changes, but Gablinger's was a lost cause.

60s Presents

New in Brew for the Sixties

Michelob was introduced in December 1961 to compete with imported beers. The fancy bottle gave it a "gourmet-type image" and made it suitable for women (this was 1961, remember) and for restaurant consumption.

Malt Liquor. The hottest new brew in 1963 was malt liquor, with 50 percent higher alcohol content than regular beer. Oh boy! Popular brands: Colt .45, Big Cat, Country Club, and Schlitz.

Hop 'N' Gator. The inventor of Gatorade used money he received from its sale to develop Hop'N'Gator, a mixture of beer and Gatorade, manufactured by the Pittsburgh Brewing Company in 1969.

Flavored Beer. Lone Star Brewing Company developed a flavored beer at the end of the decade. Available in three flavors—cola, grapefruit, and lemon/lime. Yechh!

What's New

Pop-Tops

Picture this: You're parked in lovers' lane with your date. Or you're sitting in a rowboat in the middle of a lake—just you, your fishing rod, and your cooler. Or you've managed to smuggle a six-pack into the drive-in movie. You reach for a beer and . . . uh-oh . . . forgot the church key.

In 1962, Alcoa solved that problem forever with self-opening cans. They were called snap-tops, flip-tops, pop-tops, and pull-tops. But they all amounted to the same thing: the end of the can opener and the biggest innovation in the brewing industry since the beer can.

TIME CAPSULE

To go with Pop Art and Op Art, beer drinkers discovered Pop-Top Art. By folding the flat end of one pop-top through the hole of another, clever craftoholics made headbands, necklaces, bracelets, beaded-type curtains, Christmas tree ornaments, and party decorations.

Great Moments of the 60s

River of Beer

When the Fehr Brewing Company of Louisville, Kentucky, went broke in 1964, they had to liquidate their assets—enough beer to fill 2,250,000 bottles. But they couldn't afford to bottle it, and you can't sell beer in bulk, so they dumped *all* of it into the Louisville sewers. What a waste!

Beer cans have become highly collectible. Shown here is Bill Christianson, one of America's premier beer can collectors, and three of the most valuable sixties cans. He estimates that Soul, Playmate, and 007 beer cans are worth $250 each. All of them sold for $1.00 per six-pack when they were available with beer in them.

149

Four Sixties Facts about Coca-Cola

1. "Things go better with Coke" was the first slogan that appeared on everything Coke did. They worked on it for two and a half years, and spent millions of dollars figuring out how to present it to the public. The first "things go better" jingle was sung by the Kingston Trio. This jingle was also the first in which Coke experimented with rock music. They used the Shirelles for it.

2. Here are a few of the artists who sang the Coca-Cola jingle during the sixties: Roy Orbison, Leslie Gore, The Drifters, The Vogues, Petula Clark, The Supremes, Nancy Sinatra, Ray Charles, Gary Lewis, Joe Tex, The Moody Blues, Lulu, The American Breed, Jay and the Techniques, The Fifth Dimension, Gladys Night and the Pips, Aretha Franklin, Vanilla Fudge, The Fortunes, The Tremoloes, The Bee Gees, Freddie and the Dreamers, Jan and Dean, the Coasters.

3. In 1969, Coke developed an impressionistic new red-and-white logo and it was put on everything, including Coke's truck fleet (the world's second largest after the U.S. Postal Service), vending machines, cases, containers, and an estimated 18 million Coke signs all over the world. It was called "Project Arden," after Elizabeth Arden, because it was massive cosmetic surgery.

4. Coca-Cola's sales in 1961 were $536 million. They had a good decade. In 1969, their sales had increased to a modest $1.3 BILLION.

Big Refreshment on Campus...King Size Coke! In a class by itself for cold crisp taste...and the cheerful lift that's bright and lively. You don't have to be a Senior to know...Coca-Cola refreshes you best!

FOR THE PAUSE THAT REFRESHES

Who's that sitting next to the Coke bottle?

Until cyclamates were banned, Diet-Rite was the best-selling diet cola, an important part of Royal Crown's family.

Scandals of the Sixties

Cyclamates

1960: Imagine how happy Diet-Rite Cola will make all those diet-crazy Americans who've been waiting for a low-calorie soft drink that isn't bitter-tasting. Just one calorie, and it tastes as good as the original stuff! How did they do that, anyway? Isn't modern science great!

1963: Here come the big boys with diet soda. Coke pops up with Tab and Pepsi with Patio Diet Cola. Too bad Grandma isn't here to see this. Isn't modern science great!

1965: Pepsi takes a bold step—it changes the name of its diet drink to Diet Pepsi. Its ads say: "The girls that girl-watchers watch drink Diet Pepsi." In other words, SEX. It works. Diet

Board members of the Pepsi generation.

The new wave hitting the beach all over America. Their drink:

Pepsi-Cola. Regular and Diet. Faster take-off with one. Leaner look with the other.

Honest-to-Pepsi taste with both. Go on in for a sip.

COME ALIVE! Pepsi You're in the Pepsi generation

Four Facts about Pepsi

1. 1964: "Yahoo! It's Mountain Dew!" In 1964 Pepsi bought Tip Corporation. Pepsi wanted its popular southern soft drink, Mountain Dew, to distribute nationally. It took off like a rocket, tickling the innards of Americans who loved that "good ole down-home" hillbilly image. It also spawned imitators like White Lightning and Kickapoo Joy Juice.

2. The "You've got a lot to live . . ." campaign was a smashing success for Pepsi that attracted attention from all quarters of American society. Pepsi received over ten thousand letters congratulating them. Some people even said, they were on the verge of suicide until they heard the ad. The lyrics were written by the songwriter who composed "You Light Up My Life."

3. In 1966, five years after it had "Come Alive!'" the Pepsi Generation was put to rest. It had become such a part of sixties America that even *Time* magazine eulogized it. Why did Pepsi drop such a successful theme? The times were a-changin', man. Kids didn't like to be categorized anymore. And in 1966, the clean-cut American teenager who never thought about anything but jumping up and down in swimming pools wasn't what was "happening."

4. Pepsi sales in 1961 were $176 million. In 1965 Pepsi merged with Frito-Lay, and they formed Pepsico. "Potato chips make you thirsty, Pepsi satisfies thirst," they said. That wasn't the only appealing feature of that combination; by the end of the decade, with their combined strengths, Pepsico's sales were five times as large as in 1961—they were $940 million.

Five Pepsi Slogans from the Sixties

1960: "Be sociable. Have a Pepsi."

1961: "Now it's Pepsi for those who think young."

1964: "Come alive! You're in the Pepsi generation."

1966: "Taste that beats the others cold. Pepsi pours it on."

1969: "You've got a lot to live and Pepsi's got a lot to give."

Five Coca-Cola Slogans from the Sixties

1960: "The pause that refreshes"

1961: "Zing! What a refreshing new feeling"

1963: "Things Go Better with Coke"

1967: "Coke for the taste that you never get tired of"

1969: "It's the Real Thing"

Pepsi immediately starts to move toward number one. Imagine that, a diet soda with just one calorie. Isn't modern science great!

1966: Coke, which bought Minute Maid in 1960, discovers that its chemists have been working on a citrus flavor that covers up the bitterness of artificial sweetener. Coke uses it to create Fresca, a "blizzard" of a soft drink. It's a tremendous success—and it only has *one* calorie! Isn't modern science great!

1969: Whoops. Uh, you know these diet sodas you've been drinking? Well, they're sweetened with something you've probably never heard of called "cyclamates." And, uh, well . . . we just found out they cause cancer. Isn't modern science great!

FEAR NO COLA · SEE NO COLA · DRINK UNCOLA

TOP TEN

Soft Drinks from the Sixties You Probably Never Tasted

1. Devil Shake—Pepsi's "Glitzy" chocolate-flavored drink

2. Sport Cola—The first caffeine-free cola, from Canada Dry

3. Calico Cow—Milk drink in chocolate, strawberry, vanilla, from Carnation

4. Soda Burst—Instant ice-cream soda from Birds Eye

5. Root Beer-Flavored Milk—from Dad's Root Beer

6. Geyser Water—Taken from 207-foot-deep wells, at temperatures over 255 degrees Fahrenheit. Mildly carbonated, once it cooled down

7. Vitasoy—popular drink in Hong Kong, made from soybeans

8. Pop in Pouches—imported from Canada, came in four- by six-inch poly bags with built-in straws that you punched into the bag

9. Saci—Coca-Cola's antimalnutrition soft drink. Chocolate-flavored, high-protein drink tested in South America

10. Sno-Ball—Pepsi's semi-frozen drink that came in regular Pepsi flavors

Match the Soft Drink Slogan to the Soft Drink

1. Zing! What a refreshing new feeling!   a. 7-UP

2. It'll tickle yore innards   b. Dr. Pepper

3. The Sassy One   c. Pepsi-Cola

4. Beats the others cold   d. Coca-Cola

5. BE a Mindsticker   e. Wink

6. Old-fashioned Cola taste   f. Diet-Rite Cola

7. Wet and wild   g. Mountain Dew

8. Tart and tingling   h. Royal Crown Cola

9. You'll flip at the zzzip   i. Tab

10. Distinctively different   j. Sprite

Answers

1. d; 2. g; 3. e; 4. c; 5. i; 6. f; 7. a; 8. j; 9. h; 10. b

The Inside Story: Gatorade

• Green Bay Packer coach Vince Lombardi endorsed it.

• "It beats LSD," declared actors in the Broadway musical *Hair*.

• Mixed with vodka, it gave an instant "buzz" and left no hangover.

What is it? Gatorade, an "isotonic" beverage absorbed into the bloodstream twelve times faster than water.

In 1965, Dr. Robert Cade was studying the effects of heat exhaustion on football players at the University of Florida (the team was called the Gators). He analyzed the body liquids lost in sweating and within three minutes came up with the formula for Gatorade.

Two years later, Cade sold the rights to Stokely-Van Camp. Soon, annual sales were well over $50 million and Gatorade could be found on the training tables of over three hundred college sports teams, a thousand high school squads, and all but two pro football teams. It became the acknowledged drink of athletes and a permanent part of the American diet.

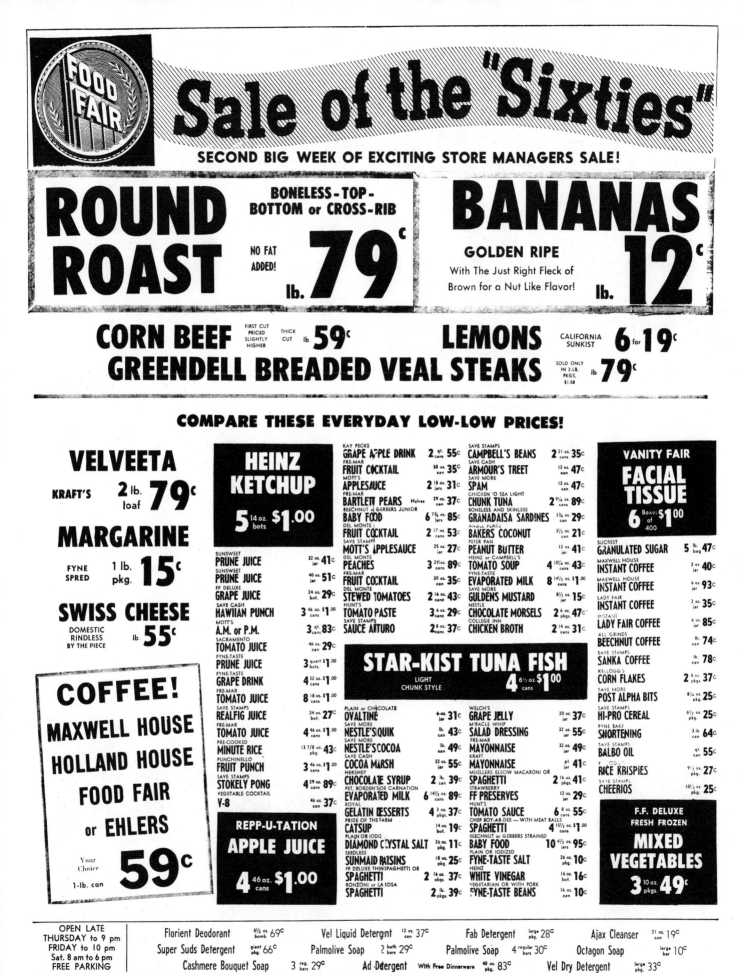

METRECAL

The Original Liquid-Diet Formula

At first, Metrecal was offered strictly as a product for doctors to recommend to their obese patients. You could only buy it at drugstores.

But America was ready for a new diet fad. "When we introduced Metrecal to the medical profession and the drug trade," commented one executive, "we honestly had no idea how far it would go." In its first year, more than $25 million worth of Metrecal was sold. And at $1.59 a can, that's a lot of diets.

The demand kept increasing. Soon it was available everywhere —supermarkets, restaurants, and even in bars, where you could get Metrecal cocktails (Metrecal and vodka).

Recognizing a fat deal, others were quick to follow with over a hundred imitations of Metrecal. Here are a few of them:

Route 900 (General Mills)

Quota (Quaker Oats)

Redi-Diet (Borden)

Minvitine (Ovaltine)

Bal-Cal (Sears Roebuck)

Sealtest 900

But as the fad died out, only one stood out as a heavyweight challenger to Metrecal—Sego. While Metrecal was pushed on the basis of health, Sego's ads stressed how much better you would look when you lost weight; in other words, SEX. It came in more flavors than Metrecal; it was like a milk shake. In the ensuing battle, Metrecal switched over to the sex-appeal approach, added more flavors and types of diet food (cookies and dinners), and, by 1966, had regained first place.

NOTE: There was no secret formula behind Metrecal's success— only a simple idea. Limit your intake to nine hundred calories a day. "You can reduce on nine hundred calories a day of anything —white bread and ice cream, even pâté de fois gras—if that is all you eat," claimed a New York nutritionist. But America ate it up anyway.

Fourteen Reasons Why You Might Go on a Diet in the Sixties

1. You want to wear a mini-skirt

2. Twiggy is your idol and you want to look just like her

3. You want to be an astronaut and you know you'll never fit in a capsule

4. Someone told you you remind them of Mama Cass

5. You're having trouble getting out of your Volkswagen

6. Every time you do the "frug," your pants pop open

7. Your Batman costume is getting a little too tight

8. Surf's up. All the kids are on the beach and you want to look like a beach bunny, not a beach ball

9. Your friends are too embarrassed to let you come with them to the peace rally

10. Just in case topless fashions catch on

11. You were nominated for "Miss Frothingslosh"

13. When you went to the New York World's Fair last summer, you heard someone say, "Look. It's a walking Unisphere."

14. You just want to join the "Metrecal-for-lunch bunch"

154

The Aerosol Gourmet

Imagine this: You're eating dinner. Someone asks you to pass the milk. You reach over and hand her an aerosol can. She tilts it sideways and squirts it into her empty glass. P-s-s-t. And she's got a glass of milk. Or: You're making a peanut butter and jelly sandwich. You spread the jelly on one slice of bread, and then reach for the peanut butter. It's in an aerosol can. You press the button and a ribbon of peanut butter squirts out onto the bread. Hard to swallow? Today it is, but after the success of aerosol cheese and aerosol whipped cream in the mid-sixties, it seemed like a sure thing. Experts predicted that the aerosol can would be as much a fixture on the American dinner table as salt-and-pepper shakers.

Scandals of the Sixties

Irradiating Food

In the early sixties, we were still fairly innocent about atomic power. Proof: Scientists thought they had found the perfect way to preserve food without refrigeration—bombard it with small doses of radiation to kill the germs that cause spoilage. This was called "irradiating" food, and people actually predicted that we were only a few years from supermarket shelves full of irradiated food.

"Most experts agree that irradiated foods will be a part of the American diet within ten years. Refrigerators will continue to be a popular piece of kitchen furniture . . . but when it comes to steaks and chops, oranges and lemons, 'atom fresh' could become the slogan of tomorrow," the *Saturday Evening Post* said in 1963.

Indeed—in 1963, the FDA gave permission to the army to serve irradiated food to U.S. troops. It was a noble experiment, beginning with bacon and fish. But in 1968, evidence came to light that radiation in food causes cancer. The FDA withdrew permission, over the objections of the army and the Atomic Energy Commission. Thank goodness.

Freeze-Dried Food

Another miracle from NASA: a way to dry out food so it shriveled to a fraction of its size and weight—until you added water; then it turned back into its original form. It was called freeze-drying.

Too good to be true? Actually, yes. Food companies found out too late that a lot of things just didn't taste good when they were freeze-dried. But it did work for some things: coffee, for instants.

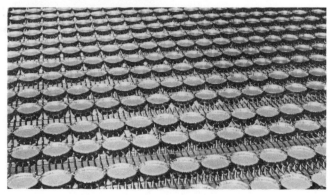

What Is It?

A mile of delicious cheesecakes from The Kitchens of Sara Lee.

Before

The Campbell Kids, 1960

After

The Campbell Kids, 1968

The Green Giant has a red face

He never figured folks would eat so many packages of his new Green Giant Vegetables Frozen in Butter Sauce. Now he's completely sold out of peas and beans. And he can't freeze any more until he grows another crop up in his Big Green Valley.

As a crystal ball gazer, the jolly Green Giant makes a good farmer. Because when he came out with his new vegetables frozen in butter sauce he figured he had enough to last for months and months.

But when a giant goofs, he does it in a big way.

As fast as grocers filled their freezers with these new vegetables, folks bought 'em, took 'em home and ate 'em. Then they came back and bought more and more. Now you can hardly find a package of the Green Giant's Little Baby Peas and Kitchen Sliced Green Beans anywhere.

Trouble is, not even the Green Giant can speed up Mother Nature. He has to wait until he can grow a whole new crop of peas and beans before he can fill up your grocer's freezer again.

The only consolation is that you can still get Green Giant Niblets Corn and Baby Lima Beans Frozen in Butter Sauce. And fortunately you can get all you want of the Green Giant's famous vegetables in cans because he knew beforehand what a big appetite you have for them so he put up plenty.

So we hope you'll accept the Green Giant's apologies for making such a bad guess on how fast his frozen vegetables would sell. But those things happen. Even to giants.

GREEN GIANT
Good things from the garden

What's new besides Ho Ho Ho? In 1960, it was frozen vegetables in butter sauce. While the Green Giant Company was still test-marketing them, the vegetables proved to be so popular that consumers bought the whole supply. It was a manufacturer's dream come true, but the company was embarrassed. They ran this ad showing a red-faced Green Giant apologizing for the shortage.

Señorita Chiquita

POPEYE MACARONI

New way for kids to eat SPINACH and love it!

(ACTUAL SHAPE)

BUITONI POPEYE

ENRICHED SPINACH MACARONI PRODUCT

FREE! TOY

Who Are They?

They're the Doublemint Twins, of course. But do you know their names?

DOUBLEMINT

Answer: Jane and Joan Boyd, the Doublemint Twins from 1959 to 1964.

SOS! HALL OF FAME

Richard Nixon: The American Phoenix

• After Nixon lost the race for president in 1960, he determined that a run for the office in 1964 wasn't a good idea. Kennedy looked unbeatable, and Nixon wanted to avoid having to run against him.

• He took time off to write his "memoirs," called *Six Crises*, which became a best seller.

• Then in 1962, he was convinced to run for governor of California against Edmund G. Brown. Nixon had never been beaten in California—he had been a congressman, a senator, and had carried the state in the presidential election. Being governor would be a good way to hide from presidential politics in 1964, especially if Nixon pledged to serve his full term (which ended in 1966). But it backfired. Everyone was convinced that he was using California as a stepping-stone. It was Brown's best issue.

• Toward the end of the campaign, as a slumping Nixon was trying to stage a last-minute comeback, the Cuban Missile Crisis hit. He was helplessly transformed back into a national leader, having to answer questions about Cuba when he tried to talk about California. Nixon felt this was the deathblow to his chances. When the election was over, he had been defeated handily. It looked like the end of Nixon.

• He met the press as he left his campaign headquarters, and held an impromptu news conference. "Good morning, gentlemen," he began. "Now that all the members of the press are so delighted that I have lost, I'd like to make a statement of my own. . . ."

• His most famous quote came from that press conference: "You won't have Nixon to kick around anymore because, gentlemen, this is my last press conference." It was *definitely* the end of Nixon.

• Now unemployed, Nixon had to find a job. He was offered the presidency of several universities, considered for the chairmanship of Chrysler, and was even suggested as the commissioner of baseball. In the end, he decided to practice law, so that he could stay active in politics. His wife, Pat, was too embarrassed to stay in California, so they moved to New York.

• Nixon hadn't practiced law for a long time and was not exactly a prestigious figure anymore. So he had a hard time finding a firm that would take him. A few friends fixed that. One of them, the chairman of Pepsi Cola, saw to it that he brought the Pepsi legal account with him. That was worth a few bucks. The Pepsi connection kept Nixon traveling frequently, opening new plants in other countries and visiting their rulers, acquaintances from his VP days. And that kept his name in the news.

• In 1964, he blatantly maneuvered to become the compromise candidate in a potentially deadlocked convention. But when Goldwater was selected as the nominee, Nixon was quick to campaign for him. He was back in politics.

• In 1966, Nixon campaigned for local Republican candidates harder than anybody. He appeared everywhere, predicting a Republican comeback after the awful Goldwater defeat. He was the only real voice of optimism the Republicans had. And when the Republicans won big in Congress and gubernatorial seats, Nixon got a lot of the credit.

• Just before the end of the 1966 campaign, Lyndon Johnson singled out Nixon as the voice of the opposition, attacking him in a press conference. Nixon was ecstatic. More than any other single event, this made Nixon the Republican hero and cemented his future in presidential politics.

• Nixon was a national figure again. Polls showed that he was among the Republican's favorites for president, despite the fact that he had been beaten the last two times he ran. Nixon was back.

Nixon

Richard Nixon, meet Marlon Brando.

Why are these men laughing?

As Nixon traveled the country in 1968, proving that political candidates could be sold to the American public like any other product, Joe McGinniss was there to record it all. The definitive statement about the "new" Nixon.

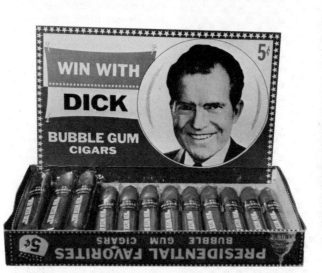

A photo of Nixon with notes on how to improve his personal appearance—let hair "grow out" on the sides.

It's "Queen for a Day" with Jack Bailey and . . . Richard Nixon?

The Poster Boom

• In 1967 some of the larger poster stores (yes, there were actually stores that sold nothing but posters) sold as many as 25,000 a month.

• Wes Wilson, a hip West Coast poster artist, sold 57,000 of them in one month in 1967.

• In 1969, it was estimated that $20 million worth of posters were sold, including 100,000 of one by Pandora Productions that had a picture of the pope on it, with the caption, "The Pill Is a No-No."

Putting posters on your wall was like joining a secret society. Adults supposedly didn't know what things like "acid" or "feed your head" meant. And they surely couldn't appreciate a picture of Jimi Hendrix.

But there were other reasons for posters' sudden popularity. With styles changing constantly, it was hard to keep up. Posters let you do that. "I think the real appeal of these posters is their disposability," said one of the most successful of the artists. "You can change them every six months without investing a fortune, and you're current." And a bookstore owner speculated: "Posters are here to stay because the audience is the college man and woman who buys posters in lieu of a hundred-dollar lithograph that they can't afford." Maybe. But we can't forget that a lot of us just liked to take psychedelic drugs and stare at the never-ending patterns in some of the posters, or watch the glow of a black-light poster in the near-dark.

160

The Inside Story:

The Beginning of the Poster Boom

In 1965 a young woman thought it would be great if her boyfriend—a New York printer—made posters with Humphrey Bogart's picture on them.

He liked the idea. So he scouted around and came up with a negative for a Bogart photo. He got it for free. Then he bought some cheap paper and printed a bunch of posters. He advertised them in places like the *New York Times* Book Review section and the *Village Voice.*

Meanwhile, back at a Greenwich Village paperback bookstore (where they also sold travel posters and art posters), a few kids came in asking for the Bogie poster. The owner hadn't ever heard of it, but took special pains to find out where he could get it. He discovered the printer and called to ask if he could buy some posters. Sure, why not? The printer kept a few, sold the rest to the storeowner, and went away for a long weekend.

When he got back, the phone was ringing like crazy. It was the bookstore owner, who had sold over a thousand posters of Bogart while the printer was gone. Could he have more? The astonished men realized they were sitting on a gold mine. They went into partnership to form Personality Posters, which featured photos of all the cult figures during the sixties—Belmondo, Brando, Harlow, Bardot . . . you remember.

161

Sonny & Cher

Dusty Springfield

The Rolling Stones, 1964

Paul Revere and The Raiders

These rock star cards came from a vending machine in the sixties. Original cost: five cents each.

JULY 6, 1968 / THIRTY-FIVE CENTS

ACME

ROLLING STONE

The Great 'Compatible' Stereo Fraud:
How Two Good Mono's Make One Bad Stereo

TINY TIM

JUDY IN DISGUISE
(WITH GLASSES)

JOHN FRED AND HIS
PLAYBOYS

CALIFORNIA
C 282

when the lights go out

WOODSTOCK

MUSIC and
ART FAIR

TINY TIM
President & First Lady

re-elect
BOB DYLAN
PRESIDENT

Sounds

"Everyday People," by Sly and the Family Stone

The Fab Four

A Monkees fan mag

A souvenir postcard from The Ginza, a New York nightclub featuring the original go-go girls dancing in cages.

Hullabaloo magazine, 1968

Top Fifteen Hits of the Sixties

1960

1. "Theme from A Summer Place," by Percy Faith
2. "It's Now or Never," by Elvis Presley
3. "He'll Have to Go," by Jim Reeves
4. "I'm Sorry," by Brenda Lee
5. "Running Bear," by Johnny Preston
6. "Cathy's Clown," by Everly Brothers
7. "The Twist," by Chubby Checker
8. "El Paso," by Marty Robbins
9. "North to Alaska," by Johnny Horton
10. "Last Date," by Floyd Cramer
11. "Stuck on You," by Elvis Presley
12. "Everybody's Somebody's Fool," by Connie Francis
13. "Sixteen Reasons," by Connie Stevens
14. "Greenfields," by Brothers Four
15. "My Heart Has a Mind of Its Own," by Connie Francis

1963

1. "Sugar Shack," by Jimmy Gilmer and the Fireballs
2. "He's So Fine," by the Chiffons
3. "Dominique," by the Singing Nun
4. "Blue Velvet," by Bobby Vinton
5. "Hey Paula," by Paul and Paula
6. "Go Away Little Girl," by Steve Lawrence
7. "Fingertips," (Part II) by Little Stevie Wonder
8. "My Boyfriend's Back," by the Angels
9. "Sukiyaki," by Kyu Sakamoto
10. "I Will Follow Him," by Little Peggy March
11. "Rhythm of the Rain," by the Cascades
12. "The End of the World," by Skeeter Davis
13. "Walk Like a Man," by the Four Seasons
14. "I'm Leaving It Up to You," by Dale and Grace
15. "Surfin' U.S.A.," by the Beach Boys

1964

1. "I Want to Hold Your Hand," by the Beatles
2. "Hello, Dolly!," by Louis Armstrong
3. "She Loves You," by the Beatles
4. "Oh, Pretty Woman," by Roy Orbison
5. "Baby Love," by the Supremes
6. "Louie Louie," by the Kingsmen
7. "There! I've Said It Again," by Bobby Vinton
8. "I Get Around," by the Beach Boys
9. "My Guy," by Mary Wells
10. "Mr. Lonely," by Bobby Vinton
11. "Everybody Loves Somebody," by Dean Martin
12. "Where Did Our Love Go," by the Supremes
13. "Can't Buy Me Love," by the Beatles
14. "Do Wah Diddy Diddy," by Manfred Mann
15. "A Hard Day's Night," by the Beatles

1967

1. "I'm a Believer," by the Monkees
2. "To Sir with Love," by Lulu
3. "The Letter," by the Box Tops
4. "Light My Fire," by the Doors
5. "Windy," by the Association
6. "Ode to Billie Joe," by Bobbie Gentry
7. "Daydream Believer," by the Monkees
8. "Happy Together," by the Turtles
9. "Somethin' Stupid," by Nancy Sinatra and Frank Sinatra
10. "I Heard It Through the Grapevine," by Gladys Knight and the Pips
11. "Incense and Peppermints," by the Strawberry Alarm Clock
12. "Can't Take My Eyes Off You," by Frankie Valli
13. "Groovin'," by the Young Rascals
14. "Little Bit O' Soul," by the Music Explosion
15. "The Rain, The Park and Other Things," by the Cowsills

1968

1. "Hey Jude," by the Beatles
2. "Love Is Blue," by Paul Mauriat
3. "Honey," by Bobby Goldsboro
4. "People Got to Be Free," by the Rascals
5. "(Sittin' On) The Dock of the Bay," by Otis Redding
6. "Love Child," by Diana Ross and the Supremes
7. "This Guy's in Love with You," by Herb Alpert
8. "The Good, The Bad and The Ugly," by Hugo Montenegro
9. "Sunshine of Your Love," by Cream
10. "Woman, Woman," by the Union Gap
11. "Judy in Disguise (With Glasses)," by John Fred and His Playboy Band
12. "Young Girl," by Gary Puckett and the Union Gap
13. "Tighten Up," by Archie Bell and the Drells
14. "Mrs. Robinson," by Simon and Garfunkel
15. "Little Green Apples," by O. C. Smith

1961

1. "Tossin' and Turnin'," by Bobby Lewis
2. "Are You Lonesome Tonight," by Elvis Presley
3. "Big Bad John," by Jimmy Dean
4. "Exodus," by Ferrante and Teicher
5. "Wonderland by Night," by Bert Kaempfert
6. "Runaway," by Del Shannon
7. "Will You Love Me Tomorrow," by the Shirelles
8. "Pony Time," by Chubby Checker
9. "Calcutta," by Lawrence Welk
10. "Please Mr. Postman," by the Marvelettes
11. "Runaround Sue," by Dion
12. "Travelin' Man," by Ricky Nelson
13. "Michael," by the Highwaymen
14. "Bristol Stomp," by the Dovells
15. "Dedicated to the One I Love," by the Shirelles

1962

1. "The Twist," by Chubby Checker
2. "I Can't Stop Loving You," by Ray Charles
3. "Big Girls Don't Cry," by the Four Seasons
4. "Limbo Rock," by Chubby Checker
5. "Peppermint Twist," by Joey Dee and the Starliters
6. "Stranger on the Shore," by Mr. Acker Bilk
7. "Roses Are Red," by Bobby Vinton
8. "Sherry," by the Four Seasons
9. "Mashed Potato Time," by Dee Dee Sharp
10. "Return to Sender," by Elvis Presley
11. "Telstar," by the Tornadoes
12. "Johnny Angel," by Shelley Fabares
13. "Soldier Boy," by the Shirelles
14. "The Lion Sleeps Tonight," by the Tokens
15. "Duke of Earl," by Gene Chandler

1965

1. "(I Can't Get No) Satisfaction," by the Rolling Stones
2. "You've Lost That Lovin' Feelin'," by the Righteous Brothers
3. "Wooly Bully," by Sam the Sham and the Pharaohs
4. "Downtown," by Petula Clark
5. "I Can't Help Myself," by the Four Tops
6. "Come See about Me," by the Supremes
7. "Let's Hang On," by the Four Seasons
8. "Turn! Turn! Turn!," by the Byrds
9. "Help," by the Beatles
10. "Mrs. Brown You've Got a Lovely Daughter," by Herman's Hermits
11. "Yesterday," by the Beatles
12. "I Feel Fine," by the Beatles
13. "I Got You Babe," by Sonny and Cher
14. "This Diamond Ring," by Gary Lewis and the Playboys
15. "My Girl," by the Temptations

1966

1. "The Ballad of the Green Berets," by S. Sgt. Barry Sadler
2. "Winchester Cathedral," by the New Vaudeville Band
3. "96 Tears," by ? and the Mysterians
4. "Last Train to Clarksville," by the Monkees
5. "(You're My) Soul and Inspiration," by the Righteous Brothers
6. "Devil with the Blue Dress On and Good Golly Miss Molly," by Mitch Ryder and the Detroit Wheels
7. "Cherish," by The Association
8. "Reach Out I'll Be There," by the Four Tops
9. "Born Free," by Roger Williams
10. "Good Vibrations," by the Beach Boys
11. "These Boots Are Made for Walkin'," by Nancy Sinatra
12. "California Dreamin'," by the Mamas and the Papas
13. "We Can Work It Out," by the Beatles
14. "Poor Side of Town," by Johnny Rivers
15. "You Can't Hurry Love," by the Supremes

1969

1. "I Heard It Through the Grapevine," by Marvin Gaye
2. "Aquarius/Let the Sunshine In," by the 5th Dimension
3. "Sugar, Sugar," by the Archies
4. "In the Year 2525 (Exordium and Terminus)," by Zager and Evans
5. "Everyday People," by Sly and the Family Stone
6. "Honky Tonk Women," by the Rolling Stones
7. "Get Back," by the Beatles
8. "Crimson and Clover," by Tommy James and the Shondells
9. "I Can't Get Next to You," by the Temptations
10. "Dizzy," by Tommy Roe
11. "Come Together/Something," by the Beatles
12. "Leaving on a Jet Plane," by Peter, Paul, and Mary
13. "Wedding Bell Blues," by the 5th Dimension
14. "Na Na Hey Hey Kiss Him Goodbye," by Steam
15. "Crystal Blue Persuasion," by Tommy James and the Shondells

A Few Hitmakers 1960-63

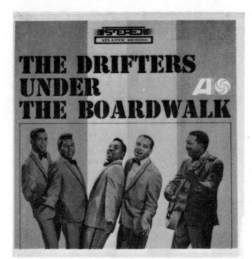

Through dozens of personnel changes, The Drifters continued to hit number one on the charts with songs like "Up on the Roof," "There Goes My Baby," and "Save the Last Dance for Me."

The Everly Brothers were big stars in the fifties, but they had their biggest-selling record ever in 1960 with "Cathy's Clown."

Gene Chandler, dressed for the part, was the "Duke of Earl."

The "last of the one-name singers," Dion, left the Belmonts in 1960 and made it big with "Runaround Sue," "The Wanderer," and "Ruby Baby."

The brilliant singer Sam Cooke was shot and killed in 1964 at the young age of twenty-nine. Some of his hits in the sixties: "Chain Gang," "Having a Party," "Another Saturday Night," and "Good News."

The Four Seasons' first hit, "Sherry," in 1962, was followed by *over twenty* top-ten records, like "Walk Like a Man," "Big Girls Don't Cry," and "Let's Hang On."

Bobby Vee got his big break when he substituted for Buddy Holly when Holly was killed in 1959. Some of his popular songs: "Rubber Ball," "Take Good Care of My Baby," and "Run to Him."

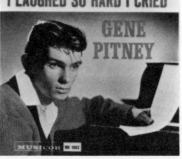

Gene Pitney, songwriter-turned-recording artist, had hits with "The Man Who Shot Liberty Valance," "I Wanna Love My Life Away," and "Town Without Pity."

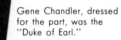

Del Shannon gave up his job as a carpet salesman when his recording of "Runaway" broke in New York and became a number-one in America. Follow-up hit: "Hats Off to Larry."

Sam the Sham and the Pharaohs swept America with "Wooly Bully" in 1965 and again with "Little Red Riding Hood" in 1966. If you're curious, Sam's real name was Domingo Samudio.

The Righteous Brothers were not brothers and their names were not Righteous. Bobby Hatfield and Bill Medley specialized in "blue-eyed soul." Featured as regulars on TV's "Shindig," their first big hit was "You've Lost That Lovin' Feelin'," produced by the legendary Phil Spector.

Dusty Springfield came over with the English Invasion in 1964. She first succeeded with "Wishin' and Hopin'," followed by "I Only Want to Be with You" and "You Don't Have To Say You Love Me."

Along with Elvis, Carl Perkins, Charlie Rich, and Jerry Lee Lewis, Roy Orbison got his start at Sun Records in the fifties. Among his hits in the sixties: "Crying," "Only the Lonely," and the classic "Oh, Pretty Woman."

Petula Clark had some of the most popular "rock" records in the world—"Downtown" and "I Know a Place"—even though she was MARRIED AND HAD KIDS!

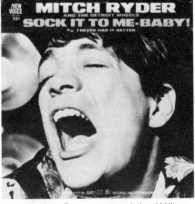

Dionne Warwick

Appearing daily on the TV show, "Where the Action Is," Paul Revere and the Raiders were adored by millions of teenagers. Among their hits: "Kicks," "Just Like Me," and "Hungry."

Producer Bob Crewe suggested that William S. Levise, Jr., change his name to Mitch Ryder and his group, the Rivieras, became the Detroit Wheels. Together they made "Devil with the Blue Dress," and "Sock It to Me, Baby."

More Hitmakers 1967-69

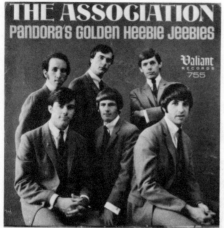

In the late sixties, Donovan went from a Bob Dylan sound-alike folk singer to top ten hits like "Sunshine Superman," "Mellow Yellow," "Epistle to Dippy," and "Hurdy Gurdy Man."

The Association's six multitalented musicians created some of rock's most intricate arrangements on "Along Comes Mary," "Cherish," and "Windy."

The Turtles started out as a surfing band called the Crossfires in 1964, and changed their name to the Turtles for their first album, which included a national hit called "It Ain't Me Babe." This was a folk-rock version of a Bob Dylan song, but their most popular records were rock songs. "Happy Together" was the biggest Turtles smash; others were: "Elenore," "She'd Rather Be with Me," "You Showed Me," and several others.

The Chicago-based Buckinghams had some of the best top-forty music of the late sixties. Their best: "Kind of a Drag," "Don't You Care," "Hey Baby, They're Playing Our Song," "Mercy, Mercy, Mercy," and "Susan."

The Young Rascals were a New York group who had their first local hit, "Ain't Gonna Eat Out My Heart Anymore," in 1965. They followed with "Good Lovin'," which was a monster in New York, but gained only moderate national success. Then, in 1967, "Groovin'" made the Rascals a national group. Some follow-ups: "How Can I Be Sure," "It's A Beautiful Mornin'," and "People Got to be Free."

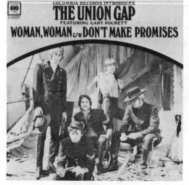

The Union Gap had a number one hit with "Woman, Woman"; they became "The Union Gap, featuring Gary Puckett," and had another number one song with "Young Girl." Then they became "Gary Puckett and the Union Gap," and reached the top again twice, with "Lady Willpower," and "Over You."

The Lovin' Spoonful originally appeared at the Nite Owl Cafe in New York's Greenwich Village. After they gathered a huge following, Kama Sutra Records signed them to a contract and their first big single, "Do You Believe In Magic?" was released in 1965. The group put out rock classics like "Summer in the City," "Daydream," "Nashville Cats," and more in the next two years. The group disbanded in 1967.

While touring with the Beach Boys in Britain in 1967, Lulu was spotted by a film director, James Clavell, who thought she would make a great actress. The result: a starring role in the movie "To Sir with Love," and one of the top hits of the year —"To Sir with Love"—which sold a million and a half copies.

FRANKIE: I saw *Beach Blanket Bingo* three times.

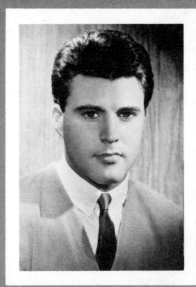

RICKY: He has dreamy eyes.

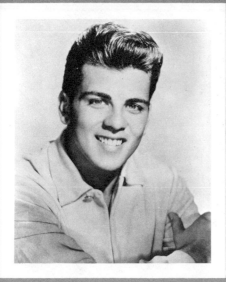

FABIAN: He can't sing, but he's cute.

*My
a
Favorite
Singers*

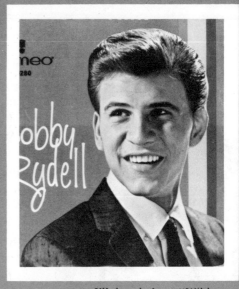

BOBBY RYDELL: I'll bet he's a "Wild One."

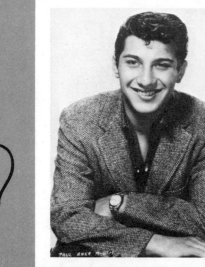

PAUL ANKA: "And they call it puppy love."

PAUL PETERSON: I love him on "The Donna Reed Show."

169

SOME OF THE GIRLS

Connie Francis. Hometown, Belleville, New Jersey

The Angels. Hometown, Orange, New Jersey

The Girls' Hits

"Will You Love Me Tomorrow," by the Shirelles, 1960

"Where the Boys Are," by Connie Francis, 1961

"Chains," by the Cookies, 1962

"My Boyfriend's Back," by the Angels, 1963

"Be My Baby," by the Ronettes, 1963

"It's My Party," by Leslie Gore, 1963

"Popsicles and Icicles," by the Murmaids, 1963

"Sally Go Round the Roses," by the Jaynettes, 1963

"I Wanna Love Him So Bad," by the Jelly Beans, 1964

"Leader of the Pack," by the Shangri-Las, 1964

"Chapel of Love," by the Dixie Cups, 1964

"Lover's Concerto," by the Toys, 1965

Leslie Gore. Hometown, Tenafly, New Jersey

The Shangri-Las. Hometown, Queens, New York

The Ronettes. Hometown, New York, New York

The Crystals. Hometown, Brooklyn, New York

Annette. Hometown, Utica, New York

The Shirelles. Hometown, Passaic, New Jersey

170

Sixties Guitars

Fender Electric XII—Twelve-string guitars enjoyed brief popularity in the sixties, a trend started by the Byrds' Jim McGuinn.

Dan Armstrong see-through guitar made of clear plastic. Favored by the Rolling Stones' Keith Richard on their 1969 U.S. tour.

Vox Mark VI: Brian Jones of the Rolling Stones used one.

Mosrite "The Ventures" guitar

Vox Phantom VI

Danelectro Electric Sitar—Its twangy sound can be heard on Joe South's "Games People Play," the Box Tops' "Cry Like a Baby," and Stevie Wonder's "Signed, Sealed, Delivered."

Gibson reverse body Firebird

Danelectro Long Horn Bass. The shape says it all.

Fender Stratocaster—another classic. The "Strat" was used by Jimi Hendrix, George Harrison, and a million others.

Gibson Les Paul "SG" (standard guitar). A classic, used by many rock greats, such as Eric Clapton.

Gibson's Flying V

Fender Mustang, named for the car. Note the "competition racing stripes."

Smooth dancing and harmony. The Temptations' first hit was "The Way You Do the Things You Do," in 1964, and their first number one was the immortal "My Girl," in 1965. In 1969, they changed their style completely, coming out with the psychedelic "Cloud 9," Motown's bid to be part of the drug music scene.

The Inside Story:
Origin of Motown

In the late fifties, Berry Gordy, Jr., was an independent producer who came up with hits for Jackie Wilson, Marv Johnson, and the Miracles. But big companies made most of the profits. So in January 1959, he borrowed eight hundred dollars and started Motown Records. Two of the guiding ideas behind Motown: make fewer records than most companies, with the emphasis on coming up with hits (top-ten hits, not rhythm-and-blues hits), and produce records that would sound good on car radios and jukeboxes. Motown's execs always listened to tapes on tinny speakers so that they could guess what the songs would sound like to the public.

In 1962, Motown had its first million-seller, "Shop Around," and it just kept getting bigger from there.

Originally backup singers at Motown, they were a group called the Primettes in high school (inspired by the Primes, who became the Temptations). Their first number-one hit was "Where Did Our Love Go," in 1964. They had twelve number-one hits in the sixties, more than any other Motown act.

Little Stevie Wonder

The Four Tops

Marvin Gaye

Some Classic Motown Hits:

"Mr. Postman," by the Marvelettes, 1961

"Fingertips" (Part II), by Little Stevie Wonder, 1962

"Heat Wave," by Martha and the Vandellas, 1963

"My Guy," by Mary Wells, 1964

"How Sweet It Is to Be Loved by You," by Marvin Gaye, 1964

"Shotgun," by Jr. Walker and the All-Stars, 1965

"Ooo Baby Baby," by the Miracles, 1965

"My Girl," by the Temptations, 1965

"Reach Out," by the Four Tops, 1966

"This Old Heart of Mine," by the Isley Brothers, 1966

★ SOUL ★

Aretha Franklin, Lady Soul

The Wicked Wilson Picket

James Brown, Soul Brother #1

Otis Redding (1941–1967) died in a plane crash just as he was on the verge of becoming a superstar. His hits: "Try a Little Tenderness," "(Sittin on the) Dock of the Bay," and "Fa-fa-fa-fa-fa (Sad Song)"

Soul Sellers

"Mother-in-Law," by Ernie K-doe, 1961

"YaYa," by Lee Dorsey, 1961

"I Don't Want to Cry," by Chuck Jackson, 1961

"Papa's Got a Brand-New Bag," by James Brown, 1965

"It's a Man's Man's Man's World," by James Brown, 1966

"Hold On, I'm Comin'," by Sam and Dave, 1966

"Knock on Wood," by Eddie Floyd, 1966

"Soul Man," by Sam and Dave, 1967

"Respect," by Aretha Franklin, 1967

"Higher and Higher," by Jackie Wilson, 1967

"La La Means I Love You," by the Delfonics, 1968

This group featured Curtis Mayfield, who wrote great songs like "Gypsy Woman," "We're a Winner," and "Keep on Pushin'."

Former lead singer of the Drifters. He hit number one with "Spanish Harlem" and "Stand By Me."

Our choice for the most beautiful soul song of the decade.

Wilson's first solo record. Followed by: "In the Midnite Hour," "Mustang Sally," "Funky Broadway."

Otis Redding's protégé. The definitive summary of soul music.

173

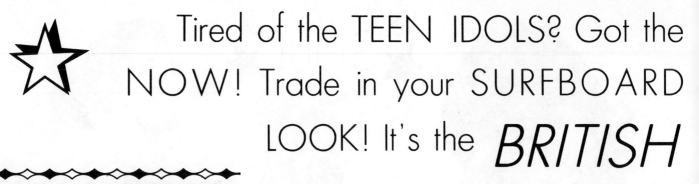

Tired of the TEEN IDOLS? Got the NOW! Trade in your SURFBOARD LOOK! It's the *BRITISH*

They're lovable! They're huggable! They're

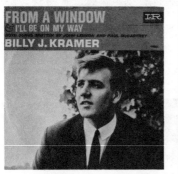

★ Highlights

SEE . . . American fast-buck artists scour the English countryside looking for NEW GROUPS to bombard the Americans with.

SEE . . . the airports jammed with adoring teenagers awaiting the arrival of THE GROUPS.

SEE . . . THE GROUPS get their clothes ripped off their backs by throngs of screaming fans.

SEE . . . the jealous American singers grow their hair long and try to imitate THE ENGLISH SOUND.

GIRL GROUP blues? All SOULed out?
and see what THE BEATLES brought in.

INVASION!!

quaint! They'll steal your heart away!

Also featuring

The Merseybeats • Georgie Fame
and the Blue Flames • Billy J.
Kramer and the Dakotas • The
Swinging Blue Jeans • The Shadows
• Cilla Black • The Tremeloes •
The Mojomen • The Rockin'
Berries • The Pretty Things • The
Nashville Teens • Wayne Fontana
and the Mindbenders • Unit Four
+ 2 • Marianne Faithfull

175

START

Amateur night at a Greenwich Village coffeehouse. You sing "We Shall Overcome," and everyone joins in. Take two steps forward.

Lose one turn while you learn the lyrics to "Blowin' in the Wind."

Joan Baez appears onstage barefoot. Take your shoes off. If you're already not wearing shoes, take two steps forward.

THE FOLK-ROCK GAME

Directions

Before beginning, throw your Ivy League suit away. Get a pair of old jeans, a work shirt, and motorcycle boots. *Do not embroider your jeans. Remember, you're a folk singer, not a hippie.*

Time magazine calls "Puff the Magic Dragon" a drug-oriented song. Could they be right? Peter, Paul, and Mary laugh all the way to the bank.

Peter, Paul, and Mary have a top-ten hit. Sing a chorus of "If I Had a Hammer."

Bob Dylan records his first album. Other folk singers, like Dave Van Ronk, accuse him of stealing their arrangements, but it doesn't matter. He's more popular than they are. Take one step ahead.

"Eve of Destruction" hits number one. Barry McGuire thinks the world is doomed. You agree. Go back three steps.

Dylan appears in the Newport Folk Festival with an electric guitar. An electric guitar? Boo him offstage.

Buy these records: "Sounds of Silence," "Mr. Tambourine Man," "Like a Rollin' Stone," "I Got You Babe." Folk rock is born. Go buy an electric guitar.

You really like folk rock. Go apologize to Dylan.

Stop at Alice's Restaurant. Get stoned, lose one turn.

Bob Dylan returns and goes country with his pal Johnny Cash.

You realize that Dylan has never written a song about Vietnam. Go back three spaces.

Sonny and Cher are turned away from a fancy restaurant because of Sonny's long hair and funny clothes. Sonny runs home and writes "Laugh at Me," a new type of protest song. Grow your hair long too.

You're in the supermarket and you hear "Blowin' in the Wind" on the piped-in Muzak. Either give up or start all over again.

Music from Big Pink, by The Band, comes out.

The Graduate features the music of Simon and Garfunkel. *Time* magazine considers them the greatest living rock poets. Whatever happened to protest music?

The Byrds go country with "Sweetheart of the Rodeo."

Dylan has a near-fatal motorcycle accident and goes into seclusion. No new Dylan albums. Go buy a Rolling Stones record instead.

Donovan graduates from Dylan imitations to Electrical Bananas

Uh-oh. Close the doors! Turn off the AM radio!

Here they come again! Those BRITISH GROUPS are back in . . . *THE SECOND WAVE*

A Heavy Musical Trip

Starring
THE "NEW" BEATLES

Costarring
THE "NEW" STONES

They started out as cute-and-cuddly moptops. But then drugs, Dylan, and dollars transformed them into . . . ARTISTS!!!

With a cast of thousands

HEAR . . . "Tommy," the first rock opera.

WITNESS . . . the beginning of the "concept album."

WATCH . . . them all get HEAVY.

SEE . . . the groups expand and multiply.

SEE . . . the jealous American groups dress up funny and try to imitate the ENGLISH SOUND.

Cream

Pink Floyd

Ten Years After

Procol Harum

The Who

Jethro Tull

Traffic

Hey! Hey! We're the MONKEES

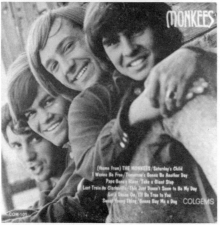

The Monkees ♪

The Monkees were not exactly what you'd call a rock group. In fact, they weren't a group at all. They were selected from hundreds of actors and musicians to play the part of a group in a TV show based on *A Hard Day's Night,* the Beatles' movie. The show was very popular. The only problem was that they could barely play their instruments. No matter. Hollywood is filled with enough great studio musicians that they could make even these guys sound good. And with that kind of help (not to mention the fact that they were on TV every Monday night at 7:30), is it any wonder that they had six *million sellers?*

But after two years on the air, the show was canceled. The Monkees "dissolved" and all we're left with are these memories.

THE SAN FRANCISCO SOUND

The Grateful Dead

The quintessential Acid Band. Members of the Dead had their musical roots in folk and bluegrass, but began playing electric music in the Bay area in 1965, calling themselves the Warlocks. They picked the name Grateful Dead in 1966 while under the influence of psychedelic drugs.

Despite the fact that they never had a number one hit (they refused to commercialize their music), the Dead developed a huge underground following which grew to millions of loyal "Dead-heads."

They kept playing free concerts after other groups gave it up. They made lots of money, but they gave a lot away. And they gave concertgoers their money's worth by playing for hours, when most of their contemporaries were playing short sets. The Grateful Dead seemed to be a symbol of the integrity of the counter culture—living proof that there was a conscientious alternative to AM pop music, and to straight middle class living.

Janis Joplin

Janis Joplin put everything she could into her performances. They became legendary.

In her first New York City concert, for example, at the Fillmore East, the hall was packed and she sang for an hour. Then she sang three encores; then, when the crowds refused to leave, she came out onto the stage and wheezed, "I'm sorry, babe, I just ain't got no more." She got a standing, stomping, screaming ovation, and then everybody went home.

The Jefferson Airplane

The Jefferson Airplane helped create the psychedelic sound that San Francisco was famous for. They were also the first San Francisco band to uncover the commercial potential in their brand of music when "Somebody to Love" hit the AM top ten in 1967.

Their lead singer, Grace Slick, was pretty, smart, and outrageous; once while Nixon was president, she tried to bring Abbie Hoffman into the White House with her (she was invited). She said it was lucky they didn't let her in—she was going to spike the punch with LSD.

By the end of the decade, the Airplane was as co-opted as the whole psychedelic scene. They were singing songs about Revolution, but riding around in limousines.

Other San Francisco Groups

Quicksilver Messenger Service

Steve Miller Blues Band

The Charlatans

The Sons of Champlin

The Peanut Butter Conspiracy

It's a Beautiful Day

Mother Earth

The Chocolate Watch Band

Rockin' Foo

Dan Hicks and His Hot Licks

Jan and Dean
"Surf City," 1964
"Dead Man's Curve," 1964

The Beach Boys
"Fun, Fun, Fun," 1964
"Good Vibrations," 1966

The Doors
"Light My Fire," 1967
"Hello, I Love You," 1968

The Mamas and the Papas
"California Dreamin'," 1966
"Monday Monday," 1966

The Ventures
"Walk Don't Run," 1960
"Hawaii Five-O," 1969

Creedence Clearwater Revival
"Proud Mary," 1969
"Bad Moon Rising," 1969

Buffalo Springfield
"For What It's Worth," 1967
"Bluebird," 1967

Led Zepplin
"Whole Lotta Love"

Vanilla Fudge
"You Keep Me Hangin' On"

Iron Butterfly
"In a Gadda Da Vida"

Deep Purple
"Hush"

HARD ROCK

♪ Jimi Hendrix, the King of Hard Rock

The Jimi Hendrix Experience debuted at the Monterey Pop Festival in 1967. Hendrix quickly became known as one of rock's finest guitarists and showmen. Onstage he didn't just play the guitar, he stroked it, caressed it, humped it, and even poured lighter fluid on it and set it on fire. "Foxy Lady," "Purple Haze," "Are You Experienced," "Axis: Bold As Love," "Electric Lady Land," "All Along the Watchtower." Three years and four albums later, Hendrix, one of the most influential rock musicians of all time, died at the age of twenty-eight of a drug overdose.

✱ Psychedelic Pop

Psychedelic Rock meets Top-Forty Pop. The result: Great AM hits like "We Ain't Got Nothin' Yet," by the Blues Magoos, 1966; "Incense and Peppermints," by the Strawberry Alarm Clock, 1967; "Talk Talk," by the Music Machine, 1966; "Psychotic Reaction," by the Count Five, 1966; and "I Just Dropped In (To See What Condition My Condition Was In)," by Kenny Rogers and the First Edition, 1968.

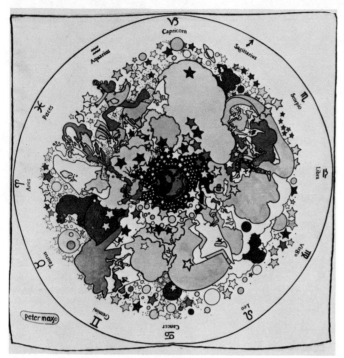

An astrological fantasy by Peter Max, printed on a scarf

60S! HALL OF FAME

Peter Max

There was a time in the sixties when you saw Peter Max's name and designs everywhere you went. In bookstores you saw his posters and books. In department stores you saw it on linen, dinnerware, scarves, clothes, clocks, and lots more. If you were in New York, you saw it on ten thousand city buses, which he had decorated. You saw it on the cover of the phone book and even in head shops. The reason you saw his name everywhere was because he made it part of his designs, and his designs were the hottest thing going. Eventually his style became synonymous with what was "happening" in America.

Peter Max could be the best example of sixties schizophrenia. He was a "groovy" artist and a "hip" businessman. If you listened to him talk, you got the impression that he was a champion of the counterculture. He said: "We're now on the verge of a golden age of infinite peace and beauty. The revolution has been won; it's happened."

This is the kind of thing you might have heard from people in communes in Big Sur or hippies hanging out in St. Marks place in the East Village in New York City. But Max was as far removed from them as his Rolls-Royce would take him. At the same time he was expressing his affinity for the "revolution," he was raking in millions of dollars designing clocks, towels, cups, posters, etc. for corporations like General Electric, the "enemies" of the "revolution."

How did he explain it? "The things I've learned under Yoga —a message of love, harmony, unity, and symmetry—I try to change into art for the masses. . . . The business people are a vehicle through which I distribute my very intimate ideas." That was what he said to *Cosmopolitan* magazine. *Business Week* magazine put it a little differently: " 'You supply the cash, the production, and the selling,' he tells (businessmen). 'I'll furnish the ideas and designs—and we'll split the profits 50–50.' " So much for the revolution.

The short-lived *Cheetah* magazine. Cover by Peter Max.

Inflatable plastic pillow adorned by a Peter Max design

Guess Whose Autographs These Are?

A.

[signature: Buny C Wallau]

B. *[signature: Martin Luther King Jr.]*

C. *[signature: Jone E Pg]*

D. *[signature: Hffgg of III 562.]*

E. *[signature: Mad Comysus]*

F. *[signature: Norman Mailer]*

G. *[signature: Apa L. Agne]*

H. *[signature: Tanapn]*

I. *[signature: Rage Maris]*

J. *[signature: Sve Have]*

L. *[signature: Sincerely Jack Riby]*

K. *[signature: Lee H Oswald]*

M. *[signature: John Carson]*

Autographs

N. *[signature: Buzz Aldrin]*

O. *[signature: Muhammad Ali]*

P. *[signature: Fidel Castro]*

Q. *[signature: Allen Ginsberg]*

R. *[signature: Sandy Koufax]*

S. *[signature: Robert F. Kennedy]*

T. *[signature: Ho Chi Minh]*

U. *[signature: Leonid Brezhnev]*

V. *[signature: Jacqueline Kennedy]*

W. *[signature: Richard J. Daley]*

X. *[signature: Neil Armstrong]*

Answers

60S! HALL OF FAME

Dr. Kildare

Richard Chamberlain starred on TV as the breathtakingly handsome Dr. James Kildare, a young intern at Blair General Hospital. Raymond Massey, who played Dr. Leonard Gillespie, Kildare's mentor, guided the intense young intern through life-and-death situations each week on this highly successful one-hour TV show. "Dr. Kildare" was a top-twenty show for three years—but that doesn't tell you how popular Chamberlain really was. Girls *loved* him. Two million teenagers alone watched Kildare every week; he got more fan mail than Clark Gable in his prime, three times as much as the star of "Ben Casey," Vince Edwards; his wholesome, Greek-god face was on the cover of every heart-throb magazine ("What is Dick Chamberlain *really* like?").

Dr. Kildare products were everywhere—games, notebooks, dolls, buttons, records. A Dr. Kildare comic book sold more than a half-million copies in six months. Even behind the Iron Curtain, Kildare was an idol. The Polish Communist party scheduled its meetings to avoid a conflict with the Wednesday-night showings of "Dr. Kildare," "for fear of playing to empty halls."

After four years, the show's ratings slipped. NBC performed surgery, cutting the series into two half-hour segments (Monday and Tuesday). But the patient lasted only one more year; the series died in 1966.

Ben Casey

A month after "Dr. Kildare" first aired on NBC, ABC premiered *its* TV medical drama—"Ben Casey." The series became the most popular show on ABC, due mostly to good-looking Vince Edwards, who starred as the "no-nonsense" Dr. Casey. His expertise as a neurosurgeon at County General Hospital seemed to justify his brusque, aggressive manner. But his mentor, Dr. Zorba, was not impressed. The two often clashed as Casey refused to "go by the book" when it interfered with his cases.

While Kildare was a beautiful, sensitive man, Casey was the opposite—violent, quick-tempered, Macho. His medical gown was always open at the top, revealing a manly tuft of hair. Psychiatrists said that his violence was interpreted as sexiness. Maybe so. Casey rivaled Kildare as a heart throb: Thirty-two million people watched him every week, and Edwards's face showed up on the same magazine covers as Chamberlain's. Ben Casey merchandise was widespread (although it didn't sell as much as Kildare), including the Ben Casey shirt, a copy of the shirt that Edwards wore. "Ben Casey" lasted five years on TV, from 1961 to 1966.

Dr. HIP-pocrates

In 1967, thirty-one-year-old Dr. Eugene Schoenfeld, a physician on the staff of the University of California (Berkeley) student clinic, began writing a medical column for the *Berkeley Barb*, an underground newspaper, because he felt that someone should be answering hippies' questions without lecturing them. His column was the most widely read thing in the *Barb*—by 1969, it appeared in fifteen underground papers around the world.

HIPpocrates (copyright 1968) Eugene Schoenfeld, M.D.

QUESTION: Our last kilo contained hundreds of chips of crushed moth balls. We have heard tell of grass cured in moth balls, but had never seen any before. The grass had a peculiar medicinal odor and a metallic taste, but it did stone us better than average. Could there be any possible harm in smoking or swallowing chips too small to see?
ANSWER: Your friendly dealer may lose a lot of customers. Moth balls usually contain 100% naphthalene. Naphthalene is fatal in quantities of 2 grams for children and 5 to 15 grams for adults when ingested at one sitting. The drug is also quite toxic when inhaled.
Some of the symptoms of naphthalene intoxication are headache, confusion, excitement, nausea, and sometimes sweating and vomiting. Death occurs when the red blood cells are destroyed and the kidneys damaged by the cellular material released by the lysed red cells.
Those suspecting they have ingested or inhaled naphthalene should see a physician in order to have a complete blood count.
QUESTION: I have heard explanations ranging from the sublime to the ridiculous -- perhaps you could shed some light on the origin of the term "pot".
ANSWER: Max Scherr, the sublime editor of the BARB, informs me that the term originated in the "beat" era when marijuana was referred to as "pod." "Pod" is apparently a reference to a part of the marijuana plant. Are there readers with other ideas?
QUESTION: I often read ads in the underground press for people wanting "French" love. Could you please tell me what this is?
ANSWER: "French love" or "French culture" refers to oral-genital relations. The French may call this "Italian love."
QUESTION: A friend of mine has been forbidden by his doctor to indulge in intercourse until a nasty bit of the clap is entirely cleared up. If any of his girlfriends should decide to employ digital manipulation of his primary sex organ to achieve orgasm and release on his part, would this result in a case of the "hand-clap"?
ANSWER: I applaud the concern you have for your friend and his friends. Gonorrhea of the hand is unknown because the gonococci bacteria favor a warm, moist, airless environment. Gonorrhea of the mouth is possible but seen rarely. Most physicians believe all sexual activity should be avoided while treatment for gonorrhea is underway.

(Note: The symptoms of gonorrhea in the male are itching, burning and pain on urination and a discharge from the urethra. Symptoms in the female may include the above but are usually less severe or absent in the early stages. Females may later develop pain in the lower abdomen and a low-grade fever resulting from spread of the infection to the uterus, tubes and ovaries.)

* * * * * * * *

Here is another letter from the turned-on mother who reported she enjoyed full sexual relations during pregnancy until labor began (her baby has a "fine sense of rhythm").
"My tiny bosom throbbed with sympathy for the flat-chested girl who wrote to you. Her problem is more cultural and psychological than physical. Although the big boob is publicly adored, some men like small-busted women.
"I used to feel inferior about my small breasts. Then I had babies and was suddenly well-endowed. So I nursed a long time and wore sweaters. The funny thing is, now that i've weaned and am tiny again, I don't feel bad any more because I know I CAN be big. I don't even like padded bras.
"I would advise 'slim' to watch the classified ads for small-breast enthusiasts, marry one of them, have kids and breastfeed a long time."

* * * * * * * * * *

Dr. Schoenfeld welcomes your questions. Write to him c/o the Berkeley BARB, P.O. Box 5017, Berkeley, CA., 94705.

Best Sellers

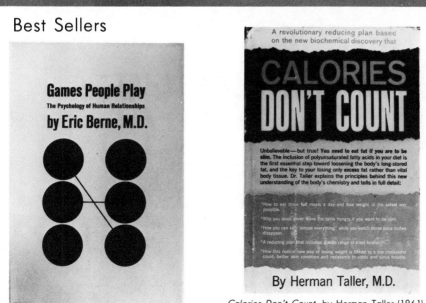

Games People Play
The Psychology of Human Relationships
by Eric Berne, M.D.

Games People Play, by Dr. Eric Berne. The chief of staff of the pop-psychology department opens the door for a flood of self-improvement books by telling you what you're doing, and why. Until this book, most grown-ups thought games were for kids.

A revolutionary reducing plan based on the new biochemical discovery that

CALORIES DON'T COUNT

Unbelievable—but true! You need to eat fat if you are to be slim. The inclusion of polyunsaturated fatty acids in your diet is the first essential step toward loosening the body's long-stored fat, and the key to your losing only excess fat rather than vital body tissue. Dr. Taller explains the principles behind this new understanding of the body's chemistry and tells in full detail:

By Herman Taller, M.D.

Calories Don't Count, by Herman Taller (1961). The messiah of the fad diets tells you how to lose weight without trying, and the federal government says "Don't!" A national scandal—the author of this number one best-seller was convicted of twelve counts of mail fraud in connection with the book.

TOP TEN

America's Favorite Doctors in the Sixties

1. *Dr. Kildare.* (Honorable mention: Dr. Leonard Gillespie)

2. *Dr. Ben Casey.* (Honorable mention: Dr. Zorba)

3. *Dr. Benjamin Spock.* His book on baby care is one of the biggest selling books in history, but in the sixties he was known for political activism, protesting nuclear testing, and U.S. involvement in Vietnam.

4. *Dr. Zhivago.* The hero of Boris Pasternak's Russian novel, which was released as a movie in 1965. Omar Sharif played the romantic lead in one of the box-office smashes of the decade.

5. *Dr. Christiaan Barnard.* Perhaps the most famous surgeon in the world. On December 3, 1967, he performed the first human heart transplant that worked (for a few days). Previous to this (1960) he gained local notoriety by transplanting a second head onto a dog.

6. *Dr. Tom Dooley.* Humanitarian and author of *Deliver Us from Evil* and *The Edge of Tomorrow*, known for founding numerous jungle hospitals. Died in January 1961, a day after his thirty-fourth birthday.

7. *Dr. Joyce Brothers.* The original "pop psychologist," a familiar guest on talk shows. She had her own daytime TV show, "Ask Dr. Brothers," in which she answered viewers' questions.

8. *Dr. Albert Sabin.* Creator of a miraculous oral polio vaccine, approved for use by the federal government in 1961.

9. *Dr. Dolittle.* The doctor who talked to animals experienced a boom in the sixties, instigated by a $15 million film—a musical extravaganza starring Rex Harrison as the good doctor.

10. *Marcus Welby, M.D.* Was it a sign of the changing times? At the end of the decade, the doctor show made a comeback; but this time instead of two handsome hunks, it was Robert Young, America's number-one father figure (from "Father Knows Best"), who played the physician.

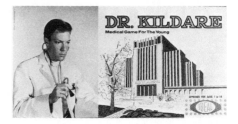

DR. KILDARE
Medical Game For The Young

187

60s! Guide to How to Look Like a Hippie

Let your hair grow long, preferably to your shoulders. (Women: to mid-back is fine.) For best effect, do not comb.

Get your head together.

Wear sunglasses so people will think you're stoned.

You're into nature now. Grow a beard. Not necessary for women, but very hip.

Love beads are a must. Shows you are sensitive and antiestablishment.

Mexican vest is a good conversation piece. Gives you a chance to talk about the "great weed" south of the border.

If you've got to wear a pullover shirt, it should be dyed long underwear unbuttoned. Tie-dye whenever possible. Always preferable: a work shirt.

A belt made of anything but leather is groovy. In this case, it is extra groovy because the belt is obviously not holding anything up. It's "just his thing."

Sew a secret stash pocket into the lining of the vest.

Raggedy old fur vest. Nice touch.

Tambourine. It shows you've got good vibes—you're really into music. Also good for panhandling.

Everyone wears jeans. The trick is to keep wearing the same pair until it's worn out. Then you can patch it. Use store-bought patches with antiestablishment slogans.

Go barefoot whenever possible, particularly where it's noticeable. Sandals are also acceptable.

60S! HALL OF FAME

Abbie Hoffman. Yippie!!!

MULTIPLE-CHOICE QUIZ

How to Talk Like a Hippie.

You've got to know the language to fit in; here's a test to get you ready. Pick A or B.

1. Blow your mind   (A) Exhale on someone's head (B) Get very high on drugs

2. Far out   (A) Great! (B) An enormous distance offshore

3. Psychedelic   (A) Pertaining to drugs (B) Selling cold cuts from a motorcycle

4. Out of sight   (A) You can't see it! (B) Terrific!

5. Spaced out   (A) Like John Glenn (B) Like Timothy Leary

6. Good vibes   (A) Lionel Hampton (B) Positive feelings

7. Be-in   (A) Vegetable, like limas (B) Joyous gathering

8. Acid   (A) For car batteries (B) LSD

9. Flower child   (A) Street vendor (B) Hippie

10. Tune in   (A) Take acid (B) Turn on television

11. Rap   (A) Discuss (B) Get a present ready

12. Roach   (A) Insect (B) Butt of marijuana cigarette

13. Joint   (A) How your bones move (B) Marijuana cigarette

14. Bread   (A) Money (B) Sandwich ingredient

15. Groovy   (A) Really fine (B) Full of little indentations

Read Up on the Counterculture Before Joining.

It's easy to join the counterculture! . . . Just do what these folks do!

OUT OF SIGHT! Looks like this spaced-out lady is tripping out on some dynamite weed. What a mind-blower! She must be zonked by now, but she keeps on truckin'. Can you dig it?

RIGHT ON! This groovy flower child knows where it's at! She's tripped out on love and peace because that's what she's into! All power to the people!

Selling underground papers is a very hip way to earn a little bread. You can do a hit of acid and just sit there and groove on the flow. Rap to a few heads, pick up some spare change. If the pigs try to hassle you, just tell 'em you're doin' your own thing.

OH WOW! What's that straight-looking chick doing here in counterculture?! Didn't somebody tell her no *kitchen* counters? Get her out of here! She makes me paranoid.

When doing your counterculture shopping, always look for the peace sign. It's a sign that an article is especially geared to the needs of the counterculture member. The peace sign is "good karma."

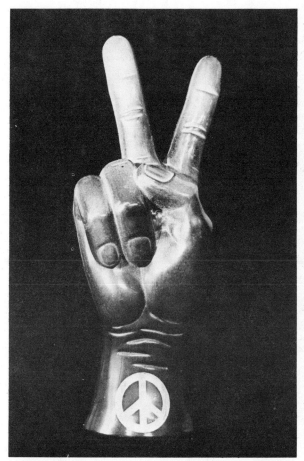

Like this lovely plastic hand giving the peace sign, for example. Put it anywhere—on your dining-room table, on top of your television, in your office.

Or this five-peace set of silverware. Now you can eat in peace.

Posters are a must for any pad, of course, but be sure to look for the genuine "peace and love" posters that counterculture members prefer. Only $1.98 per poster.

You've got to have patches on your clothes. But how can you be sure they're authentic counterculture patches?

Rule of thumb: You're "right on" with Woodstock.

Revolution is a wonderful topic for songs. Counterculture heroes make millions of dollars singing about it!

No hippie is complete without protest buttons. Now you can make your own! And they're reusable, too!

There were four "world's fairs" in the sixties.

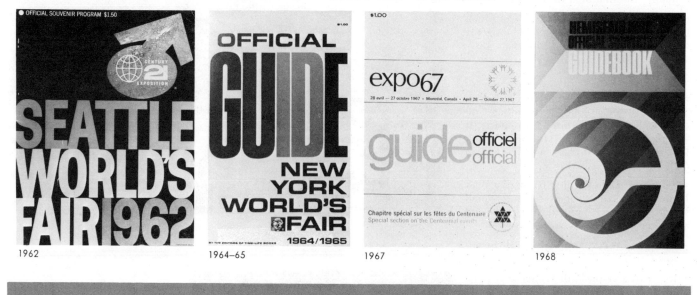

1962   1964–65   1967   1968

Seattle Century 21 Exposition

Date: April 21–October 21, 1962

Theme: "Man in the Space Age"

Originated as a plan to commemorate the 1909 Alaska-Yukon-Pacific Exhibition, which drew more than 3 million visitors to Seattle.

Highlights:

• The exposition's symbol was the Space Needle, a 600-foot-high structure with a revolving restaurant and an observation tower on its tip. The idea for it originated with a Seattle hotelman who dined in a restaurant atop a 425-foot TV tower in Stuttgart, Germany. He sent a picture postcard of it to exposition officials with the message: "Why not something like this for the fair?"

• A highly publicized monorail took visitors from downtown Seattle to the fairgrounds at 60 mph. It was a mile long and had the capacity to take eight thousand people an hour to the fair. It was widely regarded as the public transportation of the not-too-distant future.

• The U.S. "World of Science" exhibit featured a "spacearium," a multiscreen theater in which visitors could view outer space as seen from a spaceship, in a simulated space ride. "It's so realistic, the government had to install handrails for people to hold on to," said the fair director.

• AT&T exhibited telephones rigged to close windows and water lawns when you dialed your telephone number from out of town.

• General Motors showed future highways with cars under electronic control.

• A "Bubbleator"—a clear plastic globe/elevator—took people to exhibits that showed life in the year 2000.

• General Electric showed the television of the future—a color TV with a picture projected on a four- by six-foot wall panel.

• Russia did not exhibit. When fair officials requested a display of Russian space achievements, they received the curt reply: "Russia is too busy."

What is it? A cigarette lighter in the shape of the Space Needle

New York World's Fair

Date: April–October 1964 and 1965

Theme: "International Understanding"

Originated at a luncheon in 1959, at which four men were reminiscing about how great the 1939–40 New York World's Fair was.

Highlights:

• The symbol of the fair was the Unisphere, a stainless-steel globe representing the earth with satellites whirling around it. It was a gift (and PR success) from U.S. Steel. It cost $2 million dollars, was 120 feet in diameter, 135 feet high.

• The Pepsi Cola Pavilion featured a Walt Disney boat ride called "It's a Small World," in which animated dolls danced and sang in many languages.

• The Vatican Pavilion included Michelangelo's *Pieta*

• In a two-acre park, the Defense Department put on the largest exhibit of American rockets and space vehicles ever assembled outside of Cape Kennedy.

• AT&T demonstrated a "picturephone," making calls to Disneyland in which callers could see one another on a four- by five-inch video screen. Their chief engineer predicted the phones would be on the market in a few months.

• A mechanical Abe Lincoln (by Walt Disney) in the Illinois exhibit grinned, frowned, rubbed his nose, and recited speeches.

• General Motors' Futurama (the most popular display in the fair, with 30 million visitors) was an updated version of its 1939 exhibit. In 1939, patrons watched the "highway of the future"—the freeway of the sixties. In 1964, the exhibit included a moonscape with lunar crawler moving over it.

• Walt Disney's animated dinosaurs fought and roared in a time tunnel of the Ford Pavilion, in which visitors rode in 1964 Ford convertibles through the Mesozoic Era to a space-age city.

• The Chrysler display included giant "insects" made of automobile parts.

• U.S. Rubber ran a huge Ferris wheel that looked like a giant automobile tire.

• Westinghouse featured a time capsule that was to be buried and opened in 5000 years (A.D. 6964). Among the items placed in it: a bikini, filter cigarettes, a ballpoint pen, tranquilizer pills, a Beatles record, a computer memory unit, films and tapes of 1960s sights and sounds. "There's no assurance anyone will ever find this thing, but then nobody expected to find the Dead Sea Scrolls, either."

For people in Arizona who can't make it to New York in 1964, here's the next best thing.

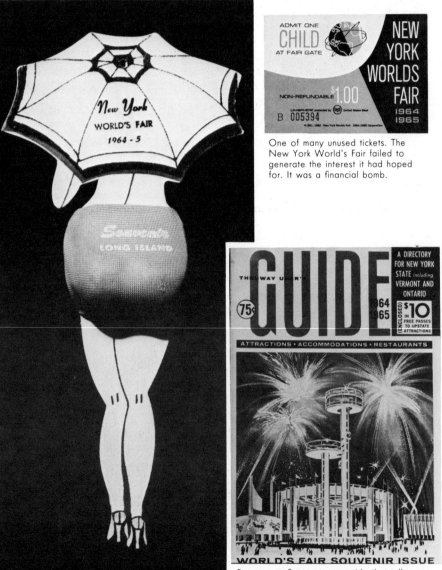

An "unofficial" souvenir—it's a pincushion.

One of many unused tickets. The New York World's Fair failed to generate the interest it had hoped for. It was a financial bomb.

For seventy-five cents—a guide that tells you how to get to the fair. Big bargain.

194

Expo 67—Montreal

Date: April 28–October 27, 1967

Theme: "Man and His World"

• At its opening, it was the world's top tourist attraction, with 1.5 million visitors in the first three days. It originated as the highlight of Canada's one hundredth birthday celebration.

Highlights:

• Soviet Pavilion: Visitors could experience weightlessness through film tricks, watch fashion shows from Riga, Kiev, and

Rah, Team. A pennant from Expo

After four years of building, the announcement Montrealers were waiting for.

Moscow, eat at restaurants stocked with eight tons of caviar and thirteen thousand bottles of Vodka, see the Bolshoi Opera, and learn about the planets in the Venus Planetarium.

• The U.S. Pavilion was a huge geodesic dome designed by Buckminster Fuller with the theme, "Creative America." It included Alan Shepard's *Freedom 7* capsule, an Apollo command module, old American artifacts (Kewpie doll, stovepipe hat), and an entire level devoted to Hollywood (the chariot from *Ben-Hur*, blowups of John Wayne, Marilyn, Marlon Brando).

• In the La Ronde amusement area, the most spectacular ride was the Gyroton, a 215-foot tubular pyramid something like a giant erector set, which plummeted riders from its peak into a simulated volcano spewing lava and wound up inside the jaws of a giant crablike monster. "We didn't know whether to put a bar or a first-aid station at the exit," said an Expo official.

• Australia displayed seventy kangaroos that were first conditioned to handle the blare from a nearby teenage band shell by being exposed to endless hours of rock 'n' roll tapes

Hemisfair 68—San Antonio

Date: April 6–October 6, 1968

Theme: "Confluence of Civilization in the Americas"

Originated as an idea at a Chamber of Commerce meeting in 1958, to be a celebration of San Antonio's two hundred fiftieth birthday.

Highlights:

• A canal was dug from nearby San Antonio River through the fairgrounds. Visitors could enter the fair on gondolas, then ride through it on flower-bedecked barges.

• The Tower of the Americas, with observation decks and two restaurants on top, was 622 feet high, the tallest in the Western Hemisphere. Glass-enclosed elevators shot people to the top in forty-five seconds. The view from the tower stretched ninety miles.

• Project Y featured continuous happenings in a group of theaters, plazas, and parks. Visitors were allowed to "do their own thing." For example, the editor of an underground newspaper was married in a "mixed-media wedding," in an inflated polyethylene church, with a minister of the Neo-American Church (LSD advocates) presiding.

• Outdoor air-conditioners cooled fairgoers as they walked or stood on line.

A commemorative coin from the Hemisfair. Remember the Alamo

• Czechoslovakia brought Kino Automat, in which viewers determined the end of a movie by majority vote.

• American exhibit featured a controversial film that included portrayals of whites shooting Indians to get their lands, a Negro family moving into a hostile white suburb, freeways jammed with cars, pollution.

Gee-tars from Mattel

Three Stooges hand puppets

A Tonka truck. Metal trucks from the sixties are collectible.

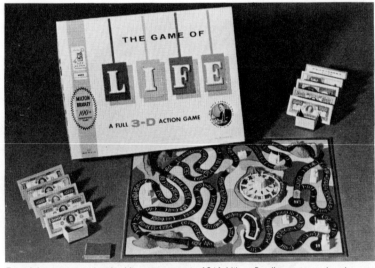

To celebrate its one hundredth anniversary, in 1961 Milton Bradley revamped and reissued its original game from 1861, the game of Life. The object of the game is to get rich.

Hey, this sounds like fun—the object of this game is to go on your dream date . . . but you don't know who your date is. He may be that handsome hunk you've been watching, or he may be that nerd who doesn't lace up his shoes. Until you open the door, you'll just have to hold your breath!

Toy guitars from the Jefferson Guitar Company

8 Toys

Kenner's "Easy-Bake oven." "Bakes with two ordinary electric light bulbs! Bake your cake and eat it too! It's quick! It's Easy! Simply add water and bake these delicious treats: devil's food cake, iced white cake, pizza, pretzels . . . ."

Flop of the Decade

"Instant Fish"

When one of the founders of Wham-O Mfg. Co. was on vacation in Africa, he camped beside a dry lake bed. One night it rained, and the lake filled up. The next day he noticed that there were fish in the lake. How could that be? Fish don't grow overnight.

When he got back to California, he asked a biologist friend of his what had happened, and found out that there was indeed a fish in that part of the world whose eggs lay dormant until they were exposed to water. Then the eggs hatched and the fish emerged.

It sounded like an incredible idea for a product—"Instant Fish." He hurriedly built huge fish tanks in the Wham-O factory and imported the fish so he could start collecting their eggs.

Meanwhile, the annual New York Toy Fair for toy store owners was taking place. And "Instant Fish" was the smash of the show. In one week, Wham-O took orders for $10 million worth of the fish. And even when they refused to take any more orders, people sneaked to the Wham-O hotel rooms and slipped orders under the door. It was a gold mine.

Except nobody told the fish. They just couldn't lay eggs fast enough. Desperate,

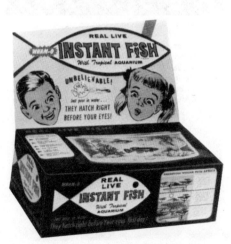

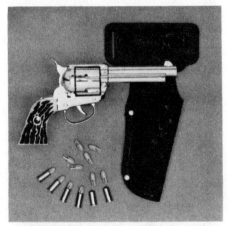

A Mattel "Fan-O-Matic" gun. Works best with "Greenie Stick-M-caps." Remember?

Wham-O tried everything—they tried covering the windows so that the inside of their plant was dark like a lake; they tried warmer room temperatures and they tried cooler; they even tried piping in romantic music. But nothing worked. Wham-O had to admit that "Instant Fish" had laid its own enormous egg. And after shipping only two hundred thousand dollars worth of the fish, they canceled all the orders.

FADS

Frisbee

Frisbee was not invented in the sixties, but it became a national "sport" when the Wham-O Mfg. Co. company rented the Hollywood Bowl in 1968 and had a Frisbee tournament, which generated tremendous national publicity.

Another thing that helped the Frisbee: America had had its fill with violent competition and the Frisbee was a peaceful, noncompetitive sport.

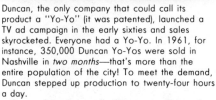

Yo-Yos

Duncan, the only company that could call its product a "Yo-Yo" (it was patented), launched a TV ad campaign in the early sixties and sales skyrocketed. Everyone had a Yo-Yo. In 1961, for instance, 350,000 Duncan Yo-Yos were sold in Nashville in *two months*—that's more than the entire population of the city! To meet the demand, Duncan stepped up production to twenty-four hours a day.

Some of the Duncan Yo-Yos you could buy: the Imperial (top of the line), the Butterfly (good sleeper), the Satellite, the Sonic Satellite (whistled), the Beginner, the Mardi-Gras (a yo-yo for girls), the Glo-Go (with a battery, lit up when it bobbed).

Superball

The Super Ball appeared in 1965, and millions were sold in the first few months. It's made of a secret rubbery compound called Zectron, which has six times the bounce of a regular rubber ball. It was developed by a scientist while he was working for a rubber company. They had no use for it, so they gave him the rights. He took it to Wham-O.

In Australia, someone made a giant Superball and dropped it from a skyscraper to see if it would bounce all the way back up. When it hit the ground, it split in half and one part of it went crashing down the street, bouncing off cars and buildings until it crashed through a plate-glass window of a store. Interesting experiment.

Despite the apparent success of the company, Duncan went bankrupt in the mid-sixties. One reason: Its patent on the term "yo-yo" was ruled invalid. The name Duncan was bought by the company that had been supplying them with plastic molds, and the Duncan was revived.

Shoop Shoop Hula Hoop

Hula Hoops were a monster 1950s toy (1958). In 1968 Wham-O tried to bring it back by putting ball bearings inside the plastic tube and calling it the Shoop-Shoop Hula Hoop (presumably inspired by Betty Evertt's hit record "The Shoop Shoop Song").

Sidewalk Surfin'

Skateboarding was an offshoot of the surfing craze. Here is a rare photo of an original California skateboard. Note the peace sign.

Twister

Even kids' toys were affected by the "sexual revolution." In 1966 Twister, described by Milton Bradley's president as "the first game in history to turn the human body into a vital component of play," was introduced.

Twister owed its immediate popularity to Johnny Carson. When it came out, Milton Bradley's PR firm brought the game to NBC and showed it to Carson's writers, who promised to get it on "The Tonight Show." Carson's guest that night was Eva Gabor. When millions of Americans saw Johnny Carson and Eva Gabor climbing all over each other, they understood ex-

actly what the game was about—SEX. The next day, toy stores were flooded with demands for the game. Over 3 million games were sold; more than ten times as many as Milton Bradley ever expected.

DIED IN THE SIXTIES
Cheap Japanese Mechanical Toys

Cause of death: Material costs made plastic more feasible for mass production and Japanese labor costs became prohibitive.

Metal mechanical toys from Japan were not considered high quality in the sixties, and they weren't expensive. But today they are among the most prized of any toys of the decade.

SPACE TOYS

DeLuxe "Operation X-500 Defense Base." Today's price: $100

Kids have always been attracted to fantasies about outer space. In the thirties and forties, their heroes were Buck Rogers and Flash Gordon. In the fifties, it was Captain Video and his Video Rangers. But in the sixties, when children who played in "outer space" were imitating real life for the first time in history, heroes had names like Alan Shepard and John Glenn. Sixties kids wanted to be astronauts, not "spacemen."

The whole country was focused on space in the sixties. And just as space travel dominated the headlines, space toys dominated the toy shelves.

Barbie Dressed as an "Astronette"

"2001" Space Clipper Model by Aurora. Today's price: $10

Battery-operated Astronaut and Windup Space Monster. Today's prices: $300 and $40

Astronaut Dime Bank. Save money with the astronauts. Today's price: $6

Space Scooter. Battery-operated mechanical toy. Today's price: $65

Men into Space game by Milton Bradley. Today's price: $15

Cape Canaveral Set featuring Shooting Rockets and Spacemen. Today's price: $100

ROBOTS

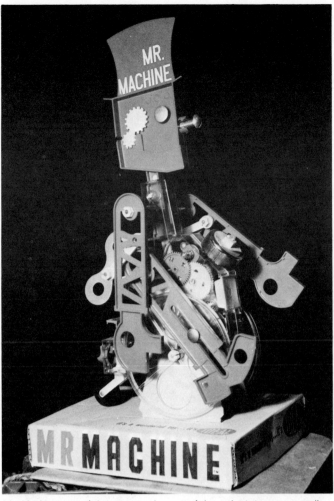

The Great Garloo

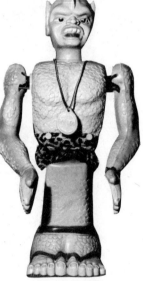

Mr. Machine, one of the most popular toys of the early sixties, was actually a comment on the condition of modern man. One day Marvin Glass, a neurotic toy designer who considered himself something of a philosopher, was having a typical argument with one of his ex-wives. Just before she hung up, she screamed at him: "You're nothing but a machine!" Glass thought about it. Maybe she was right . . . maybe the twentieth century had turned all of us into little more than machines.

Inspired, Glass designed Mr. Machine, a plastic robot with a top hat who clunked and whirred, and walked mechanically.

The Mr. Machine TV ad: "Here he comes, here he comes, greatest toy you've ever seen, and his name is Mr. Machine. . . ."

A "nauseous-green, battery-operated doll monster that stalks about, picking things up here, and putting them down over there."
—Newsweek, November 27, 1961

Robot Commando

Ideal's attack robot. His head opened up on command, revealing an arsenal of rockets that were fired by pushing a button.

Miss Popularity

WITH THE automatic Answer-PHONE

THE TRUE AMERICAN TEEN *Game*

JUDGES STAND

all girls love to play

Glamour 20

Miss Popularity must look her best. CALL your mother and ask if you may pay $15.00 for a permanent and hair style.

Concert 35

You attend a symphony concert to improve your music appreciation.

Careless -50

You have neglected your personal appearance. You must return all judge cards to the table and all vote cards to the deck.

Most Popular 50

Your classmates are voting for the most popular girl in school. CALL to see if you are elected.

Plain Pajamas 5

You may be invited to a Pajama Party. It would be wise to have these around. Pay $5.00

Break-Up -10

You have a big spat with your boyfriend. (If you have a fraternity pin or class ring you must return it to the deck.)

Sports Car 25

If you have an honor student card your father buys you a sports car.

Temper Temper -10

You lose your temper with a friend. You must CALL her for each turn until she forgives you.

Winner 25

If you have tickets to T.V. Record Hop your dancing wins first prize.

21 MOVABLE PARTS!

ALMOST A FOOT TALL!

AUTHENTIC EQUIPMENT FROM HEAD TO TOE

1964, G.I. Joe debuts

The Inside Story:
The Origin of G.I. Joe

G.I. Joe was the first successful doll for boys. He was inspired by Barbie's success. He was born one day when the staff of Hasbro was throwing some ideas around, trying to come up with new toys. Someone said: "How about a doll for boys that concentrates on accessories like Barbie; instead of fashion we can make it a soldier and give it extra uniforms and weapons."

"It was like electricity," commented a man who was there that day. "All of a sudden the room got quiet; everyone knew we had a great idea. Then everybody started talking at once." When the smoke cleared, the decision had been made to have different sets of uniforms for each branch of the service (Army, Navy, Air Force, Marines) and military gear including helmets, canteens, and lots of weapons. Joe would have pistols, knives, machine guns, a flame thrower, hand grenades, rifles with bayonets, and much more. But they knew that the secret to success would be DE-TAIL, with everything made exactly to scale. What's more, they decided to give Joe a scarred face to make him more masculine, and never to refer to him as a "doll"—only as an "action soldier."

When Joe was introduced to the toy industry, toy store owners avoided him. They did not believe that American parents would buy their sons dolls. But Hasbro stuck with it, and its first year over $30 million worth of G.I. Joe and accessories were sold—including 2 million dolls.

But in the late sixties, the increasing unpopularity of the war in Vietnam encouraged parents to prevent their children from playing soldier. Instead of continuing its steady growth, G.I. Joe's sales plummeted to less than a third of its previous level. Joe was almost wiped out. But Hasbro quietly moved with the times. To save the toy, they changed him from a soldier to an adventurer. Now he would go on missions to recover buried treasure instead of combat patrols. It worked. Soon, G.I. Joe was back in action.

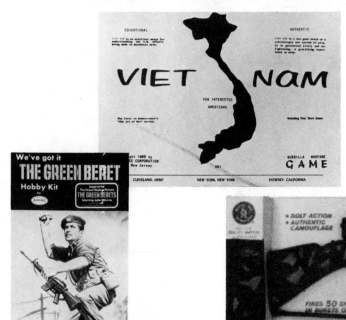

Inspired by Vietnam

Kids' toys are inspired by what's going on in the adult world. In 1961 JFK committed our first troops to Vietnam. In 1962, toys relating to Vietnam began to catch on. "We've discovered through dealer interviews and consumer mail that our customers are demanding toys about Vietnam," said the sales manager of a major toy company.

One of the first big sellers: In 1963, Mattel painted its Dick Tracy Submachine Guns camouflage green, packaged it with a poncho, toy hand grenades, and a beret, and called it a "guerrilla gun." They sold two million of them that year—twice as many as they sold the previous year when it was still a Dick Tracy gun.

Barbie

◇➤ The Barbie Story ➤◇

Barbie was introduced in 1959 and sold like crazy all through the decade until it became established as the largest selling doll in the history of the world.

Hmmm, 1959 . . . that means the first generation of Barbie's playmates are all grown up. What are you girls up to now? Are you stockbrokers? Housewives? Artists? Maybe you're stewardesses and nurses, just like Barbie.

There really was a girl named Barbie, y'know. She was the daughter of Eliot and Ruth Handler, who founded Mattel, Inc., right after World War II. Ruth was fascinated that out of all her dolls, Barbie preferred shapely paper dolls that she could dress. At the time, the standard doll was a baby doll; a girl pretended she was an adult by pretending she was a mommy. (That was a common cultural notion.) But here was something different. Barbie was pretending to be a young adult who got dressed up and went out on the town. This gave Ruth the idea that made toy history, and she created a new American institution—the teenage fashion doll. And they immortalized their daughter's name by calling it the "Barbie doll."

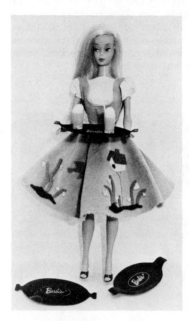

Out for a ride. Look who's driving

For Mattel, however, the success of Barbie was not in the doll, it was in the clothes. Originally the doll cost $3, but outfits cost $4–$5 each, and what self-respecting girl would have only one outfit? Let's see. If you could squeeze ten outfits out of your parents, that's about fifteen times the cost of a single doll. But then, just when you had enough outfits for Barbie, Mattel came out with a boy doll, Ken, in 1961 (named for the Handlers' son). More outfits, please. The Handlers were shocked that they sold a Ken doll for every two Barbies, when they had expected a ratio of 5 to 1. Obviously there was room for more. So here come Barbie's friends, Midge and Alan. More outfits. And Barbie wants a sports car and a dream house. And so on.

We don't want you to get the wrong impression of Barbie, though, so we would like to point out that she was "liberated" long before it was fashionable. Barbie had a career as a stewardess or a nurse or a nightclub singer or even an astronaut. Sure, she had expensive taste, but she didn't depend on her boyfriend for anything. In fact, Barbie was boss. If they ever break up, will Ken sue for palimony? He wouldn't dare.

Ken

The Barbie Family

Ken—Barbie's boyfriend

Midge—Barbie's best friend

Skipper—Barbie's little sister

Francie—Barbie's mod cousin

Allan—Midge's boyfriend

Ricky—Skipper's friend

Skooter—Skipper's friend

Christie—Barbie's black friend

Stacey—Barbie's British pal

205

DOLLS

Once Barbie had made it big, hundreds of cheap imitations sprang up. Here is Miss Babette.

What's so special about this doll? Hint: She is known as a "sexed doll."

From the TV show "Family Affair," Buffy and Mrs. Beasly

Which Dolly Is Which?
(Match the description with the doll's name)

Nancy and Kim, from Shindana, the first successful black-owned doll company.

Herbie Hippie

1. Thirstee Cry Baby

2. Hedda-Get-Bedda

3. Baby Grow-a-Tooth

4. Blabby

5. Slick Chick

6. Tipee Toes

7. Baby Bibsy

8. Kissy

9. Petite Frere

10. Marybel (the doll that gets well)

A. "Squeeze her tummy and she gurgles and coos like a baby."

B. Shuffles along, riding her play horse or tricycle, bobbing her head the whole way

C. Puckers up and smooches when hugged

D. Three faces (sick, sleeping, happy)

E. Wears a bib and drools

F. Touch her magnetic booties to her blue cradle, and she sits up and plays with a rattle.

G. One of a group of 1966 dolls called the go-go's. In a mini-skirt, of course.

H. "Anatomically correct" little boy doll (he has a penis)

I. Comes with a crutch, a cast, quarantine signs, and measle spots

J. Battery-operated, cries for over a minute, or until bottle of disappearing milk is placed in its mouth; then it stops crying and nurses.

A Kiddle mini-doll from Mattel.

Gingersnap (with a black Kewpie) was one of Remco's first "realistic" black dolls.

Answers

7-E, 8-C, 9-H, 10-I.
1-J, 2-D, 3-F, 4-A, 5-C, 6-B,

A Troll doll dressed as the Green Hornet. Would you let your daughter marry one of these?

Monstermania

If you were a boy in the early sixties, chances are you were into monsters. Frankenstein, the Mummy, Dracula, maybe you bought an occasional copy of *Famous Monsters of Filmland,* the magazine with all the great pictures from movies you never heard of . . . maybe you collected Monster Valentine Cards (a nickel a pack). Lots of toys were monster-inspired too: Creepy Crawlers, Horrible Hamilton, all the Weird-Ohs and the Rat-Finks. You might not remember it as a "craze" because it all seemed so natural. But it *was* a craze, and grown-ups were worried. "Why do kids like all those ugly things?" they wondered. "What does it mean?"

Actually it was more of a historical accident than a sign of anything psychological. It happened that in 1957 Universal Studios unearthed fifty-two old horror films (*Frankenstein* with Boris Karloff, *Dracula* with Bela Lugosi, etc.), which they sold to TV stations; the stations *showed* them to a generation of children who never even knew they existed. Kids loved them, just as audiences in the thirties and forties had. From there, the fad was strictly a matter of exploitation—as soon as "monster-products" became available, kids wanted them.

Famous Monsters

After a Philadelphia TV station was swamped by thirteen thousand youngsters who showed up for a "horror open house" in 1957, a local adman put together a quickie magazine he called *Famous Monsters of Filmland.* It was only supposed to run once, but it sold two hundred thousand copies and became the bimonthly bible of monster fans. "Most of our readers are between nine and twelve," *FMF*'s creator noted in 1964 (when readership was estimated at 1 million); "they're too old for cowboys and Indians and too young for girls. They need something to capture their imagination. After us, there's nothing but *Playboy.*"

Aurora Models

The monster merchandise boom arrived in 1961, when Aurora Plastics came out with a line of monster models (the kind you glue together), featuring Frankenstein and Dracula. "We don't make any fly-by-night monsters," a company spokesman explained; "we stick with the classics." Skeptical toy manufacturers were shocked to see Aurora's initial shipment sell out of the stores in *one* day! The monster bandwagon was off.

Soon Aurora had more monsters (the Phantom of the Opera, King Kong, the Hunchback of Notre Dame), an accessory kit with extra cobwebs and rats, and even a guillotine. Despite the growing competition, the company sold more than 10 million kits in three years. "It's the most popular line of hobby kits ever made by a U.S. manufacturer," they boasted.

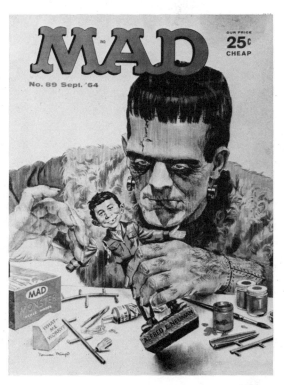

"The Addams Family"

Based on characters created by Charles Addams in cartoons which appeared in *The New Yorker,* The Addams Family was one of the best TV shows produced in the sixties. The members of the Addams family were endearing, but they were slightly eccentric. No, they were weird.

Gomez, for example, always wore the same double-breasted suit (circa 1940) and grinned like a madman. Morticia, his wife, was the urbane mistress of the household—but what a household! It was a cross between a funhouse and a chamber of horrors, with a stuffed polar bear and a suit of armor in the living room and a trophy on the wall—a sailfish with a pair of legs dangling from its mouth. Their playroom had a bed of nails and a torture rack (which Gomez used to cure his back problems).

Their children, Wednesday and Pugsley, liked to chop the heads off dolls with their mini-guillotine. Bald-headed Uncle Fester was so charged with electricity that he could light a light bulb simply by putting it in his mouth. And there was a large cast of nonhuman characters roaming the house: six-foot-nine-inch Lurch, the butler (he wasn't human, was he?), who answered most questions with a groan; Thing, a hand that emerged from a box (thank you, Thing); Pugsley's pet octopus; Wednesday's pet spider; Kitty Cat, the pet lion; Cleopatra, Morticia's African

Strangler (a man-eating plant); and Cousin Itt, four feet tall and completely covered with floor-length blond hair.

Every episode seemed to revolve around an unwitting normal human being, such as a mailman, salesman, or representative of the Board of Education, entering their home. Confronted with these bizarre goings-on, the stranger would usually end up running out of the house screaming. "Poor man," Morticia would say, "His job is getting to him."

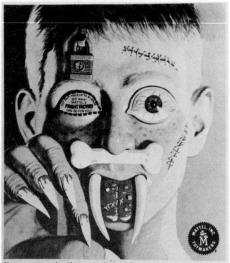

Now you can be the monster you've always wanted to be!
Mattel's Fright Factory

$ A Fast Buck $

• Cocktail stirrers shaped like monsters, called "Mon-stirs," and spoons with monsters on the handle, called "I-Scream spoons"

• Monster joke book, called *M Is for Monster*

• Soaky Bubble Bath, in Frankenstein and Wolfman containers (ad slogan: "Soapy Spooks scare you clean")

• Monster Cookies—a monstrous version of animal crackers

• Big Frankie—a twenty-eight-inch doll of Frankenstein

• Horrible Herman—a giant insect invader from outer space

• Bride of Frankenstein paper dolls

• Six-foot, life-size posters of Dracula and Frankenstein

• Weird-Ohs—a line of drooling monsters on wheels (available in models, posters, puzzles) like "Francis the Foul" and "Leaky-Boat Louie." Models were called "car-icky-tures with many fine disgusting parts to assemble."

The Inside Story: "Dark Shadows"

"Dark Shadows" began in 1967 as a standard soap opera. It was kind of mysterious, but there were no supernatural occurrences (a young woman went to Maine to be the governess in the home of a wealthy, reclusive family). Unfortunately, there wasn't much of an audience either. Its future looked shadowy—so with nothing to lose, the producers decided to try something different. They threw in Barnabas Collins, a vampire. It was the perfect touch. The show's popularity started increasing immediately, until over 6 million people watched it every day. "I suspect," said Jonathan Frid, the program's star, "that a few women wouldn't mind a bite in the neck."

The Monster Smash

Bobby "Boris" Pickett's 1962 takeoff of "Mashed Potato Time" was truly a monster hit. "The Monster Mash" sold over a million copies in fourteen weeks and has become a rock 'n' roll classic. Doing a Boris Karloff imitation, Bobby answered one of the important questions of the 1960s: "What ever happened to the Transylvania Twist?" ("It's now the Mash.")

A mechanical Frankenstein worth six hundred dollars on today's market

60s! HALL OF FAME
"The Munsters"

It had to happen . . . a situation comedy about Frankenstein. Well, not really Frankenstein; it's lovable Herman Munster—he just *looks* like Frankenstein. He works in a funeral home, of course, and commutes in a vehicle that looks like a casket on wheels. Very unusual.

Herman's wife, Lily, looks like a vampire. So does Grandpa, who spends a lot of his time reminiscing about Transylvania three hundred years ago. Their son Eddie might not *be* a werewolf, but he sure looks like one. Well, at least their niece, Marilyn, seems normal. The Munsters think she looks wierd. How would they know?

The Munsters ran for two seasons, then died, only to be resurrected soon afterward in reruns.

Monster wallets

• "Drug abuse is increasing in epidemic proportions and has become a fact of life, if not a way of life, to a sizable segment of our youth population, where we can least afford it to take root."—John F. Ingersoll, director of the Justice Department's Bureau of Narcotics and Dangerous Drugs.

• "Tune in, turn on, drop out"—Timothy Leary

TOP TEN
Drug Anthems

1. "White Rabbit," by the Jefferson Airplane
2. "Eight Miles High," by The Byrds
3. "Purple Haze," by Jimi Hendrix
4. "The Pusher," by Steppenwolf
5. "Journey to the Center of Your Mind," by the Amboy Dukes
6. "Day in the Life," by the Beatles
7. "Casey Jones," by the Grateful Dead
8. "Lucy in the Sky with Diamonds," by the Beatles
9. "Mr. Tambourine Man," by the Byrds
10. "Don't Bogart That Joint," by Fraternity of Man

Five Strange Drug Fads of the Sixties

1. *Catnip Craze.* In 1969, pet store owners suddenly saw their sales of catnip go sky-high. Reason? Someone discovered smoking catnip could be a psychedelic experience. A common roadside weed of the mint family, catnip had certain advantages over pot: It was cheaper (sixty cents an ounce as opposed to $10–$20 for pot), and legal. "My cat got turned on after I gave him this crazy stuff, so then I tried it," one youth reported. A major catnip producer rejoiced: "It sounds like it has great possibilities. Maybe it's a new outlet for the stuff." A doctor declared: "It's almost gotten to the point where they'll try anything."

2. *Banana Peel or "Mellow Yellow."* In 1967, in cozy, ladies'-page prose, the *Berkeley Barb* printed a recipe for baking the scrapings from banana peels to make a smokable substance some said gave a mild high, like weak pot. A "high" real or imagined? Real, proclaimed British pop-singer Donovan in his song "Mellow Yellow": Real, echoed hippies at a Central Park Be-in handing around a two-foot-long banana effigy as others chanted, "Banana, banana . . ." Others scoffed, especially the ones who tried it.

3. *Nutmeg.* Some said nutmeg gave an LSD-like high.

4. *Cough Medicine.* It was easy enough for kids in grade and junior high school to score this stuff and slug it down—for the codeine.

5. *Morning-Glory Seeds.* In 1963, sales of these small, bitter, brown seeds soared. A new high had been found: Rumor had it that if you injested from fifty to five hundred morning-glory seeds, you could have trances and hallucinations lasting five to eight hours. Harvard students ground up the seeds in "Elsie frappes." Three favorite seed varieties were Heavenly Blue, Pearly Gates, and Flying Saucers.

He Used Too Many Drugs

This man is spaced out, never to return.

Drugs

Millbrook

One famous place of the sixties drug culture was Timothy Leary's commune in Millbrook, New York, where there was constant experimentation with LSD. If you had gone there to stay or visit, here are the ten questions you would have been asked before they would let you join them.

1. Can you give a definition of the psychedelic experience?

2. What is the background and history of psychedelic experience?

3. Could you name some of the various agents used throughout history to produce the psychedelic experience?

4. What is LSD-25?

5. What does it do, physically and mentally?

6. Can you go into the history and controversy around LSD-25?

7. Why did you come to work with LSD-25? Could you give some of your own history?

8. What has been done with LSD so far, such as with alcoholics . . . mental patients . . . artists . . . the N.Y.U. Dream Experiment?

9. What is Millbrook? What is it doing, and where is it going?

10. Can you give some comments on the future of psychedelics?

Baba Ram Das (formerly Richard Alpert), one of the heroes and founders of the psychedelic movement

Great Moments of the 60s

LSD-Designed Hospital

To see things through a mental patient's eyes, architect Kyo Izumi took LSD—then designed a psychiatric hospital in Yorkton, Saskatchewan, in 1965. The drug made walking a normal hospital corridor a nightmare: "It seemed I would never get to the end of it," Izumi recalled. He designed a series of unimposing buildings without corridors or disturbing color schemes, and with small sleeping rooms to give a feeling of security. Concluded his co-worker Dr. Humphrey Osmond: "We can now build hospitals that at the very least do the sick no harm."

TIME CAPSULE

• Until 1967, LSD was *legal* in California.

• In 1969 there was a shortage of pot because of Nixon's crackdown on smuggling at the Mexican border. As a result, pot went from $15 an ounce to $50 an ounce.

• News item: Spiro Agnew's daughter was suspended from school while they investigated her for smoking dope.

• A head shop in Philadelphia gave a 15 percent discount to narcs.

Turning on Congress

At least one U.S. senator should "turn on," to experience what it's like; Congress should provide special parks for quiet acid trips; an "Internal Flight Agency" should be formed to license trips and map out "special journeys." These were proposals by Richard Alpert, poet Allen Ginsberg, and other witnesses arguing the benefits of mind-expanding drugs before a Senate subcommittee in 1966. Ginsberg wrote poems for the senators and told them that while on acid he found himself praying for the president.

The Caped Crusaders, 1966

The Inside Story: How Batman Got on TV

It was an accident, really. ABC was in trouble—and was looking for something—*anything*—to give them a ratings boost. Pop Art was "in," and comic books were starting to regain respectability (comic collecting got hot in the mid-sixties, fueled by Jules Feiffer's *The Great Comic Book Heroes*). So ABC bought the Batman idea. They figured that kids would enjoy it straight, and adults would enjoy it as a parody. To produce it, they got William Dozier, who had never even heard of Batman, and he got Lorenzo Semple ("the most bizarre thinker I knew") to write the script. All of them seem to agree that Batman was never intended to be anything but "camp" (something so bad it's good).

In 1965, as Dozier and crew were building the apparatus to film a Batman series—batcave, batmobile, etc.—with the intention of showing it in the fall of 1966, an amazing coincidence occurred . . . someone put together a full-length film comprised of fifteen episodes of the 1943 Columbia Batman serial. It was called *An Evening with Batman and Robin,* and it was sold out wherever it was shown. Batman became a national fad. Sensing that they just happened to be in the right place at the right time, ABC and Dozier rushed production of the Batman series. They were able to premier it on January 12, 1966, six months before it was originally scheduled, and it became the focal point of the Batmania. An instant smash.

A white hot beam of light pierces the midnight sky, sending its urgent message into the ink-black night over Gotham City, striking terror into the rotten hearts of evildoers.

Batman Dialogue
(a sample from the show)

[*As Batman and Robin swing precariously over a cauldron of boiling wax*]

ROBIN: Holy paraffin, Batman, this is going to be a close one!!

BATMAN: Too close!!!!

RIDDLER [*his raw emotions showing*]: This is my dream come true! With you two out of the way, nothing stands between me and the Lost Treasure of the Incas . . . and it's worth millions . . . millions!! Hear me, Batman, MILLIONS!!

BATMAN: Just remember, Riddler, you can't buy friends with money.

The Villains

How evil can you get? The baddest of TV bad guys, left to right, Burgess Meredith as the Penguin, Frank Gorshen as the Riddler, Julie Newmar as the Cat Woman, and Cesar Romero as The Joker

A bat-wallet

Motorized toy Batcraft

The hit version of the Bat-theme by the Marketts

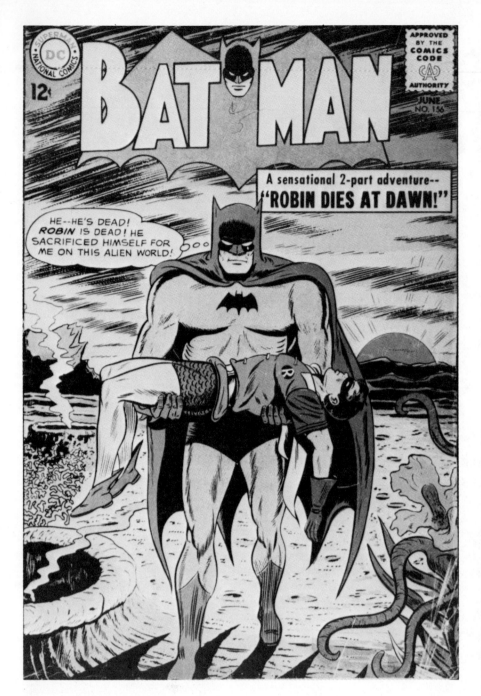

Great Moments of the 60s

Batman Goes to "Camp"

We almost lost Batman in the Batman boom. In 1966, at Batman's permanent headquarters—DC Comics—people watched in amazement as the whole country went Bat-mad. Obviously, they thought, TV had hit the perfect formula for making Batman big-time—it was camp and self-parody. So to boost their own sales, DC made the decision to turn the comic book into an imitation of the TV program, which was an imitation of the comic book in the first place. The comic book hero went from being a serious crime-fighter to acting like a member of the Three Stooges, yukking it up. Fortunately, the "New Batman" was a flop. DC had failed to realize that the people who bought comic books—the under-twelve-year-olds—took the television show seriously, too. Eventually, the Caped Crusader went back to playing it straight and regained his old audience.

Soaky strikes again . . . with Batbath bubble soap!

The Cast
Here is a list of the good guys of the Batman show:

Adam West — Bruce Wayne, a Gotham City millionaire who secretly was Batman

Burt Ward — Dick Grayson, whose secret identity was Robin (the Boy Wonder)

Alan Napier — Alfred Pennyworth, Wayne's butler (and the only other person who knew of their secret identity)

Madge Blake — Harriet Cooper, Dick's aunt

Neil Hamilton — Police Commissioner Gordon (city official who dialed the Caped Crusaders on the batphone.)

Stafford Repp — Chief O'Hara

Yvonne Craig — Barbara Gordon (the commissioner's daughter whose secret identity was Batgirl. She premiered in 1967.)

Batman and Current Events

Batman may have seemed like just a funny program to some, but actually it had an important effect on serious contemporary issues. For example:

The Generation Gap. Pierre Salinger, JFK's former press secretary, played the role of a villain named Lucky Pierre. "I have a piece of a discotheque and a football team and now a bit in Batman," said Salinger. "There is nothing else I have to do to make my kids think I'm great."

International Affairs. In Japan, the Caped Crusader was known as "Battoman."

Sex. To parry charges of homosexual overtones in the show (three unmarried men living together), Aunt Harriet was added to the Wayne household. It was instant respectability, said a show representative, because "she watches everything."

Violence. Killing on "Batman" was an absolute no-no, by order of the program's chief writer, because it would be "immoral." "This makes plotting more difficult," he said. "There isn't much for the villains to do except steal things."

Philosophy. The motto, emblazoned on Batman's crest in Latin, was "Evil Be Who Evil Does." Very deep.

Car Safety. The National Safety Council saluted Batman for always reminding Robin to fasten his safety belt. "Fasten your seat belt, Robin. We must set an example for our young people."

The Space Race. ABC faced a storm of protest when they broke into the middle of a "Batman" episode to announce the emergency landing of *Gemini 8.*

Politics. Batman was a write-in candidate for president of the student body at Ohio State in 1966.

Women's Liberation. In 1966, Big Al's bar featured a topless Batwoman who wore only a cape and a mask.

Fine Art. The Batman theme was recorded by eight different artists; in discotheques a new dance was called the Batusi.

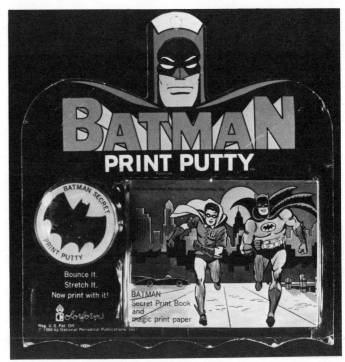

Silly Putty by any other name . . .

A Batman lunchbox

A bat-hat

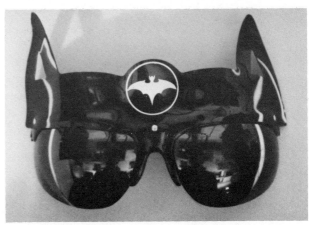

Bat-sunglasses

Holy Bat-Products!!

Almost immediately after Batman became a hit on TV, he became a hit in stores, too. In 1966, the show's first year on the air, more than sixty manufacturers made more than *five hundred* Batman products and sold more than *$60 million* worth of them! It astounded everybody. Now, said the *Wall Street Journal* incredulously, "a Batfan can have his room papered with Batpaper. He can read his Batman comics by the light of a Batlamp. He can don his Batman rain cape, Batman sweat shirt, or Batman T-shirt. He can play several Batman games or listen to eight Batman records. He can go fly a Batkite." If sales were any indication, Batman had become—in his first big year—one and a half times as popular as the previous superhero, James Bond. Here are some other Bat Products you could have bought in 1966:

- Batbath bubble soap
- Batman greeting cards from Hallmark
- Bat-wallets
- Batman peanut butter
- Batmobile models
- Mask and Cape set (by April 1966, 400,000 dozen had been sold)
- Batman sports jackets, pajamas, bathrobes, bedspreads, quilts, bathing suits, towels, slippers
- Bat-tricycles
- Batman lunchboxes and pencil cases
- Bat-puppets and Batman dolls
- Batman utility belt and Batarang (a bat-boomerang)
- Bat-jewelry

The Bat-game

On Thursday, October 20, Batman will show the winning Bat-scenes on his television show. And if one of your Bat-scenes matches, **you're a winner!** No purchase necessary to win.

Look for Batman's TV Sweepstakes display in your store, featuring Gleem toothpaste, Lilt home permanent, Liquid Prell shampoo and Hidden Magic hair spray.

HOLY BATMASK!

To get this all-new, all-color Batmask FREE, all you have to do is take your father or mother or aunt or uncle or grandmother or grandfather down to your participating G-E TV dealer. Hey! He'll even show you how it flips over and turns you into Robin.

GENERAL ⒼⒺ ELECTRIC

Just in time for Halloween—Only from General Electric TV dealers.

Don't you wish you had joined?

OFFICIAL **BATMAN** CLUB
©1966 NATIONAL PERIODICAL PUBLICATIONS, INC.

SUPERGIRL **IDEAL**

POSIN' DOLL

LINDA LEE DANVERS COLLEGE COED

The craze wasn't only for Batman—all superheroes benefited. Here's a Supergirl doll from the same period.

Flop of the Decade

"The Green Hornet"

In 1966, the fall TV season included a revival of the pre-WWII radio crimefighter "The Green Hornet." It was not only inspired by "Batman," but also staged by the producer of "Batman." Although the perpetrators claimed it wasn't meant to be camp, the dialogue was preposterous, the Hornet dressed in a silly outfit, drove an unbelievable car called the Black Beauty, and used the "Hornet gun" to stun his opponents with gas. "The Green Hornet" had nostalgia value, but could be played straight enough for kids to take seriously—and it had the potential to make a fortune in merchandising. But it wasn't popular like "Batman," the one angle that really counts. It lasted only one season.

For five cents a pack, you could buy five cards and a stick of gum in the sixties. What kind of cards? You name it—baseball, football, basketball, TV stars, political heroes, rock 'n' roll idols, monsters, astronauts. Whatever was popular. Nowadays, new cards cost thirty cents a pack, and the old ones—well, we don't want to make you cry. We know you had 'em, and we know your mother threw 'em away. Here they are again to haunt you.

CASEY STENGEL
MANAGER • NEW YORK

1960, Topps: Today's price: $4.00

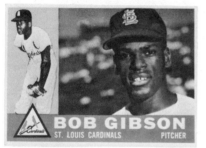

BOB GIBSON
ST. LOUIS CARDINALS   PITCHER

1960, Topps: Today's price: $4.75

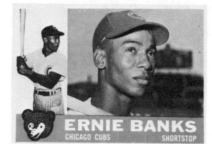

ERNIE BANKS
CHICAGO CUBS   SHORTSTOP

1960, Topps: Today's price: $5.00

YOGI BERRA
NEW YORK YANKEES   CATCHER

1960, Topps: Today's price: $4.75

STAN MUSIAL
Outfield   St. Louis Cardinals

1961, Topps: Today's price: $7.75

LOU BROCK
CHICAGO CUBS   OF

1962, Topps: Today's price: $20.00

CARL YASTRZEMSKI
BOSTON RED SOX   OF

1962, Topps: Today's price: $20.75

HANK AARON
MIL. BRAVES

1962, Topps: Today's price: $15.00

MICKEY MANTLE
N. Y. YANKEES   OF

1963, Topps: Today's price: $25.00

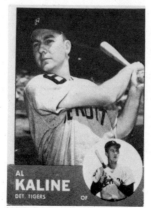

AL KALINE
DET. TIGERS   OF

1963, Topps: Today's price: $5.75

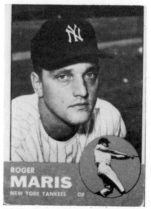

ROGER MARIS
NEW YORK YANKEES   OF

1963, Topps: Today's price: $4.00

ED MATHEWS
MIL. BRAVES   3B

1963, Topps: Today's price: $4.00

PETE ROSE — 2nd base
1964, Topps: Today's price:
$25.00

BOB CLEMENTE — outfield
1964, Topps: Today's price:
$7.00

SANDY KOUFAX — pitcher
1964, Topps: Today's price:
$7.50

3rd BASE
BROOKS ROBINSON
1965, Topps: Today's price:
$4.00

OUTFIELD
FRANK ROBINSON
1965, Topps: Today's price:
$4.75

OUTFIELD
WILLIE McCOVEY
1965, Topps: Today's price:
$3.00

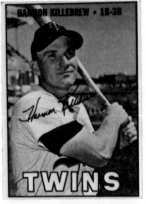
HARMON KILLEBREW • 1B-3B
TWINS
1967, Topps: Today's price:
$2.50

ORIOLES
JIM PALMER — pitcher
1966, Topps: Today's price:
$15.00

JUAN MARICHAL • P
GIANTS
1967, Topps: Today's price:
$1.75

WHITEY FORD PITCHER
YANKEES
1967, Topps: Today's price:
$2.75

TOM SEAVER — PITCHER METS
1968, Topps: Today's price:
$25.00

WILLIE MAYS — OUTFIELD GIANTS
1968, Topps: Today's price:
$8.00

STEVE CARLTON — PITCHER CARDS
1968, Topps: Today's price:
$4.50

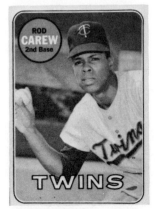
ROD CAREW — 2nd Base
TWINS
1969, Topps: Today's price:
$7.50

WARREN SPAHN
Milwaukee Braves—Pitcher
1963, Fleer: Today's price:
$4.00

DRYSDALE
1962, Topps: Today's price:
$4.00

Bryon PICCOLO
CHICAGO BEARS • RUNNING BACK

JIMMY **BROWN**
CLEVE. BROWNS
FULLBACK

GALE SAYERS
CHICAGO BEARS
RUNNING BACK

PAUL **HORNUNG**
GREEN BAY PACKERS
HALFBACK

Joe **NAMATH**
NEW YORK JETS • QUARTERBACK

ALEX KARRAS
DETROIT LIONS DEFENSIVE TACKLE

JACK KEMP
BUFFALO BILLS QUARTERBACK

KYLE ROTE
END NEW YORK GIANTS

Y. A. TITTLE
QUARTERBACK SAN FRANCISCO 49ers

PAT **SUMMERALL**
NEW YORK GIANTS
END

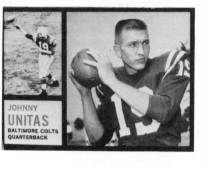

JOHNNY **UNITAS**
BALTIMORE COLTS
QUARTERBACK

BART **STARR**
GREEN BAY PACKERS
QUARTERBACK

PHILADELPHIA **WARRIORS**
CENTER
WILT CHAMBERLAIN

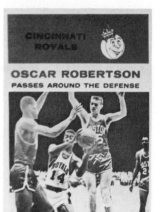

CINCINNATI **ROYALS**
OSCAR ROBERTSON
PASSES AROUND THE DEFENSE

BOSTON **CELTICS**
BACKCOURT
BOB COUSY

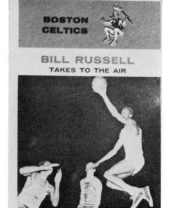

BOSTON **CELTICS**
BILL RUSSELL
TAKES TO THE AIR

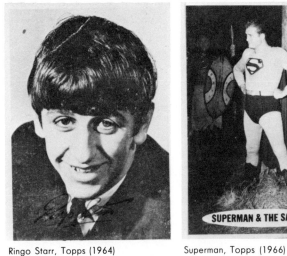

Ringo Starr, Topps (1964)

Superman, Topps (1966)

John F. Kennedy, Topps (1963)

The Man from U.N.C.L.E.,
Topps (1965)

The Beatles, Topps (1964)

Soupy Sales, Topps (1965)

James Bond, Philadelphia Gum (1966)

The Munsters, Leaf (1964)

Green Hornet, Donruss (1966)

Batman, Topps (1966)

Gomer Pyle, Fleer (1965)

The Green Berets, Philadelphia Gum (1966)

Combat!, Topps (1965)

The Civil War, Topps (1962)

SOURCES

Here's a list of sources for obtaining artifacts from the sixties, or information about them. It's not a complete list—but it's made up of people we worked with, and we feel comfortable recommending them.

MUSIC

Goldmine magazine (for info on old artists and for buying old records): Box 187, Fraser, MI 48026.

Record Prices. What're your old records worth? Jerry Osborne and Bruce Hamilton have put together a series of books called *The Original Record Collectors Price Guide.* They've got one on 45's, LPs, show music, blues, and who knows what else. They are available at bookstores or you can write to Jellyroll Productions, Box 3017, Scottsdale, AZ 85257.

Rock's Top 100. Our source for the top fifteen of each year was *Rock 100*, by Jim Quirin and Barry Cohen. Available by mail from the House of Oldies, 35 Carmine Street, New York, NY 10014.

If you were inspired by our guitars, try *Guitar Player* magazine, 20605 Lazaneo Street, Cupertino, CA 95014.

A new, up and coming music collectible is picture sleeves from the 45's. Many of the ones included in this book come from the collection of Gary King, 45 Ash Street, New Britain, Ct. 06050, who sells them (and records) by mail.

BEATLES

There are more Beatle clubs than anyone could imagine. Here are five American fan clubs you can join, listed alphabetically. They all publish magazines with the same name as the club.
1. Beatlefan, Box 33515, Decatur, GA 30033.
2. Good Day Sunshine, Liverpool Productions, 397 Edgewood Avenue, New Haven, CT 06511.
3. Strawberry Fields Forever, 310 Franklin Street #117, Boston, MA 02110.
4. With a Little Help from My Friends, 9836 Pleasant Lake #U24, Cleveland, OH 44130.
5. The Write Thing, 3310 Roosevelt Center, Minneapolis, MN 55418.

Beatle Festivals. There are conventions for Beatle lovers that go on all year round, managed by these folks. Write to them for info: Mark and Carol Lapidos, P.O. Box 436, Westwood, NJ 07675.

COMICS

Comic Prices. What're those old comics worth? Bob Overstreet was a price guide pioneer with his *Comic Book Price Guide.* Available in bookstores, or write to Overstreet Publications, Inc., 780 Hunt Cliff Drive, N.W., Cleveland, TN 37311.

Two of the many places you can get old comics: Geppi's Comic World, 612½ Edmondson Avenue, Baltimore, MD 21228. The Batcave, P.O. Box 711, Lindenhurst, NY 11757.

CARS

To our knowledge, the best source for buying 1960s cars and parts is *Hemmings Motor News*, P.O. Box 100, Bennington, VT 05201. Anyone with an old car to sell advertises there.

Their sister publication, *Special Interest Autos*, Box 196, Bennington, VT 05201, gives detailed info about old cars. Cars of the sixties are frequently included.

Car and Driver magazine is available at most newsstands. It's really not about the sixties, but it's one of the foremost magazines about autos in the world.

SPACE

One of the most spectacular museums in America is the Air and Space Museum at the Smithsonian in Washington, D.C. NASA has some information available for the public; also write to the Government Printing Office in Washington, D.C.

TOYS

Mechanical and Robots: We worked with Lloyd Ralston, who has a large mail-order business at 447 Stratfield Road, Fairfield, CT 06432.

Dolls: Pat Smith is a prolific author of doll price guides. A few of the volumes that will tell you what your sixties dolls are worth: *Teen Dolls* and the *Modern Collector's Dolls* series. They're published by Collector Books, P.O. Box 3009, Paducah, KY, but are available in most bookstores.

Chick Darrow's Fun Antiques, 1174 Second Avenue, New York, NY, has many sixties toys of all kinds, from mechanical to games. To the best of our knowledge, he doesn't do mail order.

Collectors' magazines: Antique Toy World, 3941 Belle Plaine, Chicago, IL 60618; and Collector's Showcase, P.O. Box 6929, San Diego, CA.

OTHER STUFF

How much are the old trading cards worth? Dick Sykes published a guide to non-sports cards called *The Non-Sports Price Guide.* He also sells all kinds of cards by mail. Write to him at the Rebel Peddler, P.O. Box 3092, Springfield, MA 01101.

For sports cards, there are many price guides, and a magazine called *The Baseball Hobby News,* P.O. Box 128, Glen Cove, NY 11542.

James Bond fans can join the James Bond 007 Fan Club, which publishes an attractive magazine called *Bondage.* Their address: P. O. Box 414, Bronxville, NY 19708.

The world's foremost collector and dealer of television games is Bob Cereghino. You can contact him at 1739 E. Champlain Drive, Baltimore, MD 21207.

There really is a place called the Dudley DoRight Emporium. It's run by the creators of our favorite cartoon characters, Rocky and Bullwinkle. They sell items relating to their cartoons by mail. Address: 8218 Sunset Boulevard, Hollywood, CA 90046.

Political buttons and related memorabilia has an excellent collectors' society. It's called the American Political Items Collectors (APIC), and you can contact them at 1054 Sharpsburg Drive,

Huntsville, AL 35803. There are many specialist groups within APIC. If you're interested only in Kennedy, or Goldwater, for instance, there are people whose primary interest is similar.

World's Fair Memorabilia. World's Fair Collectors' Society, Inc., 148 Poplar Street, Garden City, NY 11530.

For Movie and TV Pictures, and Movie Posters. Jerry Ohlinger's Movie Material Store, 120 West Third Street, New York, NY 10012.

If you like to read about surfing, *Surfer Magazine,* P. O. Box 1028, Dana Point, CA 92629, is the best we know of.

If you want to know more about autographs, contact The Manuscripts Society, Universal Autograph Collector's Club, Box 467, Rockville Center, NY 11576-0467.

If you want to build a fallout shelter, contact the Federal Emergency Management Administration. In the sixties, this was called the Civil Defense Department. Write to them in Washington, D.C., or call their twenty-four-hour hot line: (202) 634-6660.

How much are old buttons worth? You can use Ted Hake's books to find out: *The Encyclopedia of Political Buttons, 1896–1972,* and *The Political Button Book II, 1920–1976.* They're available from The Americana and Collectible Press, P.O. Box 1444, York, PA 17405.

Interested in beer can collecting? Write to Beer Can Collectors of America, 747 Merus Court, Fenton, MO 63026.

And if you just want to see what all this stuff looks like, there's a museum called The Popular Culture Library, Bowling Green State University Library, Bowling Green, OH 43403.

Three places we know you can get miscellaneous sixties merchandise from Twiggy pens to Dr. Kildare buttons, to Man from U.N.C.L.E. coloring books (depending on what's in stock):
• Speakeasy, 799 Broadway, New York, NY 10003.
• Artie Rickun, 7153 W. Burleigh Street, Milwaukee, WI 53210.
• Hake's Americana and Collectibles, P.O. Box 1444, York, PA 17405.